CW00515457

PARTIAL RECALL!

Brian Vincent

MINERVA PRESS
ATLANTA LONDON SYDNEY

PARTIAL RECALL!
Copyright © Brian Vincent 1998

All Rights Reserved

No part of this book may be reproduced in any form
by photocopying or by any electronic or mechanical means,
including information storage or retrieval systems,
without permission in writing from both the copyright
owner and the publisher of this book.

ISBN 0 75410 297 1

First Published 1998 by
MINERVA PRESS
Sixth Floor
Canberra House
315–317 Regent Street
London W1R 7YB

Printed in Great Britain for Minerva Press

PARTIAL RECALL!

It is certainly not my intention to misrepresent or harm anyone by references made in this book and to this end the names of some of the people referred to have been changed.

Author's Note

This book comprises reminiscences over the period 1933–1995. It is not intended as an autobiography and has nothing to do with my achievements. This is as it should be, for to keep a sense of proportion, they would be more like taking a walk up Kinder Scout than climbing Everest. They have not been stimulated by any close association to the great or famous. The best I could manage there would be a 'thank-you' letter from *Kenneth Tynan* and a quick twirl round the floor with *Vivienne Blaine* (won on a lucky draw charity ball ticket). Nor is it the record of a captain of industry, as my career in print would be more accurately described as a staff sergeant. My hope is that my reminiscences, observations and anecdotes will give an insight into those years, be of some interest, and as I have always favoured the lighter side of life, hopefully provide some amusement here and there.

Contents

Chapter One

Childhood

For me it all began in June 1930. The family home was a ground floor flat in a house in Russell Road, Holloway. I had a brother, Keith, who was six years older, and I was to complete the family unit. My father, Albert, was always referred to as Bert, and my mother, Dorothy, as Dorothy because that was the name she preferred – no abbreviations. You have to be a trifle circumspect when writing about your early years. None of us has total recall, so you rely on what you think you were told. This can create problems; my mother informed me when I was in my fifties that I had had bronchial pneumonia when I was very young, and I had thought for all those years that my brother was the one who had had it. I had been falsifying health documents for all those years with a clear conscience. Not only that, I had regaled many a person with the account of how I had visited him in hospital in the oxygen tent, going as far as to say that I saw his lips moving and moved closer to hear what he was trying to say to me, and it was, 'Take your foot off the oxygen pipe, I can't breathe.' In the light of that experience I think that it would be wise to start with the things that I do recall, and naturally enough my own memories are not very consistent until the age of three.

In the flat above were the Pitts. I have no recollection of a Mrs Pitt but that is not to say there was not one. Mr Pitt was a naval man who was awarded The Victoria Cross for his gallantry in the battle of Zeebrugge in the 1914–1918 war. In those days and at that age I knew nothing of this. He was just the man upstairs with the very gruff voice and stern mannerisms, which were part of an act that children are hardly ever fooled by. They have a sixth sense that tells them if it is really a kindly person. I used to sneak upstairs and enjoy taking part in the 'has that boy been eating my fatty bacon again' routine with threats of retribution that never, of course, took place but were all part of the ritual.

Only one other thing is in my memory from those years and that was the house next door catching fire. It was during the late evening and dark. I was gathered up out of my bed, wrapped in blanket and eiderdown and rushed out into the street where there was quite a gathering. As I recall, it was the top flat that was on fire and the fire brigade arrived in time and successfully put the fire out allowing us to return to our flat. As fires go, it was not tremendous, but one that affected me for many years. Well into my teens I would wake up in the night from an overrealistic nightmare of the house being on fire and in the cool light of day work out my means of escape should it ever occur. Thankfully the nightmares eventually left me but, to this day, whenever I use hotels or guesthouses, I always check fire doors and points of escape as a matter of routine.

The family moved to a house in Kingsbury, Middlesex, in 1933 – a move in the right direction as far as the Vincents were concerned. In those days Kingsbury was still fairly rural and our next door neighbours owned the local smithy. At the end of our turning, one side of the road was fields and at the other end was Silver Jubilee Park, which stretched across to West Hendon. This was one of two parks in close proximity and was only an area of mown grass, whereas the other, King Edward's Park, was the formal park with cricket and football pitches, putting green, flower beds and the traditional Park Keeper or, as we later referred to him, the *Oberstormführer*. There were three shopping parades within a mile's walk, all consisting of about eight to twelve shops and the main shopping centres of Neasden, Wembley and Kingsbury were a short bus ride away.

Burgess Avenue consisted of three-bedroomed houses with what now are called Georgian-style windows and medium-sized gardens. The unusual feature was that most of the houses had garages. In those days for a family to possess a car was a rarity and most of the houses in the avenue that had vehicles were owned by men who ran London licensed taxi cabs. We, the Vincents, were unique, the possessors of a motorcycle combination (a motorbike and sidecar for the uninitiated). Many memorable times were had in or via these fine vehicles, for my father was wont to change them when he saw either a better, less clapped-out bike or a more luxurious sidecar. Family excursions were made with my father at the controls, my brother on the pillion, my mother in the back seat, and myself in the front of the sidecar. What memories, picnics in the country, down to the coast for the day or off on holidays; it spelt excitement and adventure and in that sidecar I was in another world.

My father was a speedway fan; I think at one time he even contemplated having a go himself. As we lived so close to Wembley Stadium, this meant the family were all supporters of the Wembley Lions. We followed them until they sadly rode no more. Thursday night the whole family used to go; it was a fairly late night for a youngster, I suppose, but fortunately I was allowed to go. In those early days the two strongest teams used to be the Wembley Lions and Manchester's Belle Vue, battling for the championship. The teams in those days were fairly evenly balanced and it would be difficult to name a weak one. On rare occasions, if Wembley were riding against another London club in, say, the second leg of the Evening News ACU Cup, we would go to the away match. The fact that this would mean two late nights for me and the cost factor made these nights few and far between. I must have started going to these matches during 1933, and certainly regularly in 1935 through to the outbreak of war. Some of the Wembley riders I remember from those days were Lionel Van Prague (Captain), an Australian who received the VC during the war serving in the RAAF, Frank Charles, Ginger (Cannonball) Lees, Gordon (Chopper) Byers, Eric Gregory, George Wilks, Cliff Parkinson and Malcolm Craven (Reserve), who after the war became a 'World Champion' and sadly was killed in an accident on the track some years later.

On one occasion we gave a lift to two neighbours' children to the stadium. To achieve this I was in the nose of the sidecar, one of the additional passengers was on my seat and the other on my mother's lap. I must point out that at this time my mother was around the fourteen stone mark. The car park attendant waved us into our parking spot and began directing the next vehicle, then looked over in amazement when six people emerged from one motorbike and sidecar. He walked over to my father and said, 'Does London Passenger Transport know about you?'

The next day at school I would relive the night before's match and become momentarily my idols. Not all Wembley men, for even at that age I appreciated the skill, precision and relaxed style of Norman Parker (Haringay Tigers), the hair-raising and skilful riding of Ron Johnson (New Cross) winding it up round the outside with the taps wide open, and the unbelievable angles that the American rider, Wilbur Lamaroux, would achieve when cornering. The school cleaners no doubt used to wonder where the black rubber semicircular line, made by the sole of my shoe when cornering in the previous night's races, had come from every Friday. In those early years, what of my brother Keith? Well, he was six years older than me and, at that age, it was quite an age gap. We got on well enough and, as I recall, our main enjoyment at the time was baiting each other. With six years more experience in life over me he was the better baiter, though I did have my moments. The problem was his ploys were much more subtle, whereas my approach tended to be of the physical variety and the more likely to be spotted by baffled parents. When asked by your parents why you hit your brother with your cricket bat, the answer of 'because he made me look a right twit for the sixth time this afternoon' does appear, on the surface, a bit lame. It would be fair to say that deep down there were the normal feelings of brothers, but like normal brothers we did like to have a go at each other and come out on top.

Chapter Two

A Belated Entrance to the Education System

I did not attend school until well into my fifth year. I do not know how my mother prevailed upon my father, who was an eminently sensible man, that it was a good idea to delay my starting, the premise that when children usually start school they catch all the ailments like measles, chickenpox, whooping cough etcetera, but she did. The flaw in this reasoning came to light when I eventually did start about six months late. I still caught the aforementioned complaints which meant I had lost nearly a year's schooling instead of six months. Though educationally this did not get me off to a good start, it did mean that I met my lifelong friend, Malcolm Northmore, who is a year younger than me. This came about by my being moved down a year to catch up on the late start I had. It was to be through Malcolm that I eventually met my wife, June, which is a reasonable example of the random way our fate is fashioned.

School I enjoyed from start to finish. I feel sorry for people who say it was the worst experience of their life and they could not wait to leave. This does not mean that there were not times when I dreaded going, but these were only transitory periods when I was about to reap the harvest of what I had or had not done. I never resented it; if I was guilty then all I wanted to do was to get it over and done with. For the most part I could never resist life's characters. The goody-goody Fotherington Thomas brigade were never for me and still are not. The boys that I mixed with were not necessarily evil or downright villains, but they weren't the ones you would select if your main aim was good conduct points. The infant and junior schools were coeducational, but at that age we did not have a lot in common with the girls (apart from the occasional tomboy). In one class I was sat next to a plain girl who, for what reason was never explained to me, would wet her knickers at regular intervals, which was rather off-putting. A postscript to this was that about fourteen years later I was going to work on a bus and sat next to a really attractive blonde. I started taking sneaky sideways glances and finally it dawned on me that this 'cracker' was the same girl who had had the damp underwear problem as a child. My mind raced – how could I introduce myself? 'Isn't it Betty? I used to sit next to you at school and say things like – "Not again!".' The mind did not come through with a suitable line quick enough; she got off at the next stop.

Fryent School in those days consisted of two buildings. The front, original, mock-Tudor one housed the infants and the more recent two-storey building was for the juniors. There were two playgrounds and a school field, and at the time of my attendance it was surrounded on three sides by fields and a farm, the fourth side being the main road (Church Lane). The age of the children there was from five to eleven years old and in the last year the dreaded eleven-plus exams were held. Children then went their different ways and almost without exception they were then segregated. I cannot recall one local senior school that was coeducational. I am sure that as infants and juniors we were not angels and no doubt caused the odd teacher some problems but, from my experience, a teacher who moved on to take on the senior boys would not know what had hit him. The alarming speed with which children develop their Machiavellian tendencies once past eleven is truly astounding.

Empire Day was an annual event in those days. I do not remember when it actually stopped but I would hazard a guess it was after the outbreak of war in 1939. Children were asked to attend in costume if possible to represent the countries of the British Empire. In those days it was not that easy as money was not thick on the ground, but the parents showed a combination of ingenuity with more than a touch of poetic licence. We used to trudge off to school with a minority in dubious and sometimes brilliant costumes. Indian Chief (Canada), Chinaman (Hong Kong), the odd White Rhodesian (khaki shirt and shorts), no Australians in corky hats (when did they start?) and a rare grease paint job for an Indian or African. For some reason there was always a considerable number of the girls in nurses' uniforms; what the obscure relationship to the Empire was escapes me. The rest of us were in shorts and shirts and dresses, not school uniforms and all with Union Jacks to wave. We were all duly arranged in the playground on display to the parents who could attend, mostly mothers. There were speeches and we all sang patriotic songs about Britain being mighty, ruling the waves and bounds being set wider still and wider. The thing that was not so pleasant was standing about in summer clothes for an interminable amount of time on the first of May. On most of the occasions it was freezing cold, and chattering teeth would give the unusual effect of castanets in the background of *Rule Britannia* and also accounted for some of the Red Indians looking decidedly blue. Once all this rigmarole was concluded it was off for a half day's holiday, but first a quick dash to a parent for a jersey or coat if you were lucky!

I honestly believe we were receiving an excellent training to prepare us for international football hooliganism. The reason there was not a problem with it in those days was due to the fact that there were far fewer international competitions and, as more than eighty per cent of the population were lucky if they could afford a couple of days to the nearest coast for a summer holiday, who the hell could afford to troll off to an overseas football match? Whilst on the subject, when we look at the past and say, 'There wasn't any hooliganism at matches in those days!' do the statisticians take into account the low number of away supporters there were at matches? Remember, money was hard to come by and the average man worked Saturdays until at least 12.30 p.m. as part of their standard hours. So what kind of numbers could afford to not attend work and nip up to Wolverhampton to see West Ham play? My bet would be that the majority at matches were home supporters with the obvious result of fewer problems.

The most serious misdemeanour whilst at the junior school was perpetrated by the most unlikely duo of Beason and Farnes. These lads were a couple of eggheads, neither of whom had been in trouble. With no small amount of skulduggery, their own genius, and a chemistry set supplemented by some items from the chemist's, they created a bomb in an old coffee tin. This was common knowledge to the children and the plan was to blow up a concrete post in the school field. On the day it did not achieve this but it did produce a small crater and a very loud explosion, and the reverberations lasted months if not years. There were letters to their parents about their children being a menace to society. Threats about being sent to a centre for correction were fortunately not carried out but they worked. The 'Beason Farnes' outrage was a one-off in their otherwise blameless school life to the best of my knowledge.

My own black or, more accurately, blue spot during these early years was an end-of-term event. Myself and Phil Dicker were picked as ink monitors. The job was a good skive; we went round the classes collecting their inkwells in trays. We then took them to the cloakroom, washed them all out, and then returned them, clean, bright and shiny, ready for the next term. By this stage of the term, what was actually in those inkwells would have been beyond chemical analysis. As the day progressed, the more tedious aspects of the chore began to tell on us until Phil came up with a brain wave. This involved filling the two inkwells with water, putting them together with the apertures to the centre, and then shaking them like a cross between a cocktail shaker and maracas. This was a success and brightened up the job considerably, to a point where we were taking it in turns to see who could do the best 'Carmen Miranda' impersonation complete with musical accompaniment from one and vocals, dance and inkwell cleaning from the other. Coming to the end of our latest number, I looked at Phil and said, 'Blimey! Your face and shirt are covered in ink spots!' The dancing stopped and the realisation that we were in deep trouble dawned. I can't remember how efficient the technique was at cleaning the inkwells, but it was brilliantly effective at splattering ink across a very wide area. It was not just us that had been transformed, the sinks, mirrors, floor, in fact the entire room was covered in spots. The next half-hour was filled with feverish activity as, with the cloths that we had, we set about cleaning up, and finally we were relieved to have made good the damage before discovery. In fact, we thought that we had done such a good job that the school cleaners would have a cushy job that night and probably sit around having a smoke because they had never seen the cloakrooms so clean.

The next morning we were called from the class by the Deputy Head and marched swiftly to the cloakroom where he pointed with a shaking finger to the ceiling.

'How do you explain that mess?' we were asked.

It had not entered our heads that the ink had gone as high as that and we had not looked up and seen it. We were then marched to the Head's Study and left outside, the standard procedure to break down eleven-year-olds into a quivering jelly, before you gave them their just desserts. It is probably in the teachers handbook along with other useful hints like 'Sadomasochism – The Acceptable Levels'. As it turned out the punishment was not too bad. We were, however, made well aware that Fryent School was not into psychedelic ceilings and that no one should be foolish enough to trust us ever again. Perhaps we got off quite lightly.

One of the areas that Fryent did well was drama, and this tradition continued long after I had moved on. They had continuity, with dedicated teachers who put a lot of time and effort into these productions, as a result of which the school had a well-earned reputation in that area. I remember a production of *HMS Pinafore* which was excellent. The costumes, the sets, the lighting and, of course, the performances were superb. The lad who played Dead Eye Dick got rave reviews and justly so. I wonder if he ever took up the acting profession later or whether it was a one-off. The parents used to help greatly with the electrics, carpentry and painting the scenery. I am sure there was no official Parent-Teacher Association but the same result was achieved.

Because of the school tradition of drama and music, these areas were well catered for and you were gradually given more scope as you progressed to the older classes. Every year classes were split into groups which then drew up what play they wanted to do. The teachers had a watching brief to see that what was chosen was suitable and not too violent (boys' plays did have that tendency). You could use any of the school plays that were available, or you were encouraged to produce one of your own. For the 1930s I think this was quite progressive. The classes would select what they thought was the best play they had produced and these would go forward until finally on the Drama Day, once every year, there would be performances of the winning plays to the school and parents who wished to attend in the afternoon. There was then a break for tea and, in the evening, parents and older children would see the school's major production. This production, which was the official school one, was very professional and there would be several performances during the week. A nominal charge was made, with the proceeds helping to fund future productions.

The groups that I was in did get three plays through to the great day during the years I was there. Our first was *King John and the Magna Carta* – I think that was helped by the fact that they were surprised that we knew what it was and did not think it was the name of a haulage contractor. This was to be my *tour de force*, my first and last leading role on the boards. The play had to last only fifteen minutes and was written by us in a style more of 'William Brown and the Outlaws' than 'The Bard of Avon'. As in most boys' plays the dialogue was seen as a necessary evil to be squeezed in between the action.

On the day of the public performance it reached the part which was my big moment. I was not wild about the part. I had more lines than most, was nominally the lead, but not once was I scripted to enter an affray with my sword and this rankled with me. Most of the cast had been involved in a couple of sword fights already. The Magna Carta was duly offered to me to sign and with a bellowed 'You will never make me sign!' I smote the document away from me a bit too enthusiastically, for it sailed off the stage and into the audience. Children in the front row fought for the scroll, the audience burst out laughing and, on stage, King John and his noblemen cracked up. Stage management knew when to quit, they were experienced in these productions, so they brought the curtain down.

The second play was a Robin Hood effort in which I narrowly missed out on being the Sheriff of Nottingham and got a walk on part as a halberd carrier (we were strong on halberds, as there was a large stock left over from *The Yeoman of the Guard*). Not a milestone in contemporary theatre but fairly disaster-free. The third was to be our last with the school, for we were reaching the age to be off to fresh fields and this was to be our *pièce de résistance*. The parents had done us proud; there was going to be enough armour and weaponry on stage to make Laurence Olivier's *Henry V* Battle of Agincourt look like a B-film skirmish. All we had to do was knock up a bit of dialogue about this bloke nipping off somewhere in his boat, a couple of lusty battles, knock off the *Golden Fleece* and there you would have a smash hit if ever we had written one.

On the day of our performance we were amassed on stage with all our armour and weaponry, and the teachers were looking anxious. For some obscure reason there was a nervous atmosphere about the place. The first couple of battles had taken place with only minor abrasions and a few bits of additional dialogue they could have done without, but they still had this air of impending doom. Jason had a magnificent suit of armour; his father (Rodney's not Jason's) was a sheet metal worker, and had made it for him. Helmet, breastplate, shield and sword, none of your folded paper hat and two bits of wood nailed together – this was state-of-the-art armour.

'See the ship has landed.' (Last act, and Jason was back with the now blood-stained fleece). Noises of suitable awe for such an occasion came from the crowd to welcome back Jason. Offstage Jason, complete with his Argonauts and the fleece on the tip of his sword, was about to make his final and triumphant entry. Also just offstage is a large, frayed coconut mat. Jason, as he made his entry caught his sandal in the frayed mat and pitched forward onto his nose. The audience were waiting with bated breath, what a suspense job this little number had been; they now heard sounds of which the man who produced the sound effects for the *Goon Show* would have been justly proud. It was a mixture of emptying a bottle bank, discarding a number of obsolete glockenspiels into a skip and driving a bus through 'Lawleys'. Through the air from the wings came the fleece and sword followed by Jason's helmet rolling noisily across the stage and into the audience. After a pause came Jason and his Merry Argonauts and they were all killing themselves with laughter. It was our best production; the audience liked it, it was spectacular, and the staff were relieved that the bloodshed had been kept to a minimum.

Chapter Three

Outbreak of World War II

As a nine-year-old I read the papers and listened to the radio and had seen with a mixture of alarm and excitement that there would almost certainly be war. What effect would it have on us? Would my father be involved? He had fought in the army in the 1914–1918 war and been gassed. Fortunately his age, plus his occupation with the Middlesex County Council Engineers Department, meant he was not called into the services, but what did not enter my head was that my brother, who had only left school a year earlier, would be called up into the Infantry and serve throughout the Italian campaign.

Evacuation was causing the utmost confusion – whether you were evacuated or not depended on whether you were considered to be in a safe or unsafe zone. London generally was unsafe and out you went. We were borderline; we lived in Middlesex but had a London postal district. Finally the zones were agreed and the issues of evacuating children and supplying Anderson shelters began. On the opposite side of our road, which backed onto a park, they were given shelters. Our side, if anything closer to London and backing onto factories and a small army camp, was not. The factories were later commandeered for producing self-sealing petrol tanks for aircraft. Due to a method of covering the tanks with various rubber and canvas layers they sealed themselves if penetrated by bullets, for long enough for the plane to return to its base.

As we were considered to be in a safe zone and not to be evacuated, my father made hasty arrangements for my mother and me to go to Old Windsor, in Berkshire, through one of my mother's sisters and a friend. We all piled into dad's van and down to Old Windsor. My father and brother would be returning after the weekend because of their work and my mother and I would be able to stay with this kindly family in the comparative safety of the country. The timing was perfect. The next morning, the third of September, 1939, my brother and I sat on the stairs and heard on the radio Mr Chamberlain's announcement that we were at war with Germany. Almost immediately the air raid sirens sounded. I think that it was an agreed test throughout the country but people had not been warned and it caused mayhem until they sounded the 'All Clear'.

Unless you were in coastal areas, serious air raids were quite a few months away at this time. I enjoyed my spell at Old Windsor – walking by the river, excursions with my mother and no school – but it did not last. No raids came and my mother was anxious to return to Kingsbury.

She was a town-bred person and swore she could not sleep in all that quiet. She loved to hear people, traffic and the general hubbub of town. In addition to this she hated the family being split, and there was the question of school.

So back we came to number thirteen. I do not know how long all that took; I should think about two to three months at most but that is quite a long time to a nine-year-old.

By this time Fryent School was getting organised and

business was returning to normal. Lots of families that had been evacuated had by now decided to risk it and return. After all we were not next to the docks or any great industrial complex so it appeared a reasonable risk.

Chapter Four

Senior School

The school examination system was not running as normal and the eleven-plus exams were not sat by all pupils (something to do with the war, I believe). The top so many places in the 'A' classes went to the grammar and county . schools and as at that time I was in the 'B' class that meant I was destined to go to the senior school for those who normally failed their exams. As a result of this my parents arranged for me to go to a fee-paying school which was a convent school. The school was grant-assisted and to qualify had to take a number of children who were not Catholics and I was one of that number. I did not settle there and in the end prevailed upon my parents to let me go to the council school, where most of my friends were. In those days council schools did not have a lot of imagination spent on their names. The excellent seat of learning that I went to had the exciting title of 'Kingsbury Senior Boys.' Before going any further, I must say that the school did a very sound and workmanlike job with the means at its disposal. The staff were affected by the fact that all fit males between the ages of twenty and forty were in the forces. For the most part the teachers were good at their job and although the diet was reasonably basic the essentials were covered well. The principle was that they gave you the basics and beyond that it was down to you to seek further education via institutions such as evening classes.

The school was situated on the Edgware Road surrounded by factories, no such thing as a school field, only an asphalt playground. Quite an imposing building of three storeys, which I learned was originally built as Admiralty Offices. When I first viewed it, blast walls were covering the entrances and ground-floor windows, and the upper floors all had the sticky brown tape crosses on them to try to avoid flying glass from bomb blasts. Ironically, or luckily, as far as we were concerned, it was a safe place as neither the school nor the nearby factories had any serious bomb damage.

The school did not have air raid shelters as such, but the ground floor for the most part had been reinforced and had great balks of timber supporting the roof. I think it would have been fairly safe, depending on what hit it, but it did worry me a little that when I leant on one of these supports during a shelter drill it fell over. It was lucky that with its considerable weight it did not injure anyone. I assume that the timber wedges had loosened due to the heat and shrinkage. They were subsequently checked and I was relieved that I was not disciplined for breaking the shelter.

The school was a mile away from my home, and the boys from our area used to walk over Wakemans Hill to get to it. Funny that Kingsbury, which is not noted for its hills, should have had the steepest one between us and the school. There were a number of variations in the routes we could take, and these were varied based on current interest, such as the castle houses at the top of Buck Lane, or to avoid some resident we had upset the day before. In the winter when there was ice and snow I used to take the Buck Lane route in the mornings. Milk was delivered in those days by horse and cart and the United Dairies Depot was in Church Lane, just before the Kingsbury Road crossroads. The horses used to be fitted with special shoes to help them grip, and the carts had chains on their wheels. On bad mornings they would have two horses and two men with the cart, and they would sweat and strain together to get up the Buck Lane hill, and when they made it the extra man and horse would go back down to the depot. The milkman always seemed to have the same horse and there was a great affinity. When the assaults on the hill took place we would often run up with them and try to help push the cart. The milkman would yell at us and tell us to 'clear off!' – no doubt for our own safety.

The castle houses just on the crossroads at the top of Buck Lane were actually flats and built around the early thirties. They were quite unique architecturally, and to us lads they were fascinating – the imagination would run riot, especially when we ventured up into them. This would quite naturally incur the wrath of the occupants, who did not know what we were up to and objected to the invasion of their privacy. We had no harm in view, just to look out from the battlements and conjure up scenes from books by A. G. Henty, Sir Walter Scott or whoever's historical novel we had been currently reading. We were never repelled from them by other children; at that time anyway none lived there, what a waste.

The next item of interest on this route was the 'Mad Major's' wall. I am sure that the occupant of this house was neither mad nor commissioned but that was our name for him. This house had a wall that was about three foot high at one end and went to about five foot at the other end. It was about a brick's width and was butted up to a featheredged boarded fence about four foot six inches high. We could reach the top of the fence with our hands but not see over it. The object of this game was to edge along the wall facing the fence and steady yourself with your fingers clasped over the top of the fence until you got to the other end, preferably without being seen by the Mad Major and having your fingers whacked by his walking stick. Failure was very painful to the hands and had the risk of other injuries obtained falling off the wall. Why we thought it was worth indulging in this variation of Russian roulette I really do not know, but not many days passed without some bright spark saying, 'I am going to have a go at the Mad Major's Wall.' This was invariably followed with cries of 'Yeah, let's do that!' and I cannot recall ever hearing anyone voicing dissent or even saying their fingers had not healed from the last time. There was an aspect of the Major's personality which was a little disturbing. He arrived quietly; you could even say he crept up to the fence, and only when the blows were raining down on your fingers and our howls of pain were to be heard would he move to the verbal assault. This would be along the lines of 'Get off my fence, you little swines!' It surely must have occurred to him that the same message, bellowed from his back door, would have put us to flight.

Chapter Five

Blitz, The First Wave

I had not been at the senior school long before the first of the Blitz onslaughts began and we were being subjected to nightly air attack. My father had constructed an air raid shelter in the dining room as we had not been issued with an air raid shelter by the government authority. His knowledge of how to do this was very sound. The floorboards were taken up so that the shelter was on the foundations of the house, with good thick, sandbag, walls, a stout timber and sandbagged roof, and with comfortable bunks for four. He said that if the house was hit we would be all right in there, at worst having to wait to be dug out. I believed him – he was not a man who made idle boasts, and I felt as safe there as anywhere in an aerial bombardment.

That first round of the Blitz was made largely with what later would be considered as small bombs. Lots of incendiaries (which we used to call 'sparklers') and two-hundred and fifty to five-hundred pound HE bombs. The varied effects from the blast were according to the moment of detonation – some exploded on impact and others were time fused. If they were well into the ground, then the blast damage was less. If on the surface or above ground, according to the size of the bomb, the blast would effect an area of from two-hundred to three-hundred yards. Roughly, a two-hundred and fifty pound bomb would take out a house, and with a five-hundred pound one, three or four would be badly damaged. The blast areas would be affected by damage such as windows out, doors off and ceilings down. The most devastating things dropped at that time were land mines. These were around the size of a household dustbin, and were dropped by parachute with a view to exploding above ground and causing maximum damage, which was quite considerable. The worst on your nerves were the 'screaming bombs', which had some modification to the bomb flights that made them scream as they fell through the air. Fortunately this practice was dropped after a while which made things a bit better, for the first thing you heard with a normal bomb was the explosion, and by that time you knew it had missed you (even if not by much), whereas the screaming bomb gave you time to wonder if it was yours. The raids varied, but due to the heavy German losses on day raids they tended to be at night. They were made usually by *Junkers*, *Dorniers* and *Heinkels*, and as schoolboys we had memorised them and could instantly recognise them, as indeed we could our own aircraft. The distinctive drone that their engines made, largely Daimler-Benz, tipped you off as soon as you heard them. I do not know if any other power units were used but you would carry on normally in a raid until you heard that 'mm-wow, mm-wow' and when you heard that close to, you got into a shelter a bit smart.

Kingsbury obviously did not receive anything like the attention that areas like Docklands, the City and the East End received but we had more than we wanted. In the early days my brother and I marked where the bombs fell with crosses on a local street map, and by the time we stopped bothering, it was liberally sprinkled all over. Some places seemed to attract them; opposite where my friend, Malcolm, lived they had a bomb fall, then a 'doodlebug' and finally a V-2 rocket – all within two or three hundred yards of each other. The raids came in phases – you would have continuous night raids for a spell and then they would ease off. You would carry on sleeping in the shelters for a while, and almost invariably return to your beds just in time for the raids to start all over again.

The park at the other end of our road now had a pretty impressive anti-aircraft battery and we soon began to appreciate the difference in sound of what was going up and what was coming down. Most of the guns were 3.8s and one was a 4.7 which became known locally as 'Big Harry.' You knew when 'Big Harry' was being fired because your front door flew open. As people went to work or school they would remark, 'Big Harry was at it last night' and the reply was often, 'Yes, I hope it does as much damage to them as it does to us.' Another thing that made you jump out of your skin were the mobile Bofors guns. These were mounted on the back of a lorry and used to belt round the streets, pausing every now and then to let off a clip of four shells and then drive off. The problem was, if you had not seen them arrive, the first thing you knew was when they fired their four shells. Looking on the bright side it was a good cure for constipation.

This had all become part of life's routine, and we would trudge off to school past the odd gap where a house had been hit and men were busily clearing up the rubble and debris almost as though this was the natural order of things. We would stop here and there to pick up a particularly impressive bit of shrapnel or the odd shell nose-cap that we came across. This was very exciting in the beginning, but when a few tins or boxes had been filled it soon became a yawn and 'Have you seen my shrapnel collection?' became the equivalent in those days to threatening to show people your holiday slides now.

Chapter Six

Life Goes On

Kingsbury Senior was, for me, an enjoyable experience – the things we were being taught were of more interest than the suspense-filled 'Janet and John' stuff from earlier school days. The teachers were mostly men of above military service age, and some were real characters. This was well before anyone thought that corporal punishment should not be used. The school was ruled with a rod of iron, or more precisely a swishy cane, usually with Elastoplast round the end to stop it fraying. The cane was used to varying degrees by different masters but, with the exception of Mr Ridge (known to us as 'The Bump'), all used it. I must be fair and say that the eleven- to fourteen-year-olds at this school could be troublesome, and usually were. The different methods used by masters to control their classes was an interesting exercise in psychology. The ones who had to resort to the physical approach least were often very different but they all had that indefinable something. I have read that actors such as Laurence Olivier and Richard Burton had such a 'presence' on stage that it could become a problem. If they were playing the third spear carrier, that is who the audience watched instead of the leading actors. The successful disciplinarians had a similar presence. Before they said a word you knew that this was one to be handled with care – their bearing and manner told you that they should not be trifled with. The boys were appreciative of a good strict teacher who did his job well, and they enjoyed being in his class.

They were much preferred to the mass-whacking variety or the ineffective, who, once you had brought about their nervous breakdown, were pretty boring.

Mr Hunkin was a good example of the effective disciplinarian. He was my form master for a spell in my first year, due to staff changes caused by call-up into the forces, and for my last year in the school. He was also the Head Teacher, which meant that he would deal out the summary punishment to the sorry queue of miscreants, who were always there after play or dinner breaks. He was a Cornishman with quite a strong accent and used to make use of the Bible (quoting or reference – not physically). His class he used to refer to affectionately as his 'Tribe of Manasseh' and would make constant reference to people who were 'lookers and not see-ers.' This was a favourite theme of his, referring to people who looked no deeper than the surface. One day he had been holding forth on this point as usual and with the class's rapt attention – their interest was pleasing him, and everyone appeared to be caught up in his latest anecdote. There was, of course, something that we knew and he did not. The school cat was curled up asleep on his chair. If we could only keep his attention so that his eyes were on us and not on his seat. We made it; he came to his favourite phrase 'You see he was a looker but not a see-er' and sat on the cat, which did the usual thing cats do when sat on by a stocky well-built teacher. The class roared with laughter and to his credit so did he.

On another occasion a lad had been playing him up for most of the afternoon. This 'death wish' approach was not all that uncommon, the 'this is the afternoon when I am going to have the class falling about and if I get punished it will have been worth it' syndrome. His latest bit of foolery was adding the sound effects to another lad's rendition of *The Charge of the Light Brigade*. Cannon to the left of them, 'Pop' (made with the finger in the mouth). Cannon to the right of them, 'Pop.'

'Come out here Brown!'

Brown sauntered jauntily out front and stood by the class cupboard. Mr Hunkin grabbed him by his lapels and shook him ferociously in the time-honoured manner.

'So you (shake) think that's (shake) being (shake) clever (shake) do you?' At the last word he slammed him against the cupboard – on top of which was a wooden rhomboid, which tipped over and struck Brown a glancing blow on the head. The performance then given by Brown was a classic, an Italian striker would have been able to learn from it. His downfall came from overconfidence, when Mr Hunkin spotted a wink to the class in between moans.

I arrived in his class one day when he was no longer my form master and joined the queue of miscreants. When he got to me he told me to hold my hand out and gave me a stroke of the cane. He looked round and saw me still standing there.

'What are you waiting for?' he said.

'Mr Ridge sent me and said could he borrow the glue,' I replied.

The laughter from the class made it worthwhile, especially as a few days later I was in the miscreants' line in my own right and when he came to me he said, 'You can go, you have already had yours!'

Meanwhile, at home, my father had decided that we would keep chickens, which would mean we would have plenty of eggs and the odd bird for the table to help out with the rations. The family next door to us already kept chickens; they were, as I mentioned earlier, a country family, the grandfather and father having been the village blacksmiths. Breeds of chickens have no doubt changed like most things, but, in those days, next door went for the lighter White Leghorns, which were quite prolific layers, whereas we went for Rhode Island Reds and Light Sussex, which were more robust but not such good layers. We had two runs, which I helped my father to build with nest boxes, and separate nest boxes for the broody hens with their own clutches of eggs. My father was a very practical man who could turn his hand to anything and had an infectious enthusiasm. He would lay out his plans, go through them with me, and in the morning it would be, 'No laying in today, son, we have got a lot to get through.'

I would follow him out into the garden and work would begin. On average we had between thirty to forty birds, with highs and lows, as most of the cockerels were for the table and the hens, if good layers, were kept for that purpose. It certainly helped with the rations, and the sale of some of the eggs and fowls helped to finance the operation.

In the avenue, as the years went by, the boys became youths and the youths men, and it happened quite suddenly. I remember in my own case reading the papers one week when they stated that children born after a certain date would be able to get oranges. Within a few weeks the same papers stated that men born during that same period must register for military service. The young men would be called up and then reappear in the uniforms of whatever branch of the services they had been put in. You were given some choice; it was just that they did not often take any notice of it. It was rumoured that if you volunteered before you were called up you had more chance of getting in the arm of the service that you wanted, but if you waited until you were called up you went where they put you.

My brother did clerical work when he first left school and then went to the other extreme and became a panel beater (sheet metal worker) at Duples, down on the Edgware Road. They were renowned for their buses and coaches, which were to be seen all over Britain and abroad, with contracts with companies like AEC and Guy. This production had stopped soon after the outbreak of war and changed to army trucks, and part of the factory and adjoining factories had been commandeered and were now LAP (London Aircraft Production). This meant that, to my mother's relief, my brother was in a reserved occupation and would be exempt from being called up. The relief turned out to be short-lived, as, with a number of his friends, he got round the exemption and volunteered for the army. The wisdom of that move must have gone through his mind a time or two when he was landed on the Anzio beachhead in Italy. Not one of our greatest successes and one where we suffered extremely heavy casualties. His own unit of the Queens Royal Regiment, which was part of the 56th London Division, was withdrawn and sent back to Egypt to be re-formed and made up with replacements from England, before being landed back on the Italian mainland. He was in 'The Queens' throughout the rest of the Italian campaign and was transferred to the Royal Hampshire Regiment after the war in Europe ended. He was then sent to Palestine and Jordan for about eighteen months until he was demobbed. When the remustering into the Hampshires took place the men who had been in the Queens were near revolt. There was nothing wrong with the Hampshires, indeed the Hampshires men would have had exactly the same feelings about being transferred to the Queens. It is just that the army has this thing about instilling pride in your regiment – it is the only one that matters and the best in the army, and this approach works. It is not always easy but they achieve it, although it's a bit difficult when you are in the RASC (Royal Army Service Corps) as I was, and the neighbouring camps belonged to the Guards and the Royal Horse Artillery. It is therefore not difficult to see that suddenly telling people they are in a different regiment is on a par with getting a load of Chelsea supporters together and saying, 'All right, lads, from Monday on we are supporting Arsenal.' This all meant that I was not to see much of my brother over the next five years and the only contact would be by letter. I do not remember how frequently I wrote to him but it was often enough for me to remember his army number which I still remember as well as my own.

Chapter Seven

Supplementary Income

I was now at the age when I had a need to supplement my income. I did get pocket money from my parents but for my grand plans and hobbies additional income was required. Newspaper rounds never appealed, especially the morning ones, but I did help the Co-op milkman on Saturday mornings for a period. As he was trying to collect payment, I would collect the empties, stack them in crates, and make the deliveries to where he had already collected the payments on the Friday. The milkman that I helped had a large dapple-grey horse called Bob, which had three serious drawbacks, his penchant for eating people's hedges and trees, cussedness, and an ill-timed, copious output of manure.

At first I thought his disobedience was due to my lack of authority with horses, but then I was reassured by the fact that he did not take any notice of the milkman either. 'Whoa, hold on, Bob' you would shout, make a delivery and come back to find the horse halfway up the road. On other occasions you would find yourself thumping the animal and trying to drag him away by the bridle from someone's prized tree which was rapidly turning into something that resembled an umbrella without its cloth cover.

This job lasted for some months, and the extra pocket money came in handy, until one fateful day. We had just turned out of Burgess Avenue and into Townsend Lane, the milkman was making a call and I was standing on the side of the cart stacking crates. I cannot be sure of what happened but it could have been a lorry backfiring. What I do know is what the outcome was – Bob bolted. I clung to the side of the cart for dear life as the cart careered and swayed along with Bob at full gallop. We did just over a mile with the route being his choice, and he was not into the Highway Code. When we reached an area we referred to as 'bungalow town', he suddenly stopped and peacefully started chomping someone's prized hedge. An amazingly short time after the abject terror left me – I was off like a shot. My brief spell as 'milkman's aide' was at an end, and I came to the conclusion that this was an experience that was best not repeated.

That was not my last experience with a bolting horse. Some years later I was cycling round to a friend's house when I heard a crash of splintering wood and the clatter of old iron. Some idiotic lorry driver had driven into the back of a rag-and-bone cart that was parked outside a café. The horse, with only the shafts and front wheels of the cart, came thundering round the corner and up the wrong side of the road towards me. Preferring not to contest his right to be galloping up the wrong side of the road, I rode straight up the kerb and into a block of flats. From a position of safety behind a wall, I saw a bus coming in the opposite direction. The driver stopped his bus and jumped down onto the road and threw himself at the horse and, grabbing the bridle, pulled it to a standstill. He then stood patting and consoling the horse until the owner ran up and took over. I thought it was one of the bravest acts I had ever seen. It could certainly have saved someone's life, and definitely saved the horse. In all honesty, if I found myself being borne down upon by some loony horse and half a cart, going like the clappers of hell, I must be honest and say that 'Shall I throw myself at this and grab the bridle' would be a course of action that I would not seriously consider.

My next casual employment was to come from an unexpected source, the off-licence on the corner of the next parade of shops to ours. This was a picturesque little shop, mock-Tudor with leaded lights, and run by a nice genteel, blonde-haired lady whose husband, when seen on leave, was a squadron leader in the RAF and therefore worshipped by us boys. I passed there not long ago and found that the leaded lights had gone, it was painted red and yellow, and was named Boozerama. This was not an improvement and upset even a Philistine like me. On a visit one evening to collect a bottle of brown ale for my father, and a bottle of pop for myself, I picked up my next little earner. I overheard the off-licence lady say that she could not find enough spare time to exercise her dog, Patch, and would pay five shillings a week for the job. I have never been a dog-hater (with the possible exception of the one who leaves large amounts of excrement on the grass verge right by my car door) but nor was I a dog-lover. The rate of pay put any doubts I might have had to flight. To put the payment for the dog-exercising into perspective, when I started my apprenticeship some years later, the pay for a fifty-three and a half hour week was ten shillings. My eyes lit up like a cash register, I immediately asked for the job and started the next Monday.

After school I would collect Patch and he would take me for about three quarters of an hour's exercise. If I had been able to keep the job for long enough I would have had shoulders and muscles like Arnold Schwarzenegger. The dog was a black and white bull terrier with pink eyes, and pound for pound, there was no contest – he was the strongest! Every night we followed the same routine. I would pick him up and the lady would say, 'Take good care of him, give him a nice long walk, keep him away from other dogs and whatever you do, don't ever let him off his lead.'

The weeks passed and the bank balance was looking good. My physique was improving and the dog was only slightly stronger than me. We had settled into a nice routine, the off-licence lady trusted me and just passed over the dog without all the instructions, Patch now knew the route and me, and was less of a problem. Up Church Lane, into Slough Lane, across the road and into the fields owned by Kingsbury Farm, about three circuits of the fields, back out into Slough Lane and back to the off-licence. A good routine if only I had stuck to it, but I did not. My downfall was compassion for the damned dog. I kept thinking, he knows me now and does relatively all I ask him and although we both walk and trot together I bet he would love to be off his lead and have a good run. Other dogs did and, when called back by their owners, eventually came back to them. So, I did it; I slipped his lead and said, 'Go on boy, have a good run!' He didn't need telling twice – he just roared off at a speed no bull terrier has achieved before or since. He did thirty or forty laps without a break, totally ignoring my cries of 'Patch, to heel, Patch' and the odd 'Come here you stupid mutt' and I must admit some cries that were not as polite as that. Then, after one lap he did not return. Oh, my God, where was he?

Panic was setting in. I staggered round the fields until I got to the Salmon Street end, and then I only had to follow the screams and noise. When I finally got to the scene of the crime, there were two or three men, a blanket and a bucket of water, a liberal sprinkling of blood and froth, and a large Alsatian (that was still no doubt trying to figure out what had hit him) and Patch. Well, most of Patch for he had not had it all his own way. There was blood and froth all over him and a large chunk of one ear missing. I took my verbal beating from the two men and just kept repeating 'he slipped his lead,' and set off back to the off-licence.

I thought I had done a pretty good job cleaning him up with my handkerchief, his ear had stopped bleeding and I was sure he had enjoyed himself. When we got back to the off-licence one glance from the blonde lady, who promptly had what I think they mean in books by 'the vapours', and that was the end of that job. What is more, I don't think she paid me for that last week, but I did not push the matter. She was muttering something about excessive vet's bills when I hurriedly left.

Chapter Eight
Blitz, The Second Wave

There had been a lull in the air raids in the London area for a while. That is not to say they had stopped completely, but they had only been spasmodic. During this period the council had been very active and we now had street air raid . shelters. They were robustly built with reinforced concrete roofs and thick brick walls. As a result of this we were able to dismantle the shelter my father had built and return the dining room to a state closer to normality. At about the same time we received a Morrison shelter. This was a sheet metal and girder construction that would take a family of four and when not in use could be used as a table. This tended to get emergency use only. After a quiet spell, when you were caught in the luxury of your own beds and things got a bit too close for comfort, it was dive downstairs a bit smart, and into the Morrison.

When the raids began again in earnest we used the street shelter. My father saw plenty of bomb damage and, more often than not, had men working on it clearing it up. He had seen plenty of unpleasant sights and said in his opinion the street shelters were the best bet. These shelters were built to take up to six people in two compartments, one each side of the entrance. We shared ours with neighbours called Wallis, and as there were three in each family (the eldest sons both being away in the forces), that worked out nicely. I would say that we were in that shelter continuously every night for six months or more. The siren (known as Moaning Minnie) would sound an hour or two after dark and the all clear usually went about an hour before dawn. You would then emerge and find out who had caught it during the night. I think that this period was the worst we had to take with the later 'doodlebug' onslaught a close second. It was amazing how the men, women and children took it all in their stride. It was out of the shelter, wash and brush-up, breakfast (sometimes a cold one as the gas had been cut off due to bomb damage) and off to work, school, or on with the housework.

There were lighter moments, like the night we were risking it in our own beds, when the siren went. We thought we would chance it – then all hell broke loose. We scrambled into clothes that we left handy just in case, and dashed for the shelter. Olive and Mrs Wallis were there, but Mr Wallis was not.

Grace, his wife, said, 'I am worried about Alf, I'm not sure if the house was damaged but I remember him shouting to me, "Get to the shelter I'll be all right".'

My father went to look for him in the next lull and found him dazed, with a large bump on his head. Apparently, in the rush to get to the shelter, he had tucked into his trousers what he thought was his shirt but was in fact the bedroom curtain. As he dashed off he pulled the cornice pole off the wall and it struck him on the head. We all had a good laugh at his expense with his cries of 'You get to the shelter, I'll be all right' just before the cornice pole struck.

Another night, or to be precise very early morning, Alf said, 'It's a bit quieter now, how about a nice cup of tea?' and set off for the house to make it.

The fathers used to take it in turns to do this in the quieter spells. We consumed vast quantities of tea through those raids, and when the chips are down, nothing can beat the effect that a good cuppa gives. Some time passed and he returned with the tea, looking positively shaken.

'As soon as we have had the tea, Bert, you had better get on your phone to the bomb disposal squad, there is a land mine hanging outside my back door with its 'chute caught on my chimney.'

He had been standing in the kitchen making the cup of tea and when he opened the back door to throw out the tea leaves from the last brew he had bumped into the mine. This had shaken him but not to the point where he stopped making the tea. The land mines were not normally set by time fuse, they exploded on impact. Anyway we were all delayed in the morning as we could not get into the houses until the bomb disposal men had defused the mine and had taken it away.

We were also at this time getting daylight raids, and there was a new school rule: 'If the siren sounds when you are on your way to school, head immediately for whichever is nearest, home or school.' I saw kids, who I knew lived nearly a mile away, coming through the school gates when the siren had sounded, and they turned round and legged it for home. At school we were surrounded by factories, and within half a mile, was Hendon Aerodrome, from where, at one time, a squadron of 'free Poles' was flying *Spitfires*, with their black and white checks on the wings. The factories nearly all had lookouts up on their roofs, in things that looked like crows-nests. The factory workers would work on through the raids to avoid losing production, and the children worked on to avoid interfering with their education more than could be helped. When the lookouts picked up enemy aircraft getting too close they gave short blasts on their claxons, and that meant you should get to the shelters at the double.

One Sunday afternoon at about 4 p.m. the radio was on and a tenor was singing *I'll Walk Beside You*, a song that was loathed by my mother from that day on. There had been no air raid warning and people were about to have afternoon tea, the cucumber sandwiches bit, when there was an almighty explosion. I was sitting on the piano stool, but not for long. The house shook violently, and the front door flew open, followed by the sound of breaking glass. People rushed out into the street – whatever was it? The air raid siren had not been sounded, which brought several sarcastic comments. You could hear the sound of fire engines and ambulances coming from the West Hendon direction. Some people set out to walk over to see what it was, and if they could help.

To the best of my knowledge it was never established what it was. One rumour was that a bomber with its full bomb load had crashed, but this was definitely not the case, no traces of an aircraft were found. Another theory was that it was a stick of bombs that did not separate. Whatever it was I am glad it did not happen often, for that afternoon it took out most of two roads, with very heavy casualties.

I'll dwell no more on the second wave of the blitz, other than to say that 'no HE bomb fell on Burgess Avenue' and for that we were more than grateful, to say nothing of lucky.

Chapter Nine

Farewell to Kingsbury Senior School

In the second and third years at Kingsbury Senior we used to have an afternoon period spent Digging for Victory. For this we decamped to the girls' school in Old Church Lane. This had plenty of playing fields, unlike our school, and some of the area had been turned over to growing vegetables for school dinners. This we quite enjoyed. It took time to get there and made a change from school work. It also meant that we came into contact with the girls, who were now steadily moving up in our interest ratings. Last but not least, it gave us another chance for the psychological warfare with schoolmasters.

A master would stick his head round the classroom door and say, 'Okay lads, gardening tomorrow, I want bags of Dutch hoes and a couple of watering cans.'

We used to provide our own gardening implements. You can guess what was going to happen! The next day thirty-eight watering cans and two Dutch hoes would appear, and the master would shake his head in disbelief I don't know where this perverse nature comes from in children, but I don't think it has changed. That situation was considered hilarious. Woe betide any teacher who is foolish enough to be less than specific. Better still, he should give a couple of pupils the responsibility to ensure his instructions are met.

One afternoon the 'green finger brigade' were beavering away on the allotment. They were working fairly diligently, only stopping now and again to perform some piece of idiocy for the benefit of the girls (who were peeping from the windows of their classrooms). An air raid was in progress, but it had not got close enough to bother us. Suddenly whistles blew and claxons sounded, which was the 'get to the shelters' warning. The instructions were that we were to make for the nearest shelters and stay there until we were given the all clear. The shelters were the semi-underground type and adjoined the vegetable plots we were working on. They did not have electric lights in them at this stage and were badly lit by something similar to Davy lamps. When the whistles blew we downed tools and dashed, a few of us to each shelter, and joined the girls, as it happened, in the dark. It took the teachers some time to organise the lights. That afternoon brought about a change in the arrangements for the future. It was agreed that when the boys were there gardening, one shelter would be kept for their sole use. We were given lectures on our 'despicable behaviour' (a phrase much favoured by teachers) and threatened with having the privilege of slogging away gardening once a week withdrawn. It never came to that, as the separate shelter was a much better idea. We could not understand what all the fuss was about. The odd kiss and cuddle and a few moments' chaos did not seem such a crime. Then it became clearer. Some idiot had groped a teacher in the dark by mistake.

Whilst mentioning the digging for victory bit, there was another little episode that was quite amusing. Mr Hunkin's class was not actually working on gardening, but while he was taking us for a geography lesson, he dropped a very large bag of beans on the desk of one Daniel Wood. He was one of those lads of whom it would be unfair to say that 'his elevator did not go to the top floor,' but what was beyond question was that it took a long time arriving.

Mr Hunkin said, 'Divide those beans into two heaps, Wood.'

Some time passed and the class was getting twitchy. There was a fair amount of nudging going on, and more than a little concentration going into keeping straight faces. Dan, with a look of utmost concentration, was steadily counting the beans – but into one heap – '1033, 1034, 1035.' He was presumably going to find out the total, divide it by two, and count out that quantity. Mr Hunkin's gaze finally fell on Daniel, he paused, with a look of bewilderment, then bellowed like a wounded bull. This was followed by one of his most impressive 'over the top' performances. Still, Daniel survived; we all have our off days. When he left school he became a policeman (not that there is any significance in that!).

My education continued. The school had quite a formidable task with only three years to complete your education before you left at the age of fourteen. We had a metal workshop and woodwork room, both well-equipped. The main problem was that materials were hard to come by. One year we were all involved in a project of making wooden toys for young children. These were 'ducks on wheels', and when you pulled them along, their heads moved backwards and forwards. They were made from a zonking great tree trunk that arrived. We had to strip off the bark and cut it down into workable-sized pieces, before we could even start. In the finish we were quite proud of the completed toys, which were boxed up and sent to local crèches.

The science laboratory was also quite impressive, with sinks and gas taps for Bunsen burners. The only problem with the gas taps was that the kids used to keep turning them on and off, until you felt quite bad. The science teacher was a Mr Saville, who had been my form teacher in my first year. He was good at his job and fair, but a bit 'cane happy'. I think I suffered my highest ratio of canings per term, during that spell in his class. Maybe it was because we did not share the same sense of humour.

One day he was conducting an experiment with a glass container and cap. He had filled the container with, I think, hydrogen and it then involved dropping a piece of magnesium into the jar. It was not the most successful of his experiments, for I cannot remember what it was all about. What I can remember is he obviously did something wrong, delayed, or had too little or too much of the component parts perhaps. The net result was that when he dropped the piece of magnesium into the jar, there was a bang and flash of outstanding proportions. When he realised that he had still got his sight and was only missing most of his eyebrows, he peered round the laboratory looking for his class. He got the usual send-up from the boys, overdone as always with whimpering and cries of, 'Are you going to do that again, sir, or can we get back on our stools?'

Most of the masters taught specialised subjects, and were also form masters. So, for different periods, either the masters switched over or you trudged off to wherever the specialised rooms were. This system meant that you had continuity with the same teacher throughout the three years for English, history, maths etcetera. This was good news, if you had a good teacher, and bad if you did not, for it covered your whole period at the school.

Mr Holland took us for English, which also included the dreaded 'poetry', which I must admit, is the worst of the black holes in my appreciation of the arts. I love the theatre (including Shakespeare), music, and literature, but poetry, sorry, it does not get through to me. In my first year Mr Holland's instructions were to learn a poem of your own choice, with the afterthought that it must be not less than twenty lines. My choice was made with a ruler. I thumbed through my book of golden verse and found a poem with, I think, twenty-three lines and they were the shortest in the book. It was Longfellow's *Hiawatha Slays the Deer*, with the lines, 'Hidden in the alder bushes/there he waited/till the deer came.'

This stood me in good stead and I trotted it out term after term, thinking I was getting away with it. Then one term Mr Holland called my name out in a bored tone of voice, and said, 'All right, Vincent, let's get it over with, *Hiawatha Slays the Deer*, isn't it?'

The school hall was quite a good one, with lots of PT (physical training it was called then) equipment, climbing ropes, parallel bars, Swedish bars, pommel horses and vaulting boxes. This, unfortunately, was equipment I did not use for during a school medical examination it was decided that my spine was suspect, and I was instructed not to get involved in sports or exercises that could jar the spine. In fact, just to cheer me up, they gave me a mental picture of me lying on my back in plaster for eighteen months. This, of course, frightened the living daylights out of me, but as the years went by I found that I got away with more and more. I stopped worrying about it and grew confident, only sometimes worrying momentarily, if I got a particularly heavy thump on the back.

The school had virtually no involvement in sport, probably influenced by the lack of school fields. A hastily arranged cricket match was a rarity, and I cannot ever remember us being involved in a football match. At this time my favourite sport was, without doubt, cricket. Weekends and school holidays were almost entirely spent in the local park playing cricket. Malcolm and I would meet every morning with our cricket gear, join up with other like-minded lads, pick up sides, and play all day. I had my turns with the bat, but it was bowling that was my scene. I tried it all, leg breaks, off breaks and in the end settled down to being a medium to fast seam bowler. Keep the batsman from settling down, vary the length, cut them in, move them away. A bit of intimidation, but at that time the bouncer was not used. Anything on the leg side was usually severely punished and, therefore, only used in desperation. The height of my success was being picked to represent my regiment, the RASC (Royal Army Service Corps) when I was in Kenya. Although I played regularly until 1963, I cannot ever recall bowling a bouncer (intentionally). Obviously I used to play for slip catches, but nothing was as satisfying as seeing the stumps flying. I like to think that a good proportion of my deliveries, if missed, would have taken the stumps.

One morning, three of us sneaked into the school hall before morning assembly and climbed into the vaulting box, which stood at the side of the hall. Every morning it was the same routine. The boys filed in, with their classes and teachers in attendance. A couple of hymns were sung, there was a bit of a sermon from the head, and any items that affected the whole school were announced from the podium. After the announcements, the last hymn was sung and we marched from the hall.

While all this was taking place, we began to inch our way along the side of the hall, getting more ambitious as we went along. For, after all, if the boys hadn't noticed the moving vaulting box and were not having a laugh, there was no point in the exercise. Inside the box we could hear the laughter getting louder, until, finally, two teachers lifted the top off the box. 'All right, very funny, now you can get out and come with us.' This was to go before the head for punishment, the expected outcome, but worth it.

Punishment varied from teacher to teacher but was usually one of four basic items: the cane, which was the most commonly used (and funnily enough, preferred by the boys, for it was swift and did not drag on). Lines were probably the worst, as they had to be written in play and dinner breaks. The other problem with them was that you got more heaped on top, before you had finished the original ones. Conduct marks, which were, by and large, a joke. The boys, knowing they were on to a good thing, used to devote a lot of time and effort in getting across how we all hated them and appeared shattered when they were awarded. The last was detention after school, which was seldom used because of air raids, and getting everyone off the premises before dark.

My second year at the school was a good one for me. In the new class I sat next to a boy called Robert Oakes, who became a firm friend and partner in crime. My first year's exam results had been terrible. The months of missed schooling and the unfortunate spell at the convent school had taken their toll and my class position was right down at the bottom. This had pulled me up with a jerk, and the hard work I put into the second year really paid off. Not that Bob and I didn't get into our fair share of trouble. The form master, Mr Ridge, kept pointing out that our fooling around would get its 'comeuppance'. So when the end-of-year exam results came round, he skipped lightly over the first two positions as it was Bob in the number one slot and myself in the number two position. This meant that when the last year started we were in the A grade, and again we both made it into the top six.

It made a lot of difference sitting next to Bob. We both liked a laugh, but were also interested in any lessons that had not been designed to bore you to death! Prior to sitting next to Bob, I had a term of being next to a poor lad who had suffered from impetigo. To see the lad with horrific scabs all over him, which looked worse as they were painted with gentian violet, and the odd bits dropping off onto the desk occasionally, was not conducive to concentrating on your work. Another, but far more serious complaint, was mastoiditis, which could result in a very dangerous operation. They used to excavate a large semicircular crater behind the ear. Now they can usually cure this with antibiotics and no surgery is required. Thank goodness, so many of the everyday complaints that the children suffered from then, now seem to have been almost completely eradicated.

My third and last year was back with Mr Hunkin as form master. His 'over-the-top theatrics' were now rarely used. There was a mutual respect; we knew he was not to be trifled with and he was more relaxed and ready to join us in a laugh. This was also the year when we had all sorts of monitors' jobs to do one of which brought us to the brink of disaster. Bob and two others (whose names I cannot recall) and myself were given the job of getting a number of one-hundred and twelve pound bags of potatoes up to the canteen on the third floor. We carried several of them up and they were awkward to get hold of and heavy. We were completely fagged out, so we sat down and thought about it. The idea we came up with was to haul them up in the dumbwaiter. Here we had the problem of keeping the bag upright, so it did not jamb in the lift shaft. This we got round by the smallest in the party getting in the lift with the potatoes and holding them free from the sides. We got the dumbwaiter to somewhere between the second and third floor, when some master shouted, 'What are you boys doing with that lift?' Instead of answering that we were on legitimate business, we were startled and let go the ropes. The dumbwaiter, with its unaccustomed heavy load, rocketed to the ground floor with a bang. We rushed down to find potatoes all over the floor, and George, the boy in the lift, holding his head and quite badly shaken.

We then embarked on our third and last brainwave. Bob said, 'What we'll do is lift the sack onto the banister rail and slide it up.' This suggestion, which, in hindsight, had all the necessary ingredients for disaster, we readily accepted. The first of the two sacks we had left worked like a charm and the second one was moving steadily up the last slope to the top floor when it started to overbalance. We struggled momentarily, but could not hold it, and then it was gone down the stairwell. It fell the full three floors and smashed onto the quarry-tiled floor below. We dashed down the flights of stairs and when we got to the bottom there were potatoes splattered all over the place. Even worse, standing with the back door open and in a state of shock, was the school caretaker – who had been narrowly missed by a hundredweight of potatoes, dropped from three floors above. The really strange thing was that he did not drop us in it, a pastime that school caretakers are renowned for. We wondered if he was concerned that, as we had a few months to go, we might get him the next time.

End of term reached, we all said our fond farewells and, although we had all moaned about the place (referring to it as 'Colditz' and suchlike), when it came to leaving, it was with a mixture of sadness and excitement at the thought of having a go at the world outside. We did a few victory circuits of the quadrangle on our bikes, to prove we had left (at no other time would we have dared). A good number of us would be back before long, to enrol for a couple of years at night school.

I still think the school did a good job in the circumstances, bearing in mind that we left at fourteen years of age, but they could have had a little more imagination with the name! Over the years I have had to submit numerous CVs, and application forms for new positions. In the details of education section 'Kingsbury

Senior Boys' was an entry where you could not imagine the selection committee saying, 'Kingsbury Senior Boys, we must have a real high-flyer here!'

Chapter Ten

PJ and the Lodgers

In the early days, before my brother and I were old enough to be out at work, we used to have a lodger. Some people refer to them as a 'paying guest' and, to be fair, the reason we had one was to help financially. The main exception to this was 'PJ' (Percival James Wilson), my mother's brother. He was by trade a compositor, and since 1924 had been employed as a ship's printer. He was employed in this capacity by a number of shipping lines, P&O, White Star and Shaw Saville. He had travelled the world – America, Australia, New Zealand, India, and the Far East. You name it, he had been there. Whenever he was on shore leave or when he changed shipping lines, he stayed with us. On a number of occasions he decided to make a living on land, but it never worked out – he would soon be off to sea again. He was a bachelor and not only did the life appeal to him, but it was also quite lucrative. As the ship's printer you had officer status, a cabin of your own, laundry and valet service. Cigarettes and drink were cheap and entertainment free. You saw the world and met interesting people. In those days, it was the way people travelled distances; airlines were not as yet serious competition.

The ships were the large passenger ships or they would not have carried a ship's printer. He had to produce a ship's newspaper, bulletins, daily menus and programmes for events held on board, including horse-racing cards (you are right, they weren't real horses, the ships weren't that big). In addition to these duties the ship's printer was usually an able photographer, developing passengers' photographs that they had taken when ashore in different ports of call. He was also able to provide a service for enlargements, taking group photos for passengers and providing souvenir menus with photos of the liner mounted on the front. These services used to be done on the printers' own initiative, what they made in profit was theirs and could be quite a good sideline.

The only time you drew salary was either at the end of the run for your shore leave, or if you had time ashore in any interesting port of call, while the ship was being refuelled and provisioned for the return trip. For a thrifty man money could be put by for the future. PJ was not a thrifty man. What he was extremely good at was having a good time. I am sure that when he was at sea he enjoyed himself, and when he was ashore I know he did. The people he knew and mixed with, in the 'Twenties and Thirties', always had money to spend on enjoying themselves. Where it came from – a mystery – they never appeared to have jobs. This was not the case with his friends from the ship, who were usually people like the purser, the chef, stewardesses and so on. One of his friends (a Tommy Wiltshire) was straight out of a P.G. Wodehouse book. He would turn up in a green MG Open Tourer (the two-litre one, not the Midget) wearing a check suit with plus fours, a cap to match, yellow pullover and smoking a cigarette in a long holder. The only disappointment to me was he did not have a monocle. They would all pile into his MG and then go off for a day at the races.

When ashore, PJ seldom rose from his bed until about 10 a.m. but, to be fair, he was seldom back home till the early hours of the morning. When he did get up, he wandered about in his dressing gown (a very tasteful silk job with dragons on it). He only got properly dressed when he was about to go out. The reasons given for why he stopped with us were mixed. One version was that only my father and mother would put up with him. The other was that he liked stopping with us. We were an easygoing family and pretty high up the unshockable scale for that period, but I like to think it was the latter. Our house was full of curios and mementoes, oriental rugs, wooden carvings, ornamental daggers (made from Japanese coins strung together), things from Dakar, Bombay, Yokohama, all giving the house a much-travelled look. My mother was supposed to be paid something for his keep, to say nothing of his friends who were often there for meals. I am sure she was, but he was so easygoing with his money and lifestyle it was best to catch him early on, for by the time he was due back, my father had been known to pay his cab fare to get him back to his ship as PJ was spent out.

One of the 'PJ' stories was his arrival one Christmas at the home of his eldest sister, where his mother was living at the time. As usual his appearance was unheralded and out of the blue. The family was all gathered for Christmas, aunts, uncles, cousins and so forth. The whisper went round PJ was downstairs but not to let his mother know, the reason being that he was somewhat the worse for drink (like legless), and his mother would be upset. Two of his brothers-in-law, my father and Uncle Charlie headed him off and took him to the pub at the end of the road. A strange choice to sober someone up, you might think, but not so. Firstly, it was somewhere he would agree to go and secondly, it had a snooker room, a game that PJ loved. The story goes that he was only allowed one half-pint of beer, and by the time he had played three frames of snooker, he was sober enough to see his mother. Only one problem had occurred, early on in the first frame. He had been crouching down to line up a shot, lost his balance, and sat on the open fire. It was agreed by those present that there was nothing the matter with his reactions. He did not hang about getting off the fire!

He could be a bit over the top at times, turning up with a load of his cronies from the ship, and announcing that there was going to be a party. Not taking into consideration that as far as my mother and father were concerned, the next day was a normal weekday with children to get to school, and my father had to leave for work at 6.30 a.m. To have it announced at 10.30 p.m. that a party was about to start and knowing it would go on until the early hours was not all that popular. Soon after the outbreak of war it was agreed that ship's printers were not required on ships that were only carrying cargo or military personnel. He was not happy at this, and managed to get on a gunnery course due to his service in the 1914–1918 war. This came about as they were arming merchant ships – due to their being attacked by submarines – as well as from the air and with mines. He went right through the war mostly on the American run with the odd trip to Australia, South America, and Canada. You did not spend those war years on Atlantic convoys without seeing plenty of action. Fortunately, none of the ships he was on were sunk while he was on them, but three were on the next trip out. On each occasion his luck held, once for the gunnery course, once through illness, and on one even luckier occasion when he was asked to change ship. All three were sunk on the next voyage or shortly after.

Whenever he arrived home, he would always have a small crate of goodies for us to help out with the rations. American Spam, tins of sausage meat, and dried egg – what luxury! Shortly after the war ended we lost him after a short illness, he was fifty-seven years old. I can remember saying to my brother at the funeral, 'That wasn't very old was it?' and he replied, 'No, but just think of what he packed into those years; people live twenty years longer and have not done half as much!' Keith has a habit of making the odd philosophical remark like that. I had to agree with him, and it made me feel better.

In the early Thirties my mother had a knock on the door and opened it to find a man, six foot seven inches tall and with bright red hair, standing on the doorstep.

He said, 'I am told you may be prepared to take a lodger.'

My mother showed him the room, he paid a couple of weeks rent in advance and left his suitcase. His name was Fred Hunter. When my father came home, she told him of the new lodger and said that he seemed like a professional man. Well turned out and nicely spoken, he had paid two weeks in advance and left his case. Some weeks passed and Fred did not return. My parents decided to give him a bit longer and then they would have to look in his case to see if it would give them a lead to follow up. A couple more weeks passed and they decided to open the case; it was not locked and when they opened it they were surprised to find it only held a shirt and a pair of braces. Time passed and he turned up again, this time with two more suitcases and said he was sorry not to have contacted us but he had been called away. If his room was still available he would like to have it. It was, and he was with us for a number of years. He was another character, we never knew where he had disappeared to, and he never volunteered the information. My parents had a strange feeling that he had been in prison, but this was never proved or admitted. He was a very generous man, he used to take Keith and me out for spins in the most super cars and buy chocolates for my mother. My father got on well with him, apart from having to get a bit heavy about the payment of his rent, from time to time. He had a string of strange jobs – at one period he was selling surgical instruments and at another electrical goods.

He was on the GEC (General Electric Company) stand at Radio Olympia, and gave us a magnificent and much admired GEC radiogram in lieu of rent. He also had a spell at repossessing cars, where people had not kept up their repayments. For this he had a load of keys and was well able to hot-wire them if need be, if he had not got the right key. They usually worked in pairs for safety. He was a big man, well-built and in proportion with his six foot seven inches height. There could not have been many people who fancied taking a crack at him, but on rare occasions they did. People can get funny when they see their cars being driven away (even if unpaid for) not necessarily seeing the subtle difference between theft and repossession, especially if they did not have a lot of payments left to make. The laws governing hire-purchase in those days were very different from now regarding fairness.

He was a mystery man; we never really knew about his background but felt he was the black sheep of his family. He finally left us and got married and settled down, having at least one child – they dropped in to see us on a few occasions. When the war broke out some of the questions were answered, for he was immediately called up into the army as a commissioned officer. He had apparently been trained at Sandhurst and served for a period before he came to us – yet another mystery! Unfortunately we heard later that Fred had been killed in action during the landings in North Africa at Phillipville. News that we were all most upset to hear.

The next in the list of lodgers was 'Pooky Jones'. Pooky was not, you will be unsurprised to know, his real name. This was coined by my father, who said he reminded him of the character in the Popeye cartoon strip who was always eating hamburgers and wore a similar jacket. Pooky's jackets, like the cartoon character's, had sleeves intended for a man with the physical characteristics of an orang-utan, they covered his hands to knuckle length; he was definitely a contrast to his predecessor – the suave Fred. He was working at the De Havilland Aircraft Factory – as a storeman. He was a Salvation Army man, and did not endear himself to us or our neighbours, by practising on his euphonium.

My outstanding memory of Pooky was the boxing tournament. It would be hard to imagine a more timid, inoffensive man than Pooky, so it was mind-blowing to hear him announce one night at dinner that he had entered 'the DeHavilland works boxing tournament'. My father was immediately interested; he enjoyed most sport and had himself played rugby and boxed when in the army.

'Do you know anything about it?' he asked. 'Have you done any boxing before?'

Pooky answered that he had not and this would be his first go at it.

'Right,' said my father, 'we will have to get you organised!'

He immediately put our neighbour, Alf Wallis, in the picture, and number thirteen was turned into the training camp. A punchball, boxing gloves and skipping rope appeared as if from nowhere, and Bert and Alf got down to the serious business of turning Pooky into a world-beater. This was optimism of the highest order. Pooky had all the natural inbuilt aggression of a butterfly, but he was kept at it by his trainers. One night, Bert was sparring with him a bit overenthusiastically and belted him on the nose. The night's training had to be abandoned, while the duo tried to stop his nose bleeding.

The great night of the tournament arrived and Bert and Alf set out for DeHavilland's at Stag Lane with their protégé. The night, as far as they were concerned, was, all in all, not a success. When their man entered the ring, he danced around for a while, flicking out the left jab as instructed, but then the game plan changed. His opponent gave him a pretty hefty whack on the nose. Pooky dropped to the floor immediately, and would not get up, in spite of the encouragement (and threats) from his trainers. The training camp was dismantled, the trainers left the fight game and 'One Round Pooky' fought no more.

Chapter Eleven

Working for a Living

Having left school, what was I to do for work and a future career? I had no great thoughts on the subject. There was no burning desire to be an engine driver or field marshal, and if I had some natural gift, then neither the education system, nor myself had noticed it. So, when it was suggested that I take a job with the MCC (don't get excited – the Middlesex County Council, not the ones who wear the red and yellow tie) with a view to being a weights and measures inspector, it seemed worth a go. It would mean some years' training and sitting some exams to qualify, but appeared to be an interesting occupation. My interview at the divisional finance offices in Willesden was successful and I had a starting date in September.

This meant that I had time to kill and I went on a prolonged holiday. My father had arranged for my mother and me to spend two weeks at a cottage in Corfe Mullen, situated between Poole and Wimborne in Dorset. This was to be a memorable holiday. The family we were staying with – The Heckfords – were great, and made us very welcome. When we left London it was in the midst of yet another onslaught from the Germans, this time in the form of doodlebugs and rockets. The landings in Normandy had been successful and it looked, at last, as though the end of the war was in sight. My father spent the two weeks with us and then returned to London to work. Due to the good offices of the Heckfords, my mother and I stayed on for six weeks. What a holiday! We would leave Corfe Mullen every morning, catching a bus to Poole, and then there was a choice of any one of five buses to Bournemouth. When we got there, my mother would make up a picnic lunch and then it was down to the beach for the day. Each day we would get a tray with a pot of tea for two, China teapot and cups and saucers, all for a modest price – and a deposit of two shillings and sixpence. As my mother did only so many miles to the gallon of tea, this usually occurred three times every day. There was a good long area of beach cleared for bathing, and apart from the steel anti-landing craft defences and a gap they had blown up in the middle of the pier, it was holidays as usual.

This was the first time I had been in the sea since I was eight years old, as all the holiday resorts we could get to were restricted areas because they were on the coasts where a German invasion was expected. Our local swimming pool had been closed, there were no facilities at school, and I had not learned to swim. It was not surprising that with all the time I was spending in the sea, I soon could. I spent my time diving off the barge defences, learning the different strokes and improving the distances I could swim. In addition there were rounders and cricket to play on the beach with others of similar age and it was one of the happiest of times. I have always had a soft spot for Bournemouth, probably due to that very holiday. Even so, it is an area of our coast that is hard to beat; it has some of our best beaches, warmest sea and very picturesque scenery. It is also my belief that it does have, on average, the most consistently good weather in the country.

The time came for it all to end I had to get myself sorted out and prepared for making a start at earning my living. The date was drawing near for my starting with the MCC. My work outfit was purchased. I had been informed at my interview that I had a choice, either black jacket and morning trousers or black jacket and dark-grey flannels. I opted for the latter, as I thought it would look slightly less funereal. To top this off – black shoes and a plain white shirt. No coloured or striped shirts would be tolerated and only a sober tie.

This was no joke. On one occasion, due to an accident when a fountain pen leaked all over my jacket, it had to be cleaned. As it was midweek and I only had the one jacket, the problem arose of what I was going to wear. The only alternative was a brown, yellow and fawn lumberjacket. I had no choice – I went in that. There was no easy escape clause, even though it was the summer, I could not get in early and walk around in my shirt, for that was not allowed, whatever the temperature. It took just under ten minutes for me to be called in to Mr Chapman. I explained the circumstances – to no avail. He was aghast that anyone could possess such a hideous jacket, unless they worked in a North American timber forest. I was informed that it would not be tolerated a second time. If I was accident-prone then a standby jacket must be obtained. Then, having been given all the threats and warnings, I was given one day's dispensation to carry on jacketless. Even this, he explained, was preferable to that sartorial monstrosity!

When I started work I was four-foot ten inches tall, a detail that was established at my school-leaving medical. Four years later, when I had my army medical, I was six foot tall. You can see that I did not wear out many clothes at this time of my life, I grew out of them at an alarming rate. The office that I worked in was shared with two very nice ladies (typists/secretaries), a Mrs Fraser and a Miss Dawson. The excitement element of my job was not high, broadly speaking it was handling the post. Not the position I went for, but one that I was asked to carry out until the vacancy in 'weights and measures' was available.

During the day I would make frequent trips with my wire basket, out of my office, down six steps, across a landing and up six steps into the accounts office. Here a number of clerks were beavering away making out invoices for their respective areas. The areas were numbered and the numbers displayed on their desks. The invoices were all for services rendered by Middlesex County Council hospitals or home help services. I would troll along, collecting all these, and return. Out of the office, down six steps, across the landing, up six steps and back into my own office. The non-private ones were then folded into window envelopes and entered as bulk post, and the private ones had the addresses typed on a plain envelope, the invoice enclosed, and then sealed. These were entered separately in the post book. Not too exacting a task, one you would think difficult to get wrong – but not impossible! I managed to get two invoices mixed up and put in the wrong envelopes. Both people rejoiced in the name of Smith and even had the same initial. The problem was that one invoice was for a gentleman whose wife had just given birth in Bushey Maternity Hospital, and the other gentleman was paying towards his wife's stay in Shenley Mental Hospital, where she had been for some years. They were both very upset, and I had to go round to both and apologise, once the dreadful deed was traced back to me!

The months went by and one thing was becoming evident – the weights and measures job was definitely on the back burner. Some of the staff used to play table tennis every night after work, and I really used to enjoy that. Some of the youths who played were weights and measures trainees and they cheered me up no end, by explaining that over the past four years a steady stream of young men had been called up into the services. The result would be that, as soon as the war ended, they would be demobbed, making an average of four men for each job available. This certainly looked the case, and I was getting edgy. I did not know how long I could take the job I was doing, which was about as interesting as watching paint dry!

By now I had started going down less steps between the offices and was managing to jump from the fourth step, across the landing, to the fourth step on the other side. It was my ambition to clear the lot, all six steps on both sides and the landing – I was sure I could do it. Sure enough, the day came. I emerged from accounts with my wire tray full of invoices, on my return journey to my office. Decision time – this was the day! I sprinted the few strides and hurled myself across the gap. I was the thickness of the soles of my shoes from success. My shoes just caught the top of the sixth step and I went into a 'free fall' situation. The wire basket flew through the air and the invoices came fluttering down from above. Meanwhile, I was not wasting my time – I was sliding along the highly polished parquet floor on my stomach at a fair old lick. As I shot past my office door, it opened and Mr Knox, the divisional finance officer, (there was no higher 'being' in the building) stood there. The expression on his face as I shot by was impassive. One would assume that he had spent most of his life watching office boys hurtle by on their stomachs, with it raining invoices from above.

'Good morning, Vincent!' he said, and walked off.

Several months later I obtained an interview with Mr Knox, and I have to smile when I think of it. There I was, by now just five foot tall, still fourteen years of age, in my black jacket and grey baggy trousers, complaining that the job of stamp licking, which I had been doing for the last nine months, was not what I had come for, and what was my future? Mr Knox came clean and said it was highly unlikely that there would be a vacancy in 'weights and measures'. The best he could do was to arrange for me to be transferred to the wages department at Edgware.

Anything was preferable to my current boring situation, so I took the transfer that was offered.

The Edgware job proved to be marginally less boring. It meant I was a bit better off financially, for I was able to cycle there and save my bus fares. I was calculating people's wages, using a vast 'Kalamazoo' system. It consisted of large sheets (containing God knows how many wage slips per sheet) in metal binders that took up all your desk when open. Again it was the staff of MCC hospitals that we were paying out. Bushey, Shenley, Redhill and others. A sign of the times was that when we paid out Redhill Hospital, which was about half a mile further up the Edgware Road from us, we used to walk, one of the young ladies, who was going to do the actual payout, and me, carrying a large wooden case which contained all the made-up wage envelopes. Quite a considerable amount of money. Painted on the side of the case, in large white letters, was 'Middlesex County Council Wages Office'. The only words missing were 'Take Me!' By now I was marginally over five foot tall and weighed about eight stone. I don't think I would have struck terror into your fully qualified wage snatcher. Fortunately, whilst I was doing this job, nothing of this nature occurred. I was probably more in danger of being done over by a gardener or porter who thought his wages were wrong!

The staff consisted of ninety per cent young to youngish ladies, in the eighteen to twenty-six years age group, and four old men (at that age anyone over fifty seemed old). In my office it was just the ladies and me, and they really used to tease me. They would straighten their stockings, even adjust their suspenders, as if I wasn't there. I am sure they used to notice my red face and the fact that it took quite a time to get my eyes back in their sockets. The worst trick that they played on me was to send me to the workshops at Redhill Hospital, to get some Kalamazoo binders repaired.

They gave me the directions to get to the mortuary, and I fell for it. It was quite an upsetting experience.

One of my friends, John Playfoot, was training to be an estate agent and valuer with a firm in Edgware. We used to meet for lunch at a British Restaurant in Edgwarebury Lane. These restaurants did not, by and large, have a good reputation, but this one was excellent. We would chat over dinner and make plans for the evening, such as what films we wanted to see. At that time our crowd was down to the three musketeers, John Playfoot, David Pike and myself. Malcolm was at this time well tied up, still at school at Harrow High, and up to his neck in exams. John and I got into the habit of playing chess whilst we ate our lunch, which proved to be a bit of a disaster. We often got so involved that we forgot what the time was which meant scuttling off back to work, hoping no one would spot our late arrival. It was during one of these lunch hours that I was sat on the long seat at the back of a trolleybus opposite the platform for getting on and off. There were no doors on the buses' platforms in those days, and it was not unusual for passengers to jump on and off while the bus was moving. (The Health and Safety Authority no doubt stopped this practice by fitting doors eventually). The conductor was standing on the platform at the foot of the stairs, checking his tickets, when a man, certainly not in the full flush of youth, came down the stairs in between stops and angled himself across the platform at about forty-five degrees. My interest was aroused. The conductor also looked on with interest. The trolleybus was clipping along at an estimated twenty-five mph plus, and it was pouring with rain. To our amazement he dropped off the bus. He would have given Lynford Christie a run for his money, but his calculations were faulty. His body came back up into the vertical very quickly – a short pause – and then he splatted on the pavement. The conductor said 'Bloody

Idiot' and then lost interest. We were soon out of sight and did not see him peeled off the pavement. Maybe some passing Health and Safety inspector-to-be was a witness and made a mental note.

It was around this time that David Pike and I were over in the local park having a knock-about at cricket. David was two years my senior and a very useful cricketer. He was equally at home with the bat or ball. We were approached by a young man who asked us, 'Have you got any whites?' We both answered quickly that we had.

'Do you fancy turning out for us? We are a couple of men short.'

We both said that we would, and dashed off back home to change into our gear, pick up our bats, and dash back to the park.

The opposition batted first and we did not disgrace ourselves in the field. Then the club we were playing for went in to bat. They had watched David batting, and they played him at number six and he did very well. In fact he was still at the wicket when I joined him at number eleven. There was one ball left in the over for me to face, and I got all the advice. Just stand there with your bat in front of the wicket. Don't try anything clever like hitting it. (They had seen me bat as well). The odds are they won't get your wicket, if you just stand there and take guard middle and leg. Your friend will get the runs we need in the next over. As I said earlier, I played cricket for quite a few years, and never did I walk out to the crease more determined that my wicket would not fall. I took my time taking guard and waited. The bowler was nowhere to be seen, then I picked out an advancing cloud of dust hurtling towards me. I got a quick glimpse of huge feet pounding in and an arm whipping over.

When I came round in the pavilion with my broken nose and bloodstained shirt, at least my team were not blaming me. They were indignant at the treatment I had received. Statements like, 'He's only a lad. What was he trying to do – kill him!' The bowler's version was that the ball had slipped out of his hand. The result was that the first point of contact after it had left it was my 'hooter', and it was going some! I was never much use with the bat and held my place in teams with my bowling and slip fielding. That early experience, though, must have had its effect, for when I received body-line deliveries after that, I must admit that the thoughts of shall I hook it or turn it to leg were secondary to can I get out of the bloody way!

The office job with the MCC was by now reaching the point where I had achieved a level of boredom that I had previously thought to be impossible. There was no doubt in my mind that I had to find an alternative. As if in answer to my prayer, the solution to the problem was right under my nose. To be more precise, it was at the bottom of the road, a Printer's and Stationer's, with a sign in the window – 'Smart Lad Wanted'. Those were the actual words, and without more ado, I walked into the shop and was interviewed there and then. The position on offer was that of an apprentice printer. The final area of the apprenticeship to be agreed after I had spent three months each, in the composing room and machine room. The decision would then be made as to whether the apprenticeship would be as a compositor, or letterpress machine minder. The date of the apprenticeship would be backdated to the day I started. The pay was awful, for in those days teaching you a trade was considered to be part of the remuneration. Fifteen shillings for a forty-eight and a half hour week. This meant a big drop in my wages to start with, in fact it was pretty poor money for the whole seven years of the apprenticeship. The job, once you were a journeyman, was thought to be reasonable. There was also the fact that it could lead to working on national newspapers, which were very well paid. At the time I started my apprenticeship, a journeyman compositor was paid four pounds sixteen shillings per week.

My father went to see my future boss to ensure that I would receive a proper apprenticeship and that he was happy with the set-up. All was agreed, including my starting date, and all that was left for me to do was to give my notice to the MCC. No longer would the black jacket and grey trousers be obligatory workwear, and an exciting new world awaited.

Chapter Twelve

The Apprenticeship Years

The company that I signed my apprenticeship with had only recently been started up. The owner had been in business with his father and brothers before the war and decided to have a go on his own when he was demobbed. . His father had given him some of the equipment to assist him to make the start but now it was up to him. In the beginning the owner split his time between the departments, setting type, running a machine, and cutting on the guillotine. One other man, John Payne, operated a machine and, for a short time, that was the whole staff.

I was thrown in at the deep end, and in my first week began setting jobs, having had brief instruction from my boss and with a watchful eye being kept on what I was doing. One of the first tasks I was asked to carry out was to clean out all the typecases. This entailed taking every piece of type out of the case and transferring it all into the correct compartments of a clean case. This had become necessary because the printing works that they had all been in had been bombed in the war. So, after the type had been transferred to a clean case, the original one had all the brick dust removed and was dusted thoroughly ready to be refilled with type.

The job was monotonous at times, as with the case cleaning, but was interesting when setting work or running the machines. It also had its menial tasks such as sweeping up, making tea or taking parcels to the post office. The main thing that appealed was the variety and the fact that you never really knew what you would be doing the next day. This certainly was more in keeping with my temperament than the same old office routine week in and week out that I had been doing in my previous job. Some days I would be sent to 'Rudges' to drop a guillotine knife in for grinding and pick up the sharpened one. Or to one of the ink manufacturers to collect some ink we needed urgently. One of these suppliers was notorious with London apprentices for the time you spent there. You would hand in your order and then go and sit on a bench until your order was ready and your name called. All round the walls there were notices scrawled in pencil or scratched in the paint, saying things like: 'Died waiting – March '46' or 'Don't worry – they close at 5.30 p.m.'

These trips to town were a good thing, apart from getting out and about there was money to be made! There was twopence difference in the fares from Kingsbury to Hendon Central and Golders Green. Which way you went could be decided by which bus came first, an 83 or a 183, both were legitimate routes. As a hard up apprentice you caught the cheapest and booked the dearest. This meant you could pocket fourpence per round trip. Three trips in a week and you were on for a night at the cinema, price of a ticket one shilling. In addition to this, a lot of the work the firm carried out was for the dressmaking (Sorry!) gown trade. One of these companies that I used to deliver to in Regent Street often asked me to push a rack full of completed gowns to other premises which were only three or four hundred yards away. For that service they would tip me the princely sum of two shillings and sixpence. This was a lot, when you take into consideration that a week's pay for me was fifteen shillings, ten of which went to my mother towards my keep. Two of those small errands for them meant the equivalent of a weeks wage's to me.

On one occasion I had to collect some blank swing tickets from John Dickinsons at Tottenham. I arrived at the gatehouse and handed over the order. After a while a small tractor towing some trucks arrived.

'Where's your van?' I was asked.

'I haven't got one, what have I got to take?' I answered.

He pointed at a large parcel in one of the trucks. I gave the gateman what I hoped was a withering look, heaved the parcel onto my shoulder and walked off. The road was dead straight until it reached the T-junction with the main road, and that was at least three hundred yards. With the gateman and driver's eyes on my back, there was no way that I was going to put that parcel down or stop for a blow, until I was out of sight. It was one of the longest three hundred yards I have ever walked.

After some months had passed a new member of staff was taken on, he was a compositor and I would be working under him – a Mr Lawson. His Christian name was Jim, but in those days the apprentice/journeyman relationship was formal. He was referred to as Mr Lawson. I think it was about two years before I was allowed to call him Jim. When he was younger he had been a keen amateur boxer, and had taken part in the Printers' Boxing Championships that were held at the Albert Hall every year. It was all decided on the night, if you won your first bout you went on to the next. The winner had three fights on the night. Jim was still very keen on the sport and would shape up to you every now and again and throw a few playful punches at you. This quickly taught me to block or ride a punch – they weren't all that playful. I enjoyed working with him and used to be amused by some of his sayings and his philosophy. For instance, his approach to sales promotion and advertising was summed up by one phrase, 'They (the public) would buy shit if you wrapped it up!' His pet hate, which was almost obsessional, was any entertainer who involved the audience in his act. For instance, 'You all know this one – so all join in!' The performer then sings the odd word or two, while the audience sing. Jim would say, 'I pay good money to be entertained – I can sing any time I like, and I don't have to pay for it!'

The company was growing and we now had four journeymen and three apprentices (of whom I was the senior). One afternoon a lorry pulled up outside the works, with a dismantled prefabricated building on the back. The boss gave us a shout and we all went down to help offload it into the area behind the works. This was all done quite cheerfully, including ribbing Jim, when he offloaded the toilet, with such as, 'You all right Dan?', 'You're looking a bit flushed!', 'Don't let the boss catch you sitting down on the job!' The next day the boss informed the apprentices that he would acquire picks and shovels and, as it was a nice summer, we could get some fresh air and dig out the foundations. This resulted in my first foray into representing my fellow workers. The other apprentices strongly resented being used as navvies – they were print apprentices, and did not see what wielding picks and shovels had to do with print. I agreed to be spokesman and arranged a meeting with the boss.

We all trooped into his office.

'Well, what's the problem?' he asked, and I informed him that we all objected to navvying when we were supposed to be learning our trade as printers. He then asked the others, one at a time, if they objected. I stood there and could not believe my ears – as they each said they didn't mind. I am afraid that I did not learn from this experience and was to find myself in similar circumstances on many more occasions. The request for us to dig the foundations, however, was dropped, although I am sure that I was now labelled a 'troublemaker'.

The period of working within a short walk of my home was about to come to end (never to repeated). The company was growing, the 'prefab' was never erected, and we were informed that we were off to another factory site in Willesden. The new factory was certainly not 'new' and, although conditions improved the longer we were there, they were very bad at first. Only cold water was available, and that from a tap in the yard. One outside toilet across the yard and 'weevils'. The factory had been a bakery and weevils used to drop off the ceiling and amble about the place. They would get into your clothes when they were hung up during the day. Sometimes, on the way home on the bus, you noticed the passenger next to you staring at you and edging away, or even hurriedly changing seats. You would then carry out a quick weevil check, and, if you found one strolling along your collar or up your neck, you would speedily bring about its demise. People, by and large, were not overfamiliar with weevils and would understandably confuse them with another species.

When we were visited by the factory inspector, he insisted that hot water should be available in the factory and a light should be in the outside toilet. The boss went straight down to Woolworth's and bought the smallest and cheapest paraffin lamp available. He then screwed a small shelf on the wall and placed the lamp on it. On a windy day or night, as the door had a large gap top and bottom, it was very draughty in there. By the time you had lit the damn lamp, if your need was urgent, you could well have had a nasty accident. There was, of course, no heating and in the winter the boss did not have to worry about anyone spending unnecessary time in there.

We soon found that the factory was consistent, just as it was far too cold in the winter it was far too hot in the summer. To improve our working conditions we worked out our 'punkah' system. We attached string to the clamshell platen machines, so that, when they opened and closed to print, the string was pulled and released. Throughout the works we had hung large sheets of strawboard, suspended from the electrical conduit tubing. They were weighted with lead, so that they returned to their original position. Customers who came into the factory would stand and stare in amazement to see all the strings and pulleys and sheets of strawboard swinging to and fro. It looked like something that Heath Robinson dreamed up on one of his off days!

For entertainment during this period there was the cinema. In the area there were two different programmes available at both the ABC and Odeon cinemas. Two independents and one Classic – The Classic had a change of programme every three days and on Sundays. This meant that if you could afford it you could see a different film every night of the week. We certainly used to see our fair share. If I were asked to appear on *Mastermind* then 'Films 1930 to 1948', as my specialist subject would be a good bet. In addition to the cinemas there were local theatres. The Coliseum Harrow used to put on straight plays, and the Golders Green Hippodrome musicals, band shows, and variety. In those days the theatre meant a seat in the gods (the balcony) where the seats were packed in and not the place for anyone suffering from vertigo. One of the gags that artists used to do was to say looking up at the gods, 'Can you see me up there?' and then lie flat on the stage so that you had a better perspective. Memorable nights were spent there seeing big bands like The Squadronaires, Oscar Rabin, and Ted Heath. There were also variety shows with people like Jimmy Wheeler, Jimmy James, and early appearances of newcomers like Professor Jimmy Edwards and Frankie Howerd. Falling somewhere between these would be the Billy Cotton Band Show and Sid Milward and his Nitwits.

In the daytime there was cricket, cycling (touring and time trials), and ice-skating. The ice-skating was done at the Empire Pool, Wembley, which had public skating sessions two or three times a day (apart from the evenings when there were ice hockey matches being played or the training sessions). Usually when you started to skate you hired your skates and, if you found you were going to take it up and wanted to achieve any proficiency, you bought your own. This had two advantages, one, the money you were saving in not hiring soon paid for the skates and from then on reduced your costs, and two, you could skate on them. Hired skates are usually unbelievably bad, they have the blades fitted at an angle of forty-five degrees and the last time the blades were ground – they had to wait for them to finish sharpening Wallace's axe. This, I think, has a lot to do with the large number of people at public skating rinks splitting their time fairly evenly between clinging to the barrier, short-duration aerobics and lying prostrate on the ice.

We were into hockey tubes similar to the skates worn by hockey players. Figure skates were the other type available and they were designed specifically for figure skating and ice dancing. This being long before the fantastic skating performances of people like Curry and Cousins, these were considered to be weedy and effeminate by your average 'Jack-the-lads' and fit only for girlies and woofters. No doubt the amazing feats that have since been achieved by the leading exponents of the art have modified opinions, but I would not put any money on it.

During the public skating sessions there used to be two twenty-minute breaks for the ice dancers to practise. After one of these sessions there used to be periods of lunacy called 'Men's and Women's (Amazons only) Speed-Skating

Sessions'. The women's session was hair-raising enough but the men's was unbelievable. When the session started, the music played was usually *The Sabre Dance*. The macho brigade powered onto the ice and hurtled round the rink at an unbelievable speed. The ultimate was to lead the pack, at least for a few circuits. According to the number of skaters and their relative standards or lunacy rating, it either remained as a pack or got very confusing, as the fastest skaters began to lap the others. Week after week I used to sit there and think, I'll go in it tonight, but it was a definite case of he who hesitates is lost. One night I sat in the seats just behind the barrier and hesitated as usual. The pack were hurtling round at tremendous speed, and the leader was leaning so far over as he took the bends that his left hand was touching the ice. Suddenly he lost it! I think it was one of his laces that had worked loose and got under the blade of his skate. He cartwheeled across the ice, sailed right over the barrier and came down in the horizontal position on a row of seats a little way from where I sat. The first-aid men, who were always in attendance, peeled him, unconscious, off the seats and stretchered him away. That was the night when the urge to enter speed-skating sessions suddenly left me.

When I watch the figure skating and dancing on television these days and see a number of brilliant skaters fall, I think back to my skating days and remember how different the ice could be at different sessions. Sometimes it was just right, your blades gripped and you were completely confident. Other times the ice was like iron, and you had your work cut out to stay on your feet. Surely at this the highest level of competition the ice is controlled – to be just so – but, when I see the world-class skaters fall – and when they do it's usually several of them – I wonder about it!

Cycling was another pastime, touring, time trials, and road racing. The touring has very pleasant memories for the most part, but the road racing and time trials were a different matter. These consisted of pushing your body to its limits, with the obvious pain and exhaustion that that entailed, so it was much harder to see where the pleasure lay. There were similarities to distance running. The same pleasurable feeling when the body was working smoothly, the controlled effort that settled into a routine. Legs, arms, breathing, all functioning well, and the feeling of controlled, successful physical effort was very satisfying. The problems all came from pushing yourself too hard, or at least pushing yourself beyond your body's present capability.

When I used to take part in the sport we used to all race with fixed gears. The use of multiple speed gears was considered unreliable. Sturmey-Archer three speed was rejected due to its weight and the dérailleur type at that time was not considered strong enough. At critical times, such as at the start of a race, the rider's legs would thrust down with considerable force and the chain would leap off the sprocket, or worse, the gear system would fly in all directions. A freewheel was not used as at that time, the belief was that the relaxing of the muscles whilst racing was a bad thing. The winning times for a twenty-five mile race in those days were around the sixty to seventy minutes area. My best time was seventy-five minutes, and, as in all sports, a slight difference in time was the difference between success or failure. Finally, being disheartened at being a back marker, I gave up any road-racing ambitions and just continued with the touring.

The miles we used to cover were considerable. Up at about 5 a.m. and cycle to Hatfield, where the twenty-five mile race usually used to start from and finish. So it was twelve and a half miles there, a twenty-five mile race, and twelve and a half miles back. We would have some breakfast, and then decide where we were going to cycle for the day. A popular trip was to Ivinghoe in Bucks., there and back was another good fifty, so that meant one hundred miles that day and twenty-five of them spent racing. This could mean you had overdone it, especially if the day's ride was even further, and could result in you falling foul of the dreaded 'bonk'. When you were struck by this, your legs had been asked to do more than they were capable of and had gone on strike. The result was that you usually fell off your bike because your legs would not push the pedals any more, nor would they support you when the bike stopped. You would sit by the side of the road sometimes for an hour or more, waiting for the use of your legs to return, and then they were often only prepared to walk. Not a normal walk, it was as if your legs did not belong to you and you had the odd feeling that your feet were not actually in contact with the pavement. Anyone who has had this experience will, I am sure, recognise the feeling.

Normally most of our rides started by heading north out of London, as the quickest way out of town, and often on the A1. This would have been during the period 1945–48, and the A1 was not dual carriageway but single lane in either direction with an overtaking lane in the middle. Whenever traffic overtook you, it usually cut you a bit fine, and you would wobble a bit, due to the noise and rush of displaced air as it passed. Now it is three lanes in each direction for the most part and the weight of traffic would mean one continuous wobble.

By the time I was in my seventeenth year, things were changing. Most of my friends were two years older than me and had now been called up into the forces. Malcolm was the exception as he was younger than myself, had reached a crucial stage in his education, and was also heavily committed to representing his college at sport. This meant I was forced by circumstances to be a bit of a loner. So, when I bumped into some lads from my old class at school, one

Saturday afternoon, I was pleased at the prospect of some company. They informed me that they were going to a dance at Kemp's Biscuit Factory that night, said they were great, and asked me to go with them. I explained that there was a slight snag – I could not dance. This they said was not a problem, they would teach me. I spent about an hour in a local park's dried-up paddling pool, dancing (without musical accompaniment) with my ex-class mates, while they taught me the basic steps of the waltz and quickstep. Armed with this new skill I was pleased to agree to go with them.

For me the night was a success – foisting myself on a chain of unfortunate girls. I zoomed round the floor repeating time after time the basic step, over and over again, only bending it to get round the corners. To give them their due the girls were extremely tolerant. I cannot remember seeing their eyes glaze over, or any making a quick dash for the sanctuary of the 'Ladies' as I approached. This was all the more surprising as some luckless victims were danced with more than once. Nevertheless, I was hooked; it was a very enjoyable night, and it was imperative that my grasp of the Terpsichorean art was improved.

A quick word with the lads who I had gone to the dance with, and I had my answer. The next week I enrolled at the 'Mureen Elise and Lulu Lombart' ballroom dancing classes. As advised by my friends I enrolled for the intermediate classes.

They said, 'Don't go on beginners' night, you will get on much quicker at intermediate classes. They will be so embarrassed by you that they will have you doing the waltz and quickstep in no time.' The intermediate class was for the slow foxtrot and tango. The ploy was successful. I got immediate attention from Mureen and Lulu, who were aware I was at the wrong classes, but being businesswomen, also that they had me on the hook.

The dancing club had three nights a week for tuition and three nights just for dancing. The tuition nights gave you three quarters of an hour tuition and an hour and a half of dancing. The instructors (Mureen and Lulu) would take up their positions up front, and the men would line up behind one and the ladies behind the other. You were then taken through the particular steps they were teaching that night. A few run-throughs on your own without music, a few with, and then you took your partners. A couple more dry runs and then off you went. It all worked very well. 'M. and L.' would soon spot anyone in trouble, give them the concentrated bit personally, and quickly get them going. There were no wallflowers tolerated, anyone who was not dancing was descended upon and a partner found (even if it had to be themselves as partners).

There was also private tuition given, and after you had been going for a month or so, Mureen or Lulu would dance with you (ostensibly to see how you were getting on). It was actually time for the 'sales pitch'.

'You know you really do dance well, you have a natural ability – have you thought of taking your medals?' This would mean private tuition to coach you to the required standard. I did not put it to the test, but I have never regretted learning to dance. It has given me countless hours of enjoyment over the years and the Mureen – Lulu duo have nothing but my gratitude.

This was not the age of the permissive society, and the code of behaviour for all but the unprincipled was very strict. During the next twelve months, I did very well on the romance front. On your achievement scale of one to ten – ten was hectic snogging and that was it, but so what! To take home an attractive girl, have a few responsive kisses and a cuddle, and you still felt like vaulting over the gate and were on top of the world. Furthermore you were being responsible and not lumbering others with problems due to your poor behaviour.

By now, my dancing had progressed considerably since the night I attended the Kemp's dance with my two basic steps, one in the waltz and one in the quickstep. There was even a danger of my getting a bit flash, but fortunately I was taught a lesson. It was at one of the tuition and dancing nights at the club. I had a partner who, in all fairness, was 'big'. She was an excellent dancer and like a lot of ladies of, shall we say, ample proportions, very light on her feet. We took the floor for something pretty up-tempo, I think it was *The Woodchoppers' Ball*. As the dance progressed, I got more and more carried away, flashed into a corner with a half-lock, into a spin turn which I then linked into a second spin turn! This pleased my partner greatly, and this proved to be my undoing. At the very next corner I decided to go for three linked spin turns. My partner, at a conservative estimate, tipped the scales at around twelve stones, and at that time I struggled to make ten. The result was that, with a heady mixture of enthusiasm and centrifugal force, on the third spin I went into orbit round my partner's waist. We both lost control and our balance and crashed into a heap of chairs – in a cloud of French Chalk! Everyone had a good laugh at our expense and it had the right effect, unfortunately slightly too late, of getting both my feet back on the ground.

At about this time a girl whom I had danced with quite a bit, over a few weeks, asked me would I like to be her escort. She had won a double ticket to a dance at a local hotel, there was a cabaret, and refreshments were included in the ticket. I thanked her and said I would be pleased to escort her. On the night, when we got into the hall, there was a number of her friends – all girls and they all had the same tickets with drink vouchers attached. After a few dances they all gave me their vouchers and asked me to get some drinks. Off I went to the bar and got a tray full of drinks. A beer for myself and a selection that I thought the girls would like – gin and tonic, gin and orange, martinis and so forth. To my dismay, when I took them over to them, they all said they did not want them and only wanted soft drinks! Back I went for another tray, this time full of orange and lemon squashes.

I drank my beer and then made what was to prove to be the wrong decision. I was not wasting all those drinks – I would have them. Then I proceeded to work my way through them. Now, at seventeen, I had supped a few underage pints but was by no stretch of the imagination a hardened drinker. By the time the cabaret came on, let's face it, I was stoned! The second part of the cabaret was a conjuror, and not a very good one. In the state I was in, I could not resist a teensy bit of taking the mike! Management arrived, in the shape of a couple of chaps who looked like they could give Rocky Marciano a run for his money, and asked me to leave.

Though never a gambling man, I do recognise when the odds are against me, so I went to the cloakroom to get my coat. Unfortunately it then crossed my mind that the drink vouchers had not all been used. So I made my way (ill-advisedly) to the bar and saw off another pint. As I made my way back to the bar for another, some clown bumped into me and spilt beer all down my new suit (four pounds ten shillings from Burtons). Now I have never been an aggressive person, but for some reason, on this occasion, I took exception to having beer poured over me and decided to duff him up!

Shortly after this, the hotel doors opened and I shot through them onto the wet pavement, unceremoniously deposited there by the same two gentlemen who had previously asked me to leave. They seemed anxious to prove me right in my assumption that they were not to be taken lightly. At this point my luck changed for the better. One of the girls who had been with my party was in the bar on a squash-getting expedition. She saw my little fracas, got her own coat and, bless her, got me home. This was no mean feat, for, let's face it, it was one of those occasions you should learn from. I was not at my most coordinated, I doubt if my conversation could be described as sparkling; in fact, I think it was confined to a number of references to the world's inability to stay still and groans. The girl who I had taken to the dance was not overimpressed by my behaviour. She did not seem to appreciate the relevance of my inbred dislike of waste. Ella, however, the girl who got me home safely, I went out with for some months.

It was sometime after this that I met a girl, or rather a young woman, at the dancing club. She was about five years older than me and really was quite something. I called in to my home with her one night, when I had forgotten my tobacco pouch, and apparently frightened the life out of my father.

'Do you think he knows what he is doing?' he asked my brother.

'Well, if he doesn't, she looks like he soon will,' he answered.

On my scale of achievement of one to ten, I had already got to fifteen and my innocence was only saved by her husband coming home. I was not aware that she was married, and it could have been nasty. He turned up (a little the worse for the demon drink) at the dancing club – with the intention of sorting me out. Fortunately, by the time he got into the club, friends had tipped me off. I came to the conclusion that discretion was the better part of valour, and legged it!

The world and my life was about to change. My call-up papers arrived and I had to attend a medical centre at Horn Lane, Acton, to see if I was fit enough for the services. Due to the problems with the school medical regarding my spine, nobody expected me to pass and were positive that I would not have to do military service. When the day came, I went through the medical board, answered all the questions honestly, coughed when asked, provided a urine sample, and, in general, did all the things that comedians had got their laughs from for years. I must admit that no one mentioned my back, and I certainly did not. My friends were all in the services and I did not want to be the odd one out.

After the medical we were getting dressed and I remember a lad saying, 'They won't take me – I am a haemophiliac.'

'What's that?' someone asked.

'A free bleeder,' the lad answered.

'A lucky bleeder, more like it,' someone shouted.

Some days later my results came through. Not only had I passed, but I was graded A1. My papers arrived shortly afterwards. I was to report to Oudenarde Barracks, Aldershot, to join the RASC, on the 8th October, 1948.

The war had been over for a couple of years, and the only place where any fighting was taking place was in Malaya at that time, but it still gave you a strange feeling about what was ahead of you. Whatever was in store would make a change from the daily routine of a compositor's apprentice, and I was looking forward to the experience.

Chapter Thirteen

National Service

I duly arrived at Aldershot Station with a large number of other lads, all about to start their National Service. We were met by a number of NCOs who quickly sorted us out into our respective regiments. Then we were put onto three-ton trucks that transported us to Oudenarde Barracks, North Camp. The first day, like the rest of the next two weeks, went at a great pace. We were issued with denims to start with (a cross between overalls and battledress). Berets, boots, underclothes, equipment such as mess tins, boot brushes and a bewildering heap of webbing equipment. We were taken everywhere at the double and the days passed like a flash. What small amount of time that was left to us at night did not go so quickly. The webbing equipment, that we had been issued with, had been used during the war and all the brass buckles, etcetera had been treated so as not to reflect. This all had to be removed and polished with Brasso or Duraglit until they sparkled, and the webbing scrubbed clean and then blancoed. Quite a task. The RASC at that time was using khaki-green number 7, known as Durham mud. Some regiments had colours that would actually look smart – number 7 was not one of them. We thought that the main purpose of caking your equipment with this gunge was just to encourage dermatitis, or more likely, the officers knew that some months later we would be told to scrub it all off!

During what was left of the evening, you would sneak across to the NAAFI for a short break and something to eat that was less revolting than what the cookhouse was serving. Then back to the joys of polishing the brasses and 'bulling' your boots. Our barrack blocks, we were informed, were built to house troops during the Napoleonic War. I, for one, believed it. From then on they had been steadily deteriorating. The windows had bars at them and there was no glass. During the night it was freezing. The only four beds that were warm were the ones next to the combustion stove in the middle. This was stoked to the point where it shimmered with heat. One poor sprog stood too close in an effort to get warm and burnt half of his boots' toecaps away.

Shortly after we arrived, a driver backed his truck into the trestle tables that had most of the camp's china plates stacked on them. The resultant breakages meant that we were issued with old rusty tin plates, which gave us another chore. Getting the rust off them – and keeping them rust-free. The main objective of these first two weeks was to get you kitted out, make you reasonably fit, and teach you square-bashing. We were either queuing for kit issues, running for miles in PT kit, or crunching about on the parade ground learning the intricacies of moving to the left in threes, and how to about-turn. Here I witnessed things that I had been told about but not believed. The man who marched swinging the same arm as the leg (try it – it's nearly impossible). The sergeants and corporals, who used to take you for square-bashing, were affectionately known as 'drill pigs'. These were amongst the most feared of the NCOs and yet I saw them all but destroyed by the man who had trouble with the arms and legs when marching. After several days, he still could not perform an about-turn and come out of it with the right foot. One of these men in a squad can create havoc and achieve what you would think impossible – a drill pig with a nervous breakdown.

The intricacies of your webbing equipment, whilst probably not beyond a member of Mensa, could give you problems, until you were familiar with all the bits and pieces and numerous buckles and straps. You would come trotting back from a three-mile run, and the corporal would yell, 'Right, I want you all back out here in three ranks, in two minutes, in FSMO' (Field Service Marching Order). This was the whole lot – fitting all your webbing together was worth more than two minutes, let alone getting changed out of your PT kit and back into your battledress.

Any slips in putting your equipment on correctly was a case for NCO sarcasm. 'They are ammunition pouches not a bloody brassiere.' L-straps and webbing belt too loose – 'That's supposed to be a pack, not a bloody parachute.' One poor chap put his anklets-web on upside down (admittedly not easy). This, having seldom, if ever, been achieved before, rendered a corporal speechless for quite a long time, and found him wanting in the sarcastic remark department. Most of these remarks were well-practised, and handed down over years of training, such as (on discovering a speck of rust in a rifle barrel), 'What have we here – cocoa!' Or, (when drilling), 'Take one pace forward, do you feel anything? Well you ought to – I'm standing on your hair.'

A source of revenue for the squad NCOs was the cracked mug routine. When you arrived, they issued you with your own mugs, for which you paid a deposit. On your departure you handed your mug back, and if it was cracked or chipped, you did not get your money back. This fact was not pointed out to you when it was issued (because a large number of them were already cracked or chipped). They were, of course, kept specially for this purpose, the lost deposits being the NCOs' perks. This practice became so well known that it even got a mention in Parliament.

This training period only lasted two weeks and was known as primary training. You were at this point considered to be not fit for the public eye, and the only time you might have been seen was during a route march. No time was allowed for you to leave the camp area during this period.

At your medical you were asked what regiment you wanted to be in, and offered a choice of occupations, such as, dispatch rider, driver, radio operator, kamikaze pilot – that sort of thing. The principle of this was, presumably, so that the authorities could ensure you were kept as far away from your choice as possible. During your primary training another shrewd assessment was made by putting you through an aptitude test. This consisted of things like putting together a bicycle pump, which had been specially taken apart for this purpose, and answering some searching general knowledge questions. The result of this was that at the end of the two weeks you were told what they had decided you would be. Your next period of training would take place at a camp where the completion of your army training would be combined with your trade training. In my case they had decided that I should be a clerk, and for the next six weeks I would be at Dettingen Barracks, Blackdown. At the end of that period, if you were successful, you would qualify for your trained soldier, plus trade, pay. A phenomenal increase of about two pounds a week! So it was farewell to Oudenarde and its Napoleonic charm, a farewell that did not bring tears to my eyes.

Dettingen Barracks was a big improvement, you were not exposed to the elements when you were washing, and the food, while not qualifying for the 'Egon Ronay' approval, was a lot better than Oudenarde. The barrack blocks were more comfortable and definitely better heated, which was a big factor as it was winter, and it would prove to be a severe one. In the RASC you were trained as a combatant. It was pointed out that you were a soldier first, and a tradesman second. This, with the exception of the Royal Medical Corps, goes for all the support corps – Signals, Engineers, Ordnance and so forth. This would mean weapon training and assault courses, which we were looking forward to.

Our first trip to the rifle butts was in fact disappointing, largely because we were lucky if we even hit the target. Whereas we did not think we were all natural marksmen, we were surprised that we did not do better. We discovered later that this was because we had been sent onto the range with 'drill rifles'. These were ancient rifles that had not been seen by an armourer for yonks and had only been used by squad after squad for rifle drill. This also explained why I had been a bit concerned at the way my breech bolt kicked up when I fired. We were then issued with the proper weapons and our results then compared with the norm expected. There was some concern that we had actually fired the drill rifles and relief that bad results was the only problem. It was not beyond the realms of possibility that these rifles could have caused serious injury or even a fatality to the people who were firing them.

During the day there would be a variety of training sessions, some related to your trade training. It had been decided that we were to be supply clerks as opposed to technical clerks. The technical clerks were to join transport companies, and the supply clerks would go to supply depots. One of the areas of training was typing. We used to sit in rows with typewriters, which had hoods over the keyboards, to prevent you seeing the keys, to be taught touch-typing. The typing used to be done to a little tune that sounded something like *Listen with Mother*. This was played very slowly, and you hit a key with every note that was played. As you got more efficient the tempo was speeded up, and the standing joke was that, before you passed the test, you had to keep time with *Orpheus in the 'Underwood'* (Underwood being a make of typewriter at that time).

After a couple of weeks had passed, we were sent out on the assault course. The usual sort of thing – plenty of mud, brick walls to climb over, logs to run along, and water hazards to swing over. One item on the course had me worried. There was a routine where you had to throw yourself onto some barbed wire entanglements and your comrades-in-arms ran over you. Your equipment and uniform were supposed to protect you from the wire, with your rifle and arms protecting your face. Your comrades were supposed to place their foot on your pack as they ran over you – a target that they unerringly missed! Imagine being someone who during his childhood had not been allowed to do *PT* and virtually told not to step off any high kerbs, because of a spinal problem and that it might lead to spending a few years in plaster. The result was that army boots in the small of my back, with some bods weighing twelve stone or more in them, frightened the life out of me. The next morning saw me on the medical officer's sick parade. He was busily whizzing through a long line of a mixture of malingerers and genuine cases, at great speed. The odd chitty here, some gentian violet ointment there (a favourite remedy to cover everything except pregnancy, and, to the best of my knowledge, utterly useless) and, now and again, a warning to the obvious malingerer.

'Right, what's your problem?' he said.

'Well sir, I don't think I should be in the army at all, because of my spine, and the doctors did not notice it at the medical board.' I did not like the look that came over his face.

'What a load of rubbish, strip off and bend over and touch your toes,' he said.

This was a worrying moment, but there were orderlies present and I was desperate. I did as he said. There was a long pause.

'Right, I will give you a chit for light duties for today, report back here in the morning to collect your medical records and we will have you checked out at Aldershot Military Hospital.'

The next day I went to hospital, and my blood ran cold, as there were a large number of spinal cases about, including some paratroopers who had come to grief. Here they checked me out and took enough X-ray pictures to make me light up in the dark. The positions that they pushed and twisted me into, while they were being taken, made yoga look like a doddle. The result of all this was that I was informed that my spine was malformed, but apart from it looking different to other people's, was quite all right. I even retained my A1 grade. So it was back to the barbed wire and not civvy street. The only difference was – the routine did not include an underwear change! It did make me wonder why it had not been checked out thoroughly before, when I had the school medicals, but it was great to have the cloud removed from over my head at last.

One of the problems at this camp was the regular disappearance of gloves. It was winter and you needed them, you had all been issued with them, so which nerk lost his to start it all off? The fact remained that yours kept being stolen and you swiped someone else's. Kit deficiencies were like that, it was the way of the world in the services. We had a chap in our barrack room, whose name was Hooley, and his intention was to become a preacher. To be frank, he laid it on a bit thick. He was inclined to lecture people, and said his prayers kneeling by his bed in, wait for it – 'pyjamas'. Now there's bravery for you! He had achieved the double, he was the only squaddie

I saw in pyjamas and certainly the only one I saw saying his prayers out loud at the foot of his bed.

He duly lost his gloves and kicked up a right stink about the perfidy of the British soldier – especially in this particular barrack room and so on. The next morning we were about to go on parade, when a chap called Price noticed that Hooley was wearing gloves. He jumped up on the table and called us to gather round and when he had all our attention he said, 'And it came to pass that Hooley took unto himself another man's gloves.' We all solemnly added 'Amen' and went out onto parade.

At last we were considered to be respectable enough to be seen by the public, so we were allowed out of camp on Saturday night. We had now been in the army for four weeks and the thought of getting out for a night was really something to look forward to. First you had to get through the guardroom, where you were booked out – only after scrutiny by an RSM (Regimental Sergeant Major). A good number were sent back, largely for pretty trivial things, just to prove that you had to be immaculate and were breaking no regulation regarding dress.

Once out, it was off to the bright lights, a couple of beers, and as far as our small group was concerned, to find a dance. This would have been living if it was not for the fact that, at that time, there seemed to be only about six people in the whole area of Farnborough who were not in uniform. This was before you were allowed to wear civvies when not on duty. Nevertheless the evening was going well, and by 10 p.m. I had found a nice partner, a good dancer, attractive, and good company.

My mates gave me a shout, 'Come on, we have got to be back in camp by 23.59 hours.'

Not me – I was enjoying myself too much, so I said, 'Cheerio' and off they went. Just after eleven I mentioned to the girl I was with my transport problem. She reassured me that there was no problem, if I walked her home she would lend me her bike, as long as I could get it back to her on the Sunday. This I did, and off I went on the bike with just about enough time to get back to camp. It was going to be a closely run thing, for this bike was no racing machine; it had tyres like a truck and a wicker basket on the handlebars. I was pushing it as hard as I could and at the same time trying to work out what to do with the bike when I got there. About half a mile from the camp, on a nice, fast, downhill stretch, I shot past my mates (who had missed the bus anyway and had to walk). I rang my bell and gave them the 'Gee-up' as I passed, and got some pretty unsavoury replies, generally about being jammy and illegitimate. The sentry was no problem, he could not have been less interested, just another squaddie, and he could not care less about the bike. I made the deadline with about two minutes to spare, carried the bike upstairs into the barrack room and padlocked it to the bed. I didn't want that to do a disappearing act. The next day the bike was returned without my seeing the girl, who was a telephonist and on duty.

Leave was something I did not get a lot of in the army, in fact, fourteen days, embarkation leave in England and ten days, privilege leave in Kenya was the sum total in just over two years' service. This was made up for, to a certain extent, by weekend thirty-six hour and forty-eight hour passes. As I was no further away from London than Colchester, during my three months in England, I was always able to get home when I got passes. This was a mixed blessing, as the enjoyment of getting home and seeing friends and relatives was offset by the low of getting back to barracks either late at night or in the early hours of the morning. To a regular soldier the barracks might be home, but to a National Serviceman it was more like returning to a prison, with the feeling that you had precious little control over your life.

The army system of drill and extreme discipline was all directed at making you a number, a being largely incapable of thought, who just reacted to a command. (It may have changed since – but that is how it was then). I was not surprised when a friend of mine informed me that, in an officers' training manual, it said, 'Give your orders in a clear and decisive voice, and walk away.' Presumably this was in case someone raised a query as to the total impracticability of what he had been ordered to do!

It is a constant mystery to me that over the years the British Army has often survived, or even avoided total disasters, by the troops (including officers) using their initiative. One would have thought that all initiative would have been knocked out of you by training camps and the system. I have put it down to the fact that as a nation we are a 'bolshy' lot, and only go along with the system for a quiet life. When the situation is serious enough, or we find ourselves left to our own devices, we soon kick all that old nonsense into touch.

The dogma of only doing what we were ordered to do was often turned to our own advantage. This was done by doing what you were ordered, rather than what was obviously meant, or waiting for an order when it was blatantly obvious what you should do. Getting at the system was, we considered, fair game and a good source of amusement. When the corporal in charge of our squad was called over to speak to an officer, on one occasion, we marched onto the top of an air raid shelter and were about to march off the end, when spotted. The-over-the top histrionics practised by the NCOs, and the kind of offences you were put on a charge for, encouraged this approach. Three things that I was put on a charge for and received punishment of either so many days CB (confined to barracks) or fatigues were good examples. Having one steel stud missing from the sole of my boot (there should be sixteen in each sole). This was criminal negligence – they should not only be counted every night, but as one might come out whilst you were marching, presumably every few steps. Another offence was not drawing an oil bottle and pull-through from the armoury for a day on the rifle range, when I knew I would be all day at the military hospital and could not go on the range. Last but not least, the heinous crime of not getting on the duty truck to go to our depot, just because I was on the toilet with diarrhoea when the truck left. I should have done it in my trousers, after all I was wearing gaiters! You can see that it was quite simple to achieve a record in the army, and the more worrying fact was that the officer commanding meted out the punishment even when he had heard the circumstances.

The six weeks corps training ended with a passing-out parade. There was the odd person who did not pass their trade course, but they were a rarity and could be easily recognised by the scars on their knuckles – caused by their dragging on the ground. The courses were designed to ensure passes, and unless someone made a monumental error, like one of life's natural 'latrine orderlies' being entered for a course on brain surgery, failing could not occur. During the training period quite a lot of time was devoted to rehearsals for the passing-out parade. This was to be quite an occasion, the regimental band, top brass, and members of the public to be present. It was strange how you would receive a rocket on occasions for something like a minute trace of dried Brasso not cleaned from the 'back' of your cap badge or the hole in an eyelet. Yet once, in my rush to get out on parade, I forgot to put the magazine in my rifle, and went through the whole session (including an inspection) without such an obvious item being spotted.

The notices of our results were posted, and the great day of the passing-out parade came and went successfully. The Royal Horse Artillery in the next camp and the Scots Guards further down the road might have done it better, but on the day our feet were lifted the required eight inches and put down nine. Our dressing by the right was quite good, and we fixed bayonets and presented arms very smartly, I thought. In spite of all the cynicism, we felt quite proud of ourselves, as we swung past the saluting base to the tune of the regimental march.

On completion of our training we were split up, and a few friendships came to an end. A small number of us were sent to thirty-five Selection Unit in Colchester where we got our postings. Myself and two friends were to go to Kenya, and we were sent on fourteen days' embarkation leave, before reporting to the RASC Depot Battalion at Colchester. This leave was very fortunate, as it meant we would be home for Christmas, before what was surely to be the biggest adventure yet – the journey to and service in Kenya.

The first few days of my leave were spent with people, who I had not seen since my call-up, saying things like, 'You home again?' and 'When are you going back?' The bright side was that it being Christmas time there were parties and dances to go to. On Christmas Eve I was round at a friend's house, from where we went on to a local public house, where we had an enjoyable evening and sunk a jar or two (possibly, I am afraid, more than that). Not many people owned cars in those days, and they used to drink more. As long as they could find their way home all right, no great harm was done. Before I went out, my brother had mentioned to me that there was a party in the vicinity. He had given me the address and said that, if I could get there, I would be welcome.

When I arrived, it was about 11.30 p.m. and the party was in full swing. Everyone was in good spirits apart from one room, which seemed to be filled with slightly older ladies. This room was more like a wake, caused, I was informed, by an overindulgence in the gin. At one stage I found myself in the garden with a married friend, who was doing quite nicely with an attractive lady in her late twenties. The back door opened and a voice shouted out, 'Are you out there, John?'

My friend answered, coolly, 'Yes, I am down here with Brian', passed me the ladyfriend and scuttled off.

The good news was that the lady did not appear to be put out by the change of partner, and to be honest I much preferred this arrangement. Things were most enjoyable until we were disturbed by her husband. When I had taken over from John, a discussion about her matrimonial status did not appear to be what was required – so it hadn't taken place. There was a bit of a problem here, not only was a private in the RASC being more familiar with his wife than he was happy with, but he was also a warrant officer in the same regiment. I said something like, 'Oh there you are, Staff – Happy Christmas,' and beat a hasty retreat.

The fourteen days passed all too quickly, coming at the festive season it had no time to drag, with something to do for the whole period. So the time came for farewells to friends and family, as I did not know how long I would be away for. At that time your period of service was not known, as I was called up under the same act that came into being for the war. The term used was 'for the duration of the national emergency'. This was later to be changed for conscripts to 'Time and Service', which meant you had a period of two years to do and knew the approximate date of your release when you went in. This was reduced to eighteen months (the least anyone served) before it was to be finally abolished.

Colchester Depot Battalion was at Reid Hall Barracks, a recently built camp with all modern conveniences. Central heating, wash rooms with showers and baths, and something that made it unique as far as army camps were concerned – good food! Certainly, this was the best army food I had. The strange phenomenon of looking forward to meals took a bit of getting used to. The local NAAFI, and it was a good one, must have wondered what they were doing wrong. Their sales must have been among the lowest in the country, but they were no doubt saved by the fact that there were other army camps in the area. Life in this camp was one of unrest, as the men were all on draft waiting to go overseas. You went out on working parades every morning, unless you had wangled a semi-permanent position and were detailed for whatever duties were required. These ranged from kitchen fatigues, quartermaster's stores, guard duties or battalion salvage. Speaking from experience, battalion salvage was definitely one to avoid. It entailed collecting and dumping all the kitchen waste in three-ton trucks. They were not specialised vehicles, and skidding about in the back of one, on a mixture of porridge, tea leaves, and old boiled fish, was not my idea of fun.

Depot battalions were a skiver's paradise, a test of their prowess in dodging work. One old soldier (he was probably about twenty-six) slipped into the company office and filched a pile of Fire Regulation notices. These he carried about with him for weeks. He would stretch out on a bed in one of the barrack rooms, and if he heard someone coming, would busy himself with the fire notice until the coast was clear. The end result of this was that he was seen by the company commander and RSM, who were touring the blocks looking for skivers. When asked what he was doing, he said, 'Renewing the fire notices.'

'On your own?' he was asked. 'That will take far too long.' And three others were detailed to help him finish a job that no one had asked him to do in the first place.

In the forces there are more accentuated periods of highs and lows than in civvy street, and it was at this camp that I experienced an unsurpassed exercise in boredom. I had the dubious pleasure of queuing for one and a half days for tropical kit to be issued. We would queue all morning, get dismissed for a meal and, when we returned, be further away from the stores than we were when we started. This masterpiece of organisation was really quite something. There were admittedly others in the queue as well, but when you are aware that there were only twenty-three of us, it is an achievement worthy of *The Guinness Book of Records*.

Finally, all kitted out and inoculated against yellow fever, with kit all marked with our draft, we were ready for our departure. We were then informed that our draft had been delayed and we were being sent on another fourteen days' leave. We handed in our kit and were lined up outside the company office waiting to be issued with our passes and rail warrants, when an RSM arrived on the scene (bless him). They were short of men in the holding company and as a result the leave was cancelled, our kit was redrawn from the stores and we were temporarily in the holding company. The good news was that we were no longer on the working parades, the bad news was that we were on permanent guard duties. There were three guards mounted in the camp. Reid Hall – a sixteen-hour 'prowl guard', MT (Mechanical Transport) – a twelve-hour guard, and battalion quarter guard – a sixteen-hour guard and the one with all the bull, sentry boxes and the whole 'Halt, who goes there?' bit. With sentry drill and guard-changing ceremonies, this was definitely the one to be avoided. The only good thing was you got the day off after the guard duties.

By now it was January and bitterly cold, and the guard duties were of the usual two hours on, four off, rota. The experience of being half-asleep and roused to go out on guard from 2 a.m. until 4 a.m. is one that makes you appreciate the luxury of a warm bed or even four walls. During the night there would be the arrival of the guard's cocoa – this was disgusting. It arrived in a bucket, a tepid fluid, covered with an almost leather-like skin on top. You broke through the skin with your mug, dipped it in, closed your eyes and – yuk! I am sure it could have been sold to South American natives to dip their arrows in. One night I was on a Reid Hall guard, which was a prowl guard. This meant that you covered an area in ones or twos, with your rifle slung on your shoulder, as opposed to the formal sentry and paced guard. It was quiet and late, just after midnight, and I was covering the back entrance into the camp. I was sitting on the wall, my rifle leaning against it, with my greatcoat collar turned up and smoking my pipe. Any one of those things would have been enough to get me put on a charge. So, when I found myself picked out in the headlights of a jeep which swept round the corner, I was more than a trifle concerned. An officer in the jeep shouted out for instructions on how to get to the officers' mess. I crossed quickly to the jeep, snapped him up a salute, gave him the instructions, and watched them drive off, with considerable relief. They could not have spotted my rifle against the wall in the dark and could not have realised that I was supposed to be the guard, which in the circumstances was quite understandable.

On another occasion I had the unnerving experience of being on a quarter guard mounting parade, going through the drill to 'fix bayonets'. Gripping the rifle between my knees and reaching round to draw the bayonet from its scabbard, I found that there was no bayonet or scabbard (they had fallen from the bayonet frog). I went through the drill and fixed an imaginary bayonet – fortunately without detection. On this occasion I was very lucky to have a reasonable orderly sergeant (and they weren't too thick on the ground). He allowed me to go back to the parade ground where, risking life and limb, I found the missing equipment. It was an offence of the highest order to go onto a parade ground as an individual.

Whilst on my last guard in the holding company, my best battledress (uniform) was stolen. I should have been wearing it, but had gone on guard in my working battledress. The reason for this was that, when not on duty now, you could wear a tie with your tunic not done up at the neck. This meant that you pressed the revers to look smart, and I had not wanted to spoil it, as when I came off guard, I was on a weekend pass.

To my horror, when I got back to my barrack room, my best uniform had been stolen. My weekend pass was spent in my scruffy working uniform and with no small amount of concern at what my kit deficiency would cost me. As your full pay was two pounds and a few shillings, repaying the cost of a battledress would have meant quite a period of hardship.

On rejoining my draft for Kenya on my return to camp, I could not believe my luck. The very first day I was back on the working parade I was detailed to help in the quartermaster's stores. I am not without a certain amount of initiative, and by 4 p.m. my kit was back up to strength. As I had chosen it myself, it was a snazzy number in an unusual greeny shade of khaki. A much prized issue, and the only drawback was that I now only had a week or two left in this country, before I would be off to Kenya.

Once we were in the Mediterranean it would be

goodbye to battledress and time for tropical kit, which incidentally was a real term and not something dreamed up for Major Bloodnock gags – 'Tropical Kit – I love that woman!'

Chapter Fourteen

Kenya

One morning late in January we were off at last, and what a struggle, we were in field service marching order plus! This entailed you having small pack at your side, big pack on your back, your tin hat between the straps, groundsheet under it, and blankets rolled and fixed round it, two kitbags tied round your neck, your greatcoat on, and carrying your rifle. As I was struggling to climb on board the three-ton truck, a CSM (Company Sergeant-Major) who thought I was not doing it quickly enough, shouted 'Get a move on' and to add emphasis poked me in the goolies with his cane. Most unpleasant, and, if I had said what I was thinking, it would have been most unwise. When we got to the station we were marched onto the platform, and when we got the command 'Halt,' Ron Allen lost his footing and went down on his back. All the equipment that we had on or were carrying weighed so much that he could not get up, and just lay there laughing. It took two of us to get him back on his feet. At Southampton I nearly missed the boat at the last minute. I had to go to the loo on the train, and with all the kit I had on, got stuck in there.

At the docks we embarked on our boat, the *Eastern Prince*, an eleven thousand-ton ship, and I was impressed. This was not surprising as the biggest boat I had been on before was the one that went down the Thames from Richmond to Hampton Court. We did not get an inferiority complex until the evening we sailed out of Southampton and passed close by the *Queen Mary*. The tops of our funnels were level with where the passengers' entrance was – what a ship! The *Eastern Prince* was fitted out with flops. These were canvas bunks in three tiers, as opposed to hammocks, so that you could pack more in on the troop decks. We were on lower four troop deck, and when we went down the companionways, it seemed we were never going to get there. It made me glad that we were not still at war, the thought of what it must have been like trying to get out and up on deck, when a ship was mined or torpedoed, was horrific.

For meals we had a mess deck system. This was a term the significance of which only became clear when we got into the Bay of Biscay and you were carrying food back from the galley, skidding around on a mixture of spilt porridge and puke. Everyone had allotted duties on board ship, most of them not too onerous or time-consuming. In fact, the two months that I spent at sea were about the best I had in the army. Our draft was given the task of sweeping the decks of the ship every day. We would get our brooms and sweep our given areas, an unrewarding, even pointless exercise when there was a wind blowing at anything over force four. We used to go through the motions anyway until 'lifeboat stations', and after that, our time was our own. For most of the time a coastline was in view, and we would stretch out on the hatch covers and read a book or play cards. We docked in Valetta harbour, Malta, and the next stop was when we lay off Famagusta in Cyprus. There was no harbour as such and we picked up the Fourth Battalion of the South Wales Borderers from there. The sea was quite choppy, and they came out to the ship on what looked like landing craft. It was quite entertaining watching the squaddies timing their jump from the landing craft to the ship's companionway. A remarkable feat, as no one went into the sea. There were a few tin hats, a rifle or two, and a number of kitbags, but no men – self-preservation is a wonderful thing. The biggest attraction was when they dropped a fifteen-hundredweight truck in the sea – that was pretty spectacular. These men were with us until we got to Port Sudan where they disembarked on their way to Khartoum, a good spot for camels, flies, sand, and not much else.

After we left Cyprus, we were told that there was to be a film show – *The Treasure of the Sierra Madre*. This was to be shown on deck, with the side of the ship's galley acting as the screen. Entry was to be by your troop-deck berth card, on three different nights. Ours, of course, was to be the last, and brains started to tick over to think up devious plans of how to get past the military police, who were going to be a cross between usherettes and the Gestapo. I do not recall our plan but it worked. We were all sitting on the deck, cross-legged and in rows, when finally the lights went out, the music started, and lo and behold, 'Bogey and company' were on the galley wall – great! The first prize for initiative went to a group of bods who had sneaked into a lifeboat long before, and when the lights went out, the tarpaulin was rolled back, and there they were in the lifeboat seats (the equivalent of the two-and-sixpenny circle seats).

When we got to Port Said we had a couple of trips ashore and, as I recall, it was a less than enchanting place. The best rave notice I can conjure up for it would be it was an experience. The second trip ashore ended in us being chased through the docks by an irate horde of Egyptians. Quite why they were chasing us I cannot recall, but we just about managed to stay ahead of them until we reached the armed military police, who were guarding the entrance to the 'snake' that led to our ship. What has stayed in my mind is that it was one of the rare occasions that we were pleased to see military police.

Before returning to the ship we had pooled our finances and bought some rum. It was not one of the better brands, in fact it was not even in a sealed bottle – it just had a cork rammed in! This we consumed on the mess deck, from our mess tins, with a meal of bread (no butter) and a couple of tins of sardines we had. An enjoyable feast strangely enough. One of the lads had purchased a bottle of what he had been given to understand was 'Spanish Fly'. The sale of this supposedly high-powered aphrodisiac was a commercial enterprise of staggering proportions in Port Said. This was lashed into the rum of the unsuspecting Private Gosney's mess tin. He was carefully monitored through the night to see what effect it had on him. As what had been purchased was doubtlessly nothing more than coloured water, it had no effect whatsoever. This was probably a good thing, for, if it had been the real stuff, with the amount he had been given, he would have raped the whole ship's company for starters. The other danger Gosney faced was that, if it had been water from the 'Sweet Water' canal, it could have been more dangerous than the 'Spanish Fly'.

Going through the Suez Canal was an experience to be enjoyed. A large searchlight was hoisted onto the prow of the ship, and we did the first leg down to the Bitter Lakes during the night. The *Empire Orwell* troopship went past us in the opposite direction, while we were in the Bitter Lakes. Banter was exchanged, 'It's all right for you on your way home!' from us, and from them, 'You should worry – you've got a home posting!' When we reached Port Sudan we had a few days' delay, firstly to disembark the South Wales Borderers and secondly to have repairs carried out, as we had damaged our propeller on our way through the canal.

Our next port of call was Aden where we had just a few hours ashore. This I found a very depressing place, and could understand the rumours about it being a posting to be avoided at all costs. There was an air of poverty about the place, and the awfully disfigured professional beggars made it somewhere I was glad to leave. It also hosted a similar variety of fly to the Egyptian fly, which is unlike our home-grown fly (which skilfully nips off as soon as you make a move). This type fancy their chances and are prepared to take you on. You had to learn not to take food in both your hands as you needed at least one hand to keep the swines at bay.

Our journey was nearly complete now, the next port being our destination – Mombasa. It is strange now to think that it took us thirty-one days to get to Kenya, when now it is done by plane in about eleven hours. The voyage was most enjoyable, and I am glad that the journey was made before the use of air transport to move troops in any quantity. The disembarking was up to the usual armed forces standard. We had an early breakfast at 4.30 a.m. boiled cod in greasy water, served in your aluminium mess tins. Not the sort of thing to set Egon Ronay's pulse racing. This early call and meal was obviously necessary as no one left the ship until around 10.30 a.m. – what a drag!

One thing that amazed me was that, once off the ship, our kitbags and equipment, which were dumped all along the dockside, took only minutes to be found. I am not sure how many troops were on board (from several different regiments), but judging from the numbers on each troop deck it must have been over a thousand. We were taken to the transit camp at Nyali just outside Mombasa. It is now in the package holiday brochures and looks a lot different from when we arrived there. The camp boasted a couple of buildings, of a sort, but consisted mainly of *makuti*-roofed *bandas* (coconut leaf thatched huts). The scenery was lush and green with palm trees everywhere, a vast improvement on Aden.

We were unable to get our tropical kit altered to some semblance of a fit until we got to our working units. We had first put them on when the troopship got into the Red Sea. Everyone fell about, we had to be seen to be believed! It was as if the Q-stores had gone out of their way to achieve the worst fits possible. We were all swapping bush jackets, shorts and suchlike to try and get some things to wear which did not make people burst out laughing on sight. The bush hats were a hit, we all thought we were 'Chindits' when we put them on. Oddly enough, when we got to Kenya, they were only worn if you were attached to an East African regiment, and as most of us were to be posted to British Units, we hardly wore them.

When we arrived at Nyali, we were told that nobody was to leave the camp without permission. On the first night there, we all slipped out and headed for Mombasa. The military police, who obviously knew when a troopship arrived in the harbour, waited by the side of the road from Nyali. As they expected, down the road came this motley crowd, in their ill-fitting uniforms, huge bush hats and strictly adhering to the antimalaria regulations, (something that anyone who had been there awhile virtually ignored). They just rounded us up, put us on trucks, and took us back to camp. In fairness, no action was taken against us. It was strange that we did not realise how we would stand out and how easy it would be to spot us.

Life in the transit camp was about as easy as it could be in the army. We paraded in the mornings, were told our postings had not come through, and were dismissed for the rest of the day. We then lounged about and went down to the beach for a swim. The area was known for sharks, and wooden piles had been driven into the sand out to the coral reef. Although you could not see it, we were assured that the sharks could not get over it and it was safe to swim. Funnily enough, every now and again when you were swimming, something would brush against you, probably some seaweed, but the thought of a shark would cross your mind (and this was before the film *Jaws*). This accounted for the not infrequent impersonations of Johnny Weissmuller, the Olympic swimming champion, who later played Tarzan. Chaps would achieve speeds doing the crawl, which they had never thought they were capable of, to get out of the sea. Then, realising their error, they tried to look casual, 'Me, I always come out of the sea like that!' There were rumours about bods who had swum the other side of the reef and lost a leg in a shark attack. Some wag amended the routine orders for going sick to, 'If attacked by a shark you should report sick to the MO, with your small pack, a change of underclothes, shaving gear, and plimsole.'

The rumour was that the postings in East Africa command were all good ones – with the exception of one – 'Mackinnon Road'. Finally the postings came through, the RSM called out your name and the last three of your army number, and you fell in with that group. My name was called for the group that was going to the Seychelles. This was a plum, and a much sought-after posting. A sergeant with a check list went through our names and details.

'Right, Vincent, you are a technical MT (Motor Transport) clerk?' Before I realised it, I heard myself saying, 'No, Sergeant, I am a supply clerk.'
Quick checks were made, and I was swapped with an MT clerk in the Mackinnon Road group. All I had to do was keep my mouth shut and I blew it!

Chapter Fifteen

Mackinnon Road

The Mackinnon Road ran from Mombasa to Nairobi and the camp of that name was approximately eighty miles from Mombasa. It was a vast ordnance base, which was for storing equipment that had come out of Egypt and from India. You name it and it was there in large quantities, trucks of all kinds, guns, invasion barges and so forth. Presumably it stayed there and finally rotted there or became obsolete. At that time it was being held in case the need for it arose again. The Royal Engineers were there putting up buildings for stores and camps, and building roads. The Royal Army Ordnance Corps looked after the stores, and the Royal Army Service Corps provided supplies and transport. When we arrived it had been in operation for about a year and it was supposed to be a nine-month hardship station. There was no water, so that had to be brought in daily by RASC water tankers, and we were clearing areas of the bush, to put up our tent lines for accommodation.

The ground was like granite, and digging a monsoon ditch round your tent required a pneumatic drill, which we did not have. Hence the regulation fifteen-inch deep ditch was more like five inches at most, and when the long rains came hardly a tent stayed up and it was chaos. The lessons were learnt the hard way and, before the ground dried rock hard again, the ditches were a good fifteen inches deep. We also drove branches into the ground and made a frame to lash the tent guy ropes to instead of using tent pegs. This was to prove successful and time well spent. It was pretty miserable to find after a few weeks of pouring rain, that your kit box was standing in six inches of water, your boots were up on the bed with you, so they didn't float away, and during the night your tent had collapsed on top of you. A six-man IP tent, with a double roof and ridge poles, was not a light construction – especially when it landed on you soaking wet.

The Central Camp housed a number of units and we each had our own tent lines, one communal cookhouse and a mess hall which was built with mud walls about three foot six inches high, with poles supporting the usual *makuti* roof. No such things as windows – this was to make sure the African flies had good access. You had to continually brush them aside to eat your meals, probably one of the reasons why dysentery was rife. Toilet facilities in Kenya at that time were not of the best, especially in the army. The first one I had to use was in Mombasa and was really one of the better ones that I encountered. When I turned to close the wooden flap I was rather unnerved to see a large green lizard peering at me from over the seat on which I had been sitting only seconds before. The urinals in the camps tended to be a variation of the Desert Rose variety, and consisted of a rolled sheet of corrugated iron, fixed to the wall at an angle, so that it drained into a funnel driven into the ground at one end. Here my height was an advantage, as the corrugated iron used to rust through before it reached the funnel. This tended to be at the lower level – the six-footers were all right, but the under-five-foot-eight bods used to have the unpleasant experience of finding their gaiters had just been filled.

During one period there were so many men with dysentery that the military hospital was unable to cope and was only taking the worst cases. Like many others I was having a rough time of it, trying to carry on working with too frequent interruptions, usually without any warning. It was most unpleasant for all concerned. We were issued with binding pills, which were so large it was like trying to swallow manhole lids. These did not seem to have any effect for several days but, when they did, it was generally agreed that it was as if you had been using old cement bags for toilet paper. You were then worried that you had the opposite problem, but after the experience you had just gone through, the one word that had been struck from your vocabulary was 'laxative'.

The unit I had been posted to was a supply platoon. We had tents for offices and the stores were constructed by wooden stakes driven into the ground to support the usual *makuti* roof. Barbed wire was strung round the poles and there were lockable doors. The stores were stacked at what was considered to be more than an arm's length from the wire to prevent pilfering. The Africans used to get round this by pushing what they wanted, with long poles, into the area that they could reach, to be stolen. We were well understaffed, the war establishment for the unit was one-hundred and thirty men and at one time we were down to only twenty-nine. Discipline had become almost non-existent. We used to have amazing working parades where we would saunter on to parade as a complete shambles. We prided ourselves that we did not have two people whose uniform was the same. We had unbelievable scenarios like, 'Have you shaved this morning, McCallum?'

'No Staff!'

'Well you should you know!'

One of the clerks who had been with the unit only a short time before I arrived was so outrageous that, even under this lax regime, he was able to split his service fairly evenly between being on 'jankers' and in the military hospital. He returned from a spell in hospital, a couple of weeks after I had arrived at the unit, and on his first working parade was back in trouble. Sergeant Counter looked at him despairingly. He looked him straight in the eyes and said, 'Hipwell, you are a shower of shit – what are you?'

Hipwell replied, 'I must be a mirror, Sergeant!' That did it!

My duties with the unit were assisting in broad terms with the accounting for the supplies we received. The ration scales had to be calculated for each unit we supplied in the area. Records had to be kept of all supplies issued, and all supplies received, and the balance of stocks that we held had to be agreed. This was accomplished with a staff of an officer commanding (a captain), a second-in-command (a second lieutenant), two warrant officers, two sergeants, two corporals, clerks, drivers, storeman and issuers. The bulk of the transport was carried out by East African Service Corps companies, and the storemen had African labourers to assist. The African labour units were on government contract and lived in a camp in the area. Each day they were detailed to the different units where they were required; they used to march in early in the morning, and you would hear them singing as they marched along, usually a part song, *Jambo Safari*.

The first Saturday I was with the unit we were told in the morning that, as we were so short of staff, the clerks would have to help out with the stores duties in the afternoon. This we did, and I was more than a little surprised with the job I was given. That was to take thirty three-ton trucks with Askari drivers down to the railway sidings, unload a train there onto the trucks (there would be labour available there) and get the supplies back to the depot. This I found, shall we say, a challenge. I was eighteen years old, a private, and had been in a foreign country for two or three weeks at most, and could not speak more than a word or two of Swahili. In a remarkably short time I found that there was plenty of train left to unload, but no trucks. Fortunately I had taken note of the transport company's flashes on the trucks, and knew that it was 993 EAASC (East Africa Army Service Corps). So I went into the RT (Railway Transport) office at the station and rang their company HQ. When I explained the situation to him, the sergeant at the other end was very sympathetic. He said he would round them up and send them back, and gave me my first practical Swahili lesson. Make sure before they drive off you speak to the driver and say, *'Wewe kurudi hapa!'* ('You return here') and it worked. It is a strange thing that in any foreign country there is always a selective method of learning a language. Phrases like 'You can knock off now' or 'We will pay you double for that' are always understood. Whereas 'Pick-up those one-hundred and twelve pound bags and stack them over there' will produce instant bewilderment.

I used to like the greeting which usually went on at some length:

'Jambo.' ('Hello.') The answer to this would be

'Habari.' ('How are you,' or 'What news.')

'Msuri.' ('Good.')

'Msuri sana.' ('Very good.')

'Msuri kabesa.' ('Excellent.' – literal translation: 'absolutely.') End of ritual.

A lot of the Kenyan Africans' names were tied in with the British occupation and influence. Names like King George were popular, and some were even stranger than that. We had a chap called Typewriter Smith, and one I have good reason to remember called Weary Willie Moshima. The earlier part of his name, I believe was culled from the old comic paper *Chips.* He was the cleaner at the new supply depot that we moved to. One of his tasks was to clean the toilets, quite good toilets, as army toilets in the African bush go. It was a three-seater with partitions and doors, vastly superior to the twelve seater with no partitions or doors that we had at the Central Camp. These toilets were constructed over pits, and the method of keeping them relatively hygienic was to burn them out. Diesel oil was poured down into the pit and then set alight, a task requiring a reasonable level of skill. People had been known to visit them at night, and as they were unlit, foolishly light a piece of paper to see that there was nothing harmful cruising around the seat area. This, it should be noted, is a practice to be avoided and could only be surpassed in its horror if, at the same time as you were checking with the lit paper, the lid over the seat area was lifted. Things hurtled out of that pit that the people at the Natural History Museum would only dream of, if they were on hallucinatory drugs. Strong men were known to be traumatised by this experience.

When only weeks away from getting the ship back to England to get demobbed, I had cause to use the upmarket toilet at the supply depot. I entered the toilets and noticed to my pleasure that they had just been cleaned by Weary Willie Moshima. Everywhere was nice and clean and there was a hygienic smell of disinfectant. This was obviously going to be one of those rare occasions to savour. I settled myself down comfortably in trap number three, only to find myself becoming what must have looked like an early British attempt at putting a man on the moon. This was occasioned by a reasonable-sized explosion and a tongue of flame shooting up from between my legs. This I may say did nothing to improve the appearance of my scrotum – as many a medical officer observed over the next four or five weeks.

'My God!' they would say. 'What have you done to yourself?' as they looked at something that resembled a brown paper bag that had got too close to a blowlamp. Seldom did I have time to explain that I had done nothing (if you exclude trying to break the high jump record from a sitting position) and that it was Weary Willie, bless him, who had poured the diesel oil into the latrine and then gone to get some matches. He had returned, lifted the lid on trap number one, not knowing that number three was occupied, thrown the flaming brand down and shut the lid.

The supply depot for the first few months was situated in what we referred to as 'the garrison'. It was, for the most part, where the working units and camps were, as opposed to the living accommodation. Two major conveniences were there – the NAAFI and the cinema. There were small canteens in the camps, which were run, for the most part, by the army personnel themselves, but the provisions and goods on sale were purchased from the main NAAFI. The cinema was an AKC one, run by the army, and had a weekly change of programme. The building was quite good, it had been built by the Royal Engineers and was of a corrugated iron and girder construction. It had a projection room, decent screen, and rows of fixed seats. The cladding of the walls did not reach the ground or the ceiling, which left gaps of between two to three feet. This had the advantage of providing good ventilation, which was necessary, as the temperatures were usually ninety degrees Fahrenheit, or higher, and if they were showing a horror film, the real bats, that were flying around in the cinema, added to the atmosphere. The NAAFI was the only place where you could get your Tusker lagers chilled, and for that you had to get there pretty early, as they were usually being sold so quickly that they were only passing through the icebox.

The Engineers were up to their necks in work, building camps, roads, stores, and laying a pipeline from the river Tsavo to the camps. This would save us having to transport water in tanker lorries and issuing it in jerry cans. I remember the great day when the water was turned on. There was one small snag, the time of the year was right at the end of the dry season. This was when most rivers looked like small ditches, trickling through the middle of the river beds. The ground was like granite, and if you leant on a tree, it collapsed in a dust heap. Six weeks later it would have been fine, at least for the next nine months, but at this particular time, what emerged from the taps bore a closer relationship to cocoa than water, as it contained so much of the red mud from the river Tsavo. Not to be churlish, it was soon to be a great improvement and only to be spoilt briefly when an elephant sat on the pipeline (which ran above ground) and the REs had to find where the break was and repair it. The troops who were in the Tsavo area all used to look like Red Indians and their uniforms were discoloured all due to the staining powers of that red mud and dust.

Another thing that used to affect your colour when you first arrived in Kenya was the mepacrine tablets that you took to prevent getting malaria too badly. These, after you had been taking them for a while, made you look like you had a bad bout of jaundice. A book was issued to you on the troopship to enlighten you on these matters. It went under the title of *Health for the British Soldier in the Tropics*. This had bags of good stuff in it. You were cheered up no end by the information on malaria; it listed three main types – malaria, malignant malaria, and spinal malaria. It then went to some lengths to explain the different types. The first was unpleasant, rather like influenza, the second was much the same, with the nasty additional fact that, once you had it, it would keep recurring, and the last, but definitely not the least, tended to be 'terminal' in a matter of hours. What was disturbing was the symptoms were all exactly the same, so you would lay shivering in your bed with a splitting headache, sweat pouring out of you and your teeth chattering, with the knowledge that you had one of the three. When you awoke the next morning, you knew you had one of the other two!

After a few months the good news was that the mepacrine was to be replaced with Paludrine. This had two things going for it, it was a better preventative, and it did not send you yellow. Thank you, the medical profession, a positive improvement. At about the same time as the Paludrine tablets arrived, so did a new colonel, and a couple of new practices were instituted by him that we could have done without. An early morning parade to be held at six in the morning, at which you would be handed your Paludrine tablet to take, and then some physical training for you to enjoy before you had your breakfast. The other one was a colonel's parade for all the RASC units in the area, to be held on what was supposed to be a sports field every Saturday morning. The climax of this was a march past a saluting base, where the colonel (bless him) would take the salute. It probably will not come as a surprise to you that neither of these innovations were very popular, but the PT and tablets number took pride of place in the hate league. A siren would sound at a quarter to six, and you would get out of bed, slip on your boots and shorts, and stagger up to the transport park. There you were formed up under the command of an NCO, and the orderly officer of the day would take the parade. There was a roll call, tablets were issued and exercises were organised, and you blundered about half-asleep in the dark bumping into each other and swearing.

One morning the duty officer was a new arrival, very young and with a high-pitched squeaky voice. The usual routine was gone through, and when we formed up in our units again to be dismissed, the 'sprog' officer started some long tirade about how long it had taken us to get on parade.

'I'm orderly officer again tomorrow,' he squeaked, 'and I will expect an improvement.'

He squeaked on and on, and finally the sergeant in charge of Group Workshops (who had been in the army when this officer was running around in nappies) muttered, 'I've had enough of this,' came smartly to attention, and gave the command, 'Group Workshops dismiss!'

This was quickly followed up by all the other NCOs in charge of units, resulting in the whole parade being dismissed, leaving 'Squeaky' leaping irately about with no one taking any notice of him.

We said to the sergeant, later, 'Surely there will be trouble over that.'

He answered, confidently, 'No, there won't, there's no way he is going to report that he had a parade walk off in front of him – he would never hear the last of it.'

The colonel's parades did not last all that long, for, as they had to be attended by all the units in the area, the commanding officers of each of the units were quite probably against them. After all, they all had work to do, and no doubt resented the time spent by ninety per cent of their men attending a parade every Saturday. Another thing that did not help was the numbers of men fainting on parade. They were held at the hottest part of the day, and the EAASC units had their Askaris on parade. The colonel used to arrive to take the salute when most of us had been on parade for about three quarters of an hour, and by that time you could see men's tunics changing colour with sweat. The temperature was well up in the nineties or more, and the Africans were more used to it than the BORs (British Other Ranks), who were falling down in large numbers due to the heat. The end result, for whichever reason, was that they were abandoned and we were all grateful.

Chapter Sixteen

The New Supply Depot

Our new supply depot was making good progress and we knew that we would shortly be making the move there. Our commanding officer went home on release, and the lieutenant who had been our second-in-command took over temporarily. He took over the OC's (Officer Commanding) office, which was one of a series of tents linked together, and we all watched fascinated while he fixed up a contraption with staples, string and wire. This he completed with a tin of pebbles suspended just behind his personal clerk's (Hipwell's) desk. He disappeared into his office, pulled the string and the pebbles jangled. He then walked into the main office and said to Hipwell, 'What do you think of my new bell, Hipwell?' and Hipwell (not the most circumspect of people you will recall) answered, 'Pathetic!'

In the main office at the old depot there were two large wicker laundry baskets. What was different about these was their contents. They were full of Army Council Instructions and Army Routine Orders. These were amendments and updates dating back so far that some of them quite possibly contained instructions on the care of pikes. When these were received in army offices they were to be incorporated and used to update the master copies that were held. We were more than a little concerned that, if they ever came to light, someone would have so much 'jankers' to do that he would qualify for his pension before his release came up, or possibly a worse fate – he would have to do all the amendments. We all agreed that during the move the baskets would have to go. When the great day came and there was general chaos, we carried the baskets round to the toilets and hurriedly stuffed them all down the traps into the pit. Time was running out and we had to put in an appearance before we were missed, so Wendholt was the one who we left to get the diesel and set light to them. We were all clock-watching and getting worried, when we spotted a huge black cloud rising over the toilets, and into the office walked Wendholt. He looked all set to go on in a minstrel show and was sadly lacking in the eyebrow department, but his grin made it obvious that the amendments would never be seen again.

At the new supply depot we got the replacement for the commanding officer. Rather a strange choice, he was a cavalry officer, and was totally unfamiliar with the running of a supply depot. This meant that he had the second-in-command just where the second-in-command wanted him. Having said that, he could have been far worse. The depot was duly visited by top brass from command HQ. One of the staff officers got out of the staff car as it entered the depot and before he even acknowledged the guard of honour he touched the whitewashed stones that were all round the perimeter, and remarked, 'That surprises me, they are dry!'

The new depot was quite splendid we had our own railway sidings, large store buildings (that were a cross between Nissen huts and aircraft hangers), an ice house, huge cold stores for the meat and so forth, and our own bakery. There used to be an early morning detail which consisted of some storemen, a couple of clerks, and some butchers. This was to receive fresh fruit, vegetable and meat deliveries, and work out the ration issues for the day.

Wendholt was one of those on regular early detail, and due to this, did not appear on a parade for months. Some time in the past, due to a skin complaint, he had obtained a chitty that excused him shaving. This he kept in his pocket, and grew a pretty impressive beard. This made him really stand out – I believe there are only two people in the whole of the British Army who, due to tradition, are allowed to have a beard. I think it was over a year before he was rumbled and then the beard had to go.

If you were one of the early morning detail or duty clerks (which meant you had been there through the night), you made your way over to the butchery at about six o'clock. There a feast awaited you – the butchers knew how to live – there was bacon, kidneys, sausages, fried eggs, fresh bread, that had been baked during the night, with oodles of butter, and mugs of fresh tea. Once you had seen that lot off, you cleaned your mouth out with a fresh pineapple, and it was worth being on duty all night.

One of the problems on duty clerk was rats. We had a good supply of rats in the area, both at the depot and at the tent lines. Not my favourite species! The first night I was on duty at the depot, I made my bed up in the office. The bed was of a general issue, and consisted of a bed frame which rested on two triangular supports that kept it about six inches off the ground. I was woken during the night by noise – it was rats. They had knocked the waste paper basket over and were chewing the paper, playing football, and fighting on the floor round my bed. I could see their beady eyes in the dark, and as they were at virtually the same height as I was when lying in bed, it was off-putting. I was lying there, trying to think of how to get rid of them, so that I could get my boots on (the most important thing) and put on the light. In the end I went for it, made a lot of noise, loosened my mosquito net and managed to get my boots on. They made a good noise and made you feel more prepared to argue with rats, once your feet were in them.

The next time I was on duty there, I pushed the table up to the wall and made my bed up on that, to give me a height advantage. I fixed my mosquito net to the wall frame and thought that would be the answer, but I was wrong. That night I awoke to find that they were having a fine old time, running along the wall frame and using my mosquito net as a ski run. The net was the type which had a hanger at the head end and tucked in round your feet, which made it a nice slope for the rats to slide down. I tried whacking them as they slid down, but in the end had to go through the noise, boots and then light routine, to get rid of them. Success was finally achieved by fitting the net to the light flex in the middle of the office, with the bed on the table. It did not get rid of the rats, but they could play around, without disturbing you.

Down on the transport park at our depot, there was a 350cc AJS motorcycle that was used by one of the sergeants during the day for getting to and from the railway station. Whenever I was on duty clerk and there at night, I used to have a go at riding it. I had messed about with my father's motorbikes, but had never ridden one. This was great fun, I used to start it up and ride round the depot's perimeter road, getting the hang of how to change gear. This became more hazardous at one time, as the clutch cable had broken. This meant you would start the engine up with the bike on the stand, put it into first gear, ease it off the stand, and you were away, if you had the revs right. If you had them wrong, you either stalled the bike or fell off. This was good experience for, when you were riding it, you could change gear without the clutch, but you had to be dead right with the revs or you sailed through the air with greatest of ease.

One morning I was sitting in the supply office, when the OC came in and said, 'Anyone here who can ride a motorbike?' I immediately said yes, with visions of getting a number that got me out of the office.

'Right,' he said, 'take this crash hat and gloves, and scrounge a lift down to the station. Report to the RT officer and tell him you have come to pick up Sergeant Riley's bike. He has had an accident and broken his leg.'

No need to ask twice, I was off like a shot, and got a lift from one of our drivers. When I got to the station, I reported as instructed and was shown where the bike was. Now I was quite concerned that someone might suspect that my experience of riding motorbikes was virtually non-existent, and even more worried, when I had a hell of a job trying to start it. When the engine burst into life, I knew that, whatever I did, I must not stall it. Everyone was looking at me out of the RT office door, curious, no doubt, as to why I had such a job starting it. The result was that I overcooked it on the throttle and, when I let the clutch out, I headed straight for the office at an alarming rate. The transport park area was only dried mud and the surface was just like sand. I laid the bike over and turned at a hectic angle, with one foot on the ground, and gave it a bit more on the throttle (the old speedway memories coming to my aid). It worked like a charm, and I shot through the gates, going like the clappers of hell. The only problem was that the wheel spin, when I gave it some stick to pull the bike round, had shot a couple of hundredweight of sand in through the office door. I should imagine they were thinking, 'He's either bloody good – or a mad bastard.' In fairness it was the latter. Tootling along on my way back to the depot, I spotted one of our bods walking towards the camp. I pulled in and asked him if he wanted a lift. He said, 'Great' and jumped on the pillion, we rode back into the depot and down to the MT park in great style, but there things deteriorated. I don't know why, for I had been doing quite well, but when we entered the car park, everything seemed to happen at once, including hitting a heap of chains and some buckets. We both came off, but no damage was done. Gosney (the lucky recipient of the lift) criticised my motorcycling skills at some length, and seemed to be a bit put out, when I said I thought I had done pretty well – for my first attempt!

Chapter Seventeen

Malindi, and the CO's Wedding

Things were going nicely at this point, we had even had a few replacements turn up to strengthen our numbers. There had not been a lot of trouble, a few cases of malaria and one bad case of rheumatic fever that had resulted in the man being sent back to England, but then we had a bad outbreak of typhoid in the area and we lost a number of men. I was on firing party twice at funerals, and once as a bearer. Experiences that I could have done without. On the brighter side, I had played in a number of cricket matches for my unit and wound up being picked several times for the RASC area team. This was to go on for the rest of my time in East Africa. It meant quite a few trips down to Mombasa for weekends, to play matches against other regiments. On these occasions I usually had the exacting job of bringing on the lime juice, or fielding for any injured player. In one match I actually made the team and during my spell with the ball took four wickets.

'That should do it,' I thought. 'That should get me into the team proper, instead of twelfth man.'

But the first-choice bowler, a chap called Larkin, got over his ankle injury by the next match, and I was back on the lime juice!

The next thing to cause interest was the area sports event. They were 'press-ganging' people into taking part in the sports meeting, which would be between all of the units in the Mackinnon Road area. This covered field and track events, plus a boxing tournament in the evening. They approached me to see what I would enter and I chose the 880 yards event. I had not done any competitive running since my schooldays, and decided that the competition in the 100, 220 and 440 yard events would be fierce. This was to prove a wise decision, as we had a chap called Whitworth, who, prior to being called up, was at Loughborough training to be a PT instructor. He entered all three of those events and won the lot, plus the long jump. I trained extremely seriously for my event. The night before the sports meeting, I said to a friend of mine, 'Let's go down to the sports field, I had better see how far 880 yards is.'

We went down there, and I was told it was two laps of the track. My friend held my cap and belt, and I ran the distance. The next day at the meeting, to my surprise, I won the event. This was later to be followed up by going down to Mombasa to take part in the East Africa Command championship meeting.

Whitworth, the chap who had cleaned up at the sports meeting, was one of the replacements who had just come out to the unit. I remember being in the washhouse doing my smalls. The 'dhobi wallahs' used to wash and press our uniforms, but we considered it wise to wash our own underclothes and socks, to avoid a complaint known as 'dhobi itch'. With the luxury of water now on tap, this only took a few minutes, and they dried in no time. I was listening to piano music, and very nice too. A number of classic pot boilers – Grieg's piano concerto, followed by Tchaikowsky's *Fifth*. To my surprise a passage was repeated, I thought for a minute the needle had stuck, but soon realised that it was the piano in the canteen being played. I left my washing and went in to find it was Whitworth playing. He was very accomplished, and played a number of pieces that chaps had requested (the canteen now being full). The next thing we knew, he was singing to his own piano accompaniment a selection of Paul Robeson pieces. You have guessed it – the voice was superb. To round off the morning's entertainment people said, 'That's all right, but can you play boogie' – he could and proceeded to do so, extremely well. He obviously was in great demand, and provided all of us with excellent entertainment, but I would not say he was popular. Popularity seldom goes hand in hand with being extremely good at something, but with being good at so many things – never!

There was a short period of chaos in the Mackinnon Road area at this time. For when our replacements came, Group Workshops had also received new men. Some of these were drivers who had done their MT course on fifteen hundredweight Bedfords and that was it. They did not find it too difficult transferring to three-ton lorries, but ten-ton Matadors and tank recovery vehicles were something else. For a few months it was commonplace to see a trail of destruction caused by these lads, and you were very wary if you spotted a fresh, young, untanned face in the driver's cab.

We used to drive back from our working units to the Central Camp for our lunch and this often turned into a race to beat the others there. Early arrivals got shorter queues and cleaner tables, and if you were lucky, fewer flies. One day we were doing the 'Grand Prix' bit with Driver Lonsdale at the wheel and losing the race. He looked round and grinned.

'Don't worry, we'll get there first, I'm going in the back way!'

This was not supposed to be allowed; there was a large ditch at that end of the camp with a bridge of sorts going over it. This had a notice on it stating that vehicles of more than one ton should not cross it. We hurtled over it at something like fifty miles per hour, there was a terrible noise, and when we looked out of the back of the truck we saw that the bridge had collapsed. Fortunately our impetus had carried us over before it went. We were at the cookhouse first, no one spotted the vehicle that caused the problem, and Driver Lonsdale got away with it.

The command sports were held at Port Reitz RAF station on the outskirts of Mombasa. The night before the meeting, I went into town to the pictures, not a wise choice as it turned out. The film was so boring that in the interval I went into the bar for a drink and stayed there. The idea of going to the cinema was to pass the evening without having too much to drink as I was running the next day. Then there was to be one of those coincidences that you just do not think could happen. Some months before I was called up, I met Phil Dicker, a lad I was at school with, and had a chat. He told me that he had joined the merchant navy, and had decided to do this rather than go into the armed services. As long as he completed three years, it would count as his National Service, and he preferred it that way. So when he walked into the cinema's bar, in the uniform of the RASC Waterborne Section, I could not believe my eyes. He was also surprised to see me; it turned out that he had caught some complaint that meant he had to stay ashore for a period, and before he could get another boat he had been called-up. Due to his service in the merchant navy he was able to get into the Waterborne Section, and was quite enjoying, his service, carrying out duties in Mombasa harbour. We had a good evening, the only problem being the amount of lager consumed and the time I got back to Port Reitz.

I was given a shake by a friend the next morning at well after 10 a.m. He said, 'You had better get your gear on, they are calling the 880 yards.'

This shook me. I put my things on, rushed to the washhouse, splashed cold water on my face and made for the track. When the race was started I stayed with the pack until the third bend, and then started to put more pace on and move away. One other competitor went with me, and he appeared to slow down and looked finished, so I headed for the finish. As I went into the last bend, I could hear footsteps coming up behind me, and then saw it was the same chap coming alongside. Down that last straight, I was giving it all that I had got. The second-in-command from my unit was running alongside the track shouting encouragement to me, and in trying to increase my speed I nearly fell (the legs just would not go any faster). As we went over the line he had the advantage and it was annoyingly only inches. I remember one of the officials saying to me, as I ran through, 'Are you all right?' and then I passed out. When I came round, they found me a chair to sit on until I recovered. When I felt better, I went off in search of something to eat. I would not wish to be unfair to the chap who beat me, but without the late night and the lager, I think I would have made it. There was a ceremony at the end of the meeting, and I did get a prize for being runner-up. Funnily enough, it was a penknife-cum-pipe smoker's companion, and at that time I did smoke a pipe. I kept it for years without using it, until one day I picked it up to cut some string and the blade fell off – well I was only second!

Christmas came round without any marked drop in temperatures to warn you, and I found myself on Christmas Eve night on duty clerk at the supply depot. When it came to the time to get the guards' cocoa (yes, even in Kenya the foul cocoa was still to be had), I agreed to go with Driver Lonsdale to fetch it in the truck. Unofficially, we also had agreed to get into the canteen and purchase a load of lager to bring back for the guard and ourselves to drink. When we got to the Central Camp we collected the cocoa and put it in the back of the truck, and then went into the canteen and bought the lager. Things seemed to be going with a bit of a swing in there, so we decided we would put the beer in the truck and pop back for a couple before we returned to the depot. This was probably not wise, but it was Christmas. We got a seat at a table and were drinking our beer, when it occurred to us that some of the bods had obviously partaken of quite a lot. A few tables away, there was a group who had been having the type of beer that made them want to sing. This in itself was not all that unreasonable, but I think it was what they, or to be more specific, what he was singing and how. The song I had never heard before and, fortunately, not since. It had the line in it which I do remember, it was 'As my mother taught me to sing!' The chap who was performing it (an Irishman), in fairness, was not a very good recommendation for his mother's tuition. Someone a couple of tables away remarked on this and followed it up with an empty bottle. He was a better shot than the Irishman was a singer, and it struck him on the head. I have seen lots of films with brawls that break out in bars and thought them to be exaggerated. Not so, the place was a complete shambles, with everyone knocking seven bells out of each other, in a matter of seconds. The NAAFI Staff, who were now running the canteen, were trying to get the shutters down over the bar, but before they could get them down, I saw someone thrown over the top.

Lonsdale said to me, 'Let's get out of here, they are bound to have phoned for the MPs.'

We were both extremely fortunate to get out of there, without being clobbered by someone or something. We ran to our truck, Lonsdale started it up and headed out of the vehicle park. Our blood ran cold as we saw the second-in-command of our unit waving his arms about in our headlights. Lonsdale said, 'We didn't see him' and drove straight at him, and he dived out of our way.

We thought, 'He may not believe us later, when we say we didn't see him, but that was a better risk than letting him get in the truck and finding it full of beer.' The Central Camp had the pole-type barriers with a disk in the centre at the entrances and exits. We belted through, but had the misfortune of the ropes catching on our headlights, which brought the barrier down on the cab roof. Lonsdale was usually one of those slow-speaking and leisurely people who took an age to do things. I was now seeing him in a new light. He got out of the cab, threw the broken barrier in the ditch, and we were off in seconds.

As soon as we got to our depot, we drove round to the butchery. I had the keys and we put the beer in the cold store as planned. Then we dropped the cocoa off to the guard and parked the vehicle. The second-in-command came down to the depot and spoke to Lonsdale who stuck to his story of not having seen him. I don't think he believed him but he accepted it. When he had gone, we started on the beer and were worried that we had to look sober when the orderly officer made his rounds. We need not have bothered; when he finally got to us, he was well away himself and even had a job signing the guards' log.

Our canteen remained closed over the Christmas as punishment for the trouble on Christmas Eve, but this was not too much of a problem; it just meant we had to go to the main NAAFI down at the garrison. This had the military police in attendance, just in case, but there was no more trouble.

There was a scheme in operation in East Africa Command at that time that enabled you to apply for transport and supplies, if you wanted to go off on your own to have a look around the country. It had to be authorised by your CO and there had to be an NCO in charge of the party. Three of us plus one corporal decided to have a go at this, and succeeded in getting approval for a weekend. These schemes were eventually withdrawn because of the trouble that the men caused. Some of the complaints were quite unbelievable like throwing bricks at crocodiles to frighten them off, so that they could get a swim at Misumu Springs! The mind boggles at what else was being done to upset the order of things. Chasing the rhinos, or being beastly to the lions perhaps.

Funnily enough, when we first got to Kenya, coping with snakes and animals like lions was uppermost in our minds. In fact, there were virtually no problems of this kind at all. Mombasa was the only place resembling a town near us and that was about eighty miles away, but the garrison and surrounding depots were apparently quite enough to discourage most wildlife. When you come to think of it, with electric lights, floodlights, construction work and lorries belting about all over the place, it was not surprising that we only saw them when we got away from the camp areas. Lions used to be quite evident at Tsavo, some miles up the road, and the lads up there on the water-pumping station used to see them pretty regularly. Just down the road from the Central Camp, between us and the garrison by the side of the Mackinnon Road, ran the railway lines. There was a shrine there, dedicated to railway workers who had lost their lives by being attacked by lions, while the tracks were being laid. That was well back in time and they were in a far more dangerous situation.

Animals in their natural state have enemies and sources of food that are natural to them, and noisy people with their even noisier machines are far more likely to be seen as something to avoid than attack. In fact, the Masai, when they are looking after their cattle, are known to walk towards lions and make a fair amount of noise, to make them clear off. For the most part, it works, with the odd failure now and then (so don't try it yourself). Most animals will only go for you if you disturb them, and that includes snakes. What we did treat with respect were herds of elephants. As you are no doubt aware, they are vegetarian, but when a large number of them are on the move, you don't want them ambling through your tent lines. We used to have lookout towers to keep an eye out for such problems. We did have one poor old lion walk into the camp, and an overenthusiastic NCO went to the armoury to draw a rifle and ammunition to shoot it. The story went that, by the time he had got the necessary approval and dragged the sergeant armourer away from his tea break, the lion had died of natural causes!

For our weekend we had a fifteen hundredweight truck, complete with its Askari driver, and some rations for the weekend. We had decided to go to a place on the coast called Malindi. It turned out to be quite an experience. It took us most of the day to get there, as the road was the same as the Mackinnon Road, made by clearing the bush and scraping the mud flat. The difference was that it was not in the same kind of use, and therefore did not receive such good maintenance. After fifty or sixty miles of being thrown about and shaken all over the place in the back of a truck, you felt as if you had done three times the distance. For the most part, it was just the bush on each side of you with small African villages here and there. You really felt that this was Africa, especially when we got to the Kilifi river ferry. This was quite small and could take about three trucks and a few people. We drove onto it and got out and sat on the bonnet or stood by the truck, and it was really Saunders of the river stuff. The ferry pulled across the river by a chain. A man was in charge, we knew that for he had an old hat on with 'Chief' written on it, and from time to time he blew into a conch shell, making a noise like a ship's siren. The team of men who pulled it across would walk along the side of the ferry, pulling the chain through, and when they got to the end, they walked back to repeat the procedure. While this was going on, they were all singing, and when they got to the front of the ferry, before they grabbed the chain and started back, they did a solo part of the chant and a bit of a dance. It was a great experience, I can remember thinking, 'This beats waiting for a tin of ink at Winstones!'

When we got to Malindi, it was getting fairly late and we were looking for somewhere to make camp for the night. We had gone past a flash hotel about a mile back, but could not find anywhere to pull off the road. As soon as we saw a clearing with a good stretch of grass instead of bush, we pulled over and started sorting ourselves out. We had just got a fire going to brew up when a jeep came speeding over the grass towards us. The driver asked us what we thought we were doing, and when we answered that we were having a brew up and making camp, he said, 'I wouldn't if I was you, this is the Hotel Sinbad's airstrip.' He gave us the okay to have our cuppa, and suggested we then found somewhere more suitable. This we did and found a spot not much further on. After we rustled up something to eat, we decided to visit the Hotel Sinbad for a drink in the evening. We changed into civvies, which was not too exacting, we just put on a civvy shirt with our KD slacks and that passed muster. We felt it best not to go in uniform, as being in the army put you about one step up from being an African, and in those days that was not good news. The hotel was not too staggering, it was early days, but they did offer glass-bottomed boats and speargun fishing. This did not interest us, largely because it would have cost us about six months of our pay to do it.

One man who befriended us there was both good company and very kind to us. He asked us where we were staying, and when we said that we were in the back of a truck, he gave us details of how to get to a bungalow he was having built near the beach, telling us it was nearly finished and we were welcome to use it. This we did – we moved in to it the next morning, made a base camp there, and immediately went for a swim. Frankly, this was a disappointment. We were looking forward to a nice refreshing swim, but found that the temperature of the water was much the same as jumping into a warm bath. That night we spent back at the Sinbad and thanked the man who had let us use the bungalow. We had a few drinks with him, telling him we had eaten before we came out. This was true; there was no way we could afford their prices on army pay. We decided to have a swim before we turned in. It was a nice moonlight night, there was no one about, and we swam in the nuddy. Two strange things happened that night. Firstly, when we came out of the sea, we found that the beach was covered in millions of tiny crabs – the whole beach seemed to be moving. Secondly, when we got back to the bungalow to turn in, there were no lights, and we discovered that our nether regions were luminous with phosphorescence from the sea.

The next morning we were off on our journey back to camp. The Kilifi ferry was once again an enjoyable experience, and our Askari driver met some people he knew. We noticed that he was joking and laughing with them, and drinking something out of a wooden cup with a straw, and we thought no more about it, until some time later. Once over the river we were off on the road again, and it was not long before we started to get concerned at the speed we were doing. We noticed that not only were we approaching speeds more suitable to a 'Grand Prix' than driving on mud roads, but the driving was also becoming very erratic. It finally finished up with us sailing off the road, and we were very fortunate that the truck didn't actually turn over. We then had to sort things out. The driver had been drinking a native strong beer called 'pombi' out of that cup, and it was obviously a pretty lethal drop of stuff. We put him in the back of the truck to sleep it off, and discussed who was going to drive the truck. None of us had a licence, which was a snag, but two of us were prepared to have a go, myself and Corporal Whitehouse. It was agreed to give the job to Alan Whitehouse as he had more experience than me. (My experience at that time was a few goes round the depot in a three-ton truck).

Corporal Whitehouse proved to be up to the job and we had a reasonable run back to camp. For the sake of appearances and to avoid our Askari getting into hot water, we passed the driving back to him once we were sure he had got over the lunatics' broth. His driving having returned to normal, there were no more hair-raising exploits in the last few miles.

One evening I found that I had run out of tobacco, and the canteen at the camp did not have any. This was pretty careless of me because tobacco was so cheap that we bought it in half-pound tins (at the exorbitant cost of four shillings a tin). The cost of tobacco and cigarettes with the lower duty in Kenya was so much cheaper than in England. Fifty Senior Service were only five shillings and pipe tobacco about sixpence an ounce. It is funny how soon something like that becomes the norm. When we first arrived, troops who had been out there for some time were smoking African cigarettes like Three Spears and Bears Elephants. When these were offered to the newcomers to try, they took a couple of drags on them, coughed, spluttered, and said, 'Why on Earth are you smoking those?' The answer was simple – 'They only cost two-and-a-half cents for ten!' The story about these African cigarettes was that a squaddie found himself in the factory where the cigarettes were manufactured. Watching them being prepared, he noticed that they were made from two parts cattle dung to one part tobacco. One of the overseers saw him standing there and walked over to him.

The squaddie said, 'The way those cigarettes are made really does surprise me.'

The overseer answered, 'Didn't you know there was dung in them?' and the squaddie answered, 'I knew there was dung in them – it was the tobacco that surprised me!'

I did not get any 'takers' for joining me in the walk down to the garrison. It was about a mile away and a duty *gari* (truck) usually took us down and brought us back, but I had missed it. So I decided to walk down on my own. The road passed several camps on the way and had quite long stretches of nothing but the bush on either side. There was no real worry about animals giving you trouble, and I was armed with the response if challenged by any Askari guards of '*Mzungu Rafiki*' (European friend). This was to be on the safe side. The guards were probably briefed on an English reply, but just in case – I had the right answer in Swahili. Having been on guard numerous times myself, it had crossed my mind what a strange ritual the guard challenge was. 'Halt, who goes there?' Would you honestly expect the answer, 'Foe,' or alternately someone with a gun pointing at you answering 'Friend' – just before they shot you! Still, if you found yourself confronted by an Askari waving a *panga* (bush knife) under your nose, it would be just as well to be prepared.

At that time there had been several unexplained incidents, with accidents that had caused loss of life, men being mugged or violently attacked. This had been put down to misadventure, but in the light of later experience could well have been the beginning of the 'Mau Mau' problems. Certainly as far as I was concerned, this would have been a shock to me, for I found the Kenyan Africans a friendly, cheerful and trustworthy people, and could easily nominate a number of nationalities that would have given me far more worry as to their reliability.

On this occasion, I would be a liar if I said I enjoyed the walk. Once you were away from the camp areas, there were the strange noises from the bush to worry about. In addition to this, just off from the side of the road, some yards into the bush, there were men running and calling to each other. All you could see were the burning torches that they were carrying. It was unnerving to put it mildly, and it would be sufficient to say that, when I reached the garrison, I purchased my tobacco, had a few Tusker lagers, and waited for the duty *gari* to get back to camp. The walk down to the garrison on your own after dark was an experience that I did not repeat.

The 'Forthcoming Events Diary' now had a new date entered into it – 'The CO's Wedding'. Our commanding officer was to be married to a nurse on the staff of the British Military Hospital, and a number of men from the unit were invited to both the ceremony and the 'knees-up' that would follow. The invites were based on a representation from all ranks and, for some reason, when it got to privates, there were only two invited. Surprisingly I was one of them.

The great day came round and it was quite something. The CO was resplendent in the dress uniform of the Cavalry Regiment that he had been seconded from, and as the temperature that day was pushing one hundred degrees Fahrenheit, how he stood wearing a blue serge uniform, with the collar done up to the throat, could qualify as the eighth wonder of the world. The fact that he was wearing spurs was another item not overlooked by those who were into ribald comments.

When the ceremony, which included a guard of honour complete with an arch of crossed swords, was over, the guests made their way to the BMH where the reception was to be held. On arrival there, we were all offered drinks by some staff sergeants who were in charge of the refreshments. Now who made their appointments I do not know, but it should go down in history alongside other great military blunders like 'the charge of the Light Brigade.' The first little item that came to my attention was that the staff sergeants giving out the drinks were, for the most part, showing signs that they had got off on the celebrations before us. This was a situation that they intended to remedy as quickly as possible by giving out the martinis in half-pint glasses. The food was very good and was doing a good rearguard action soaking up the booze. The champagne was poured into our glasses by the steadily deteriorating staff sergeants, and the speeches went off quite successfully. The wedding cake was dished out, and it was all very well done.

The next item in the programme was to be a dance. A very good little Italian band had arrived and were now playing. I was most surprised when a sudden attack of democracy overtook the second-in-command of our unit. He came over to me with a nurse on his arm, and after exchanging some pleasantries with me, I was asked by the nurse if I would like a dance. This shook me a bit as 'nursing sisters' in the services held the equivalent of officer rank. Nevertheless, I enjoyed the dance, which was a quickstep, and had the nerve some time later on to go back for a second helping and asked her for a waltz, and was accepted.

Up to this point nothing had gone wrong. A few people were looking decidedly the worse for the demon drink, but the other ranks were behaving quite well. I was having a chat with Wendholt, who was there representing the corporals, when one of the staff sergeants came up to us and asked would we give a hand with SQMS (Staff Quarter Master Sergeant) Wiley. We foolishly agreed, for we knew this SQMS, he was one of ours and we also knew that he weighed at least sixteen stone – probably more. When we got to him he was out like a light, and we were asked to get him into a truck over on the vehicle park for onward transition to his unit. This was not easy to do in his semiconscious state, and we struggled out of the canteen and past the dance, on our way to the vehicle park. His arms were round our shoulders and our arms were round his waist, to support him. His feet were dragging in the dust and he was mumbling incoherently.

On our way, we passed some seated officers from other units in the area. They were majors or above and I am sure that I saw some caps with the red ribbon that denotes staff officers round them. The problem was that I heard some derogatory remarks made as I passed, which were along the lines of 'Those men are drunk' 'Disgusting' 'Bad Form' and that sort of thing. When we got to the truck and heaved the SQMS, now unconscious, aboard the truck, Wendholt said, 'I'll go back with him and might as well stay there – it's getting late.'

I then made my way back to the dance on my own. The main reason for this was that I took exception to the remarks the officers had made. I certainly was not drunk. I stayed on and had a few more beers and a few more dances. The band really was quite good, and I was enjoying the night. Now, in all fairness, by this time I was getting a touch affected by the drink. I come to that conclusion because I remember joining the band and singing *Blue Moon*, and singing in public when sober was not something I was given to doing very often.

The next morning I woke up in bed in my tent back at Central Camp. I thought that I must have had a lot to drink the night before because I had the sort of head that would make you ask the canary to stop stamping about in his cage, and I had a mouth like the bottom of the cage. I said to the lads in my tent, 'I don't remember coming back last night' and they said, 'I don't suppose you would, an RAOC truck picked you out in its headlights, lying in the middle of the road, and brought you back. You had apparently fallen out of the truck you were in originally without anyone noticing.'

I replied, 'Now that's what I call careless, and not only that – I think someone was bad down my bush jacket.'

Chapter Eighteen

They Who Dared
(would have lost)

The supply office had a partition between us and the commanding officers, but the windows in it had not been glazed. Consequently, we could hear a lot of the conversations that took place. Late one morning we heard enough of a telephone conversation to let us know that there was a problem of some urgency taking place. The CO shouted, 'Someone get me Sergeant Williams straight away,' and when he came into the office the CO said, 'Get twelve volunteers together, take them up to the Central Camp, draw rifles and sidearms from the armoury and come back here to pick me up, as quick as you can. There is a riot going on at the Mauritian Pioneer Company!'

Wendholt, at this point, made what I considered a rash request, 'Is it okay for us to volunteer, sir?' he asked, and the answer he got was, 'Yes.'

Well, it rather put us on the spot, and we all volunteered. This left Sergeant Williams with only another eight to find, which he soon did. We all jumped into the back of a three-ton truck and were of to the Central Camp. The sergeant took us into the armoury and we were issued with rifles, bayonets, and steel helmets. We fitted the bayonet frogs onto our web belts, to hold the bayonets, slipped the steel helmets over our shoulders until we were asked to put them on, and got back on the truck. We then drove back to the supply depot and picked up our second-in-command, who was now wearing a revolver on his belt, as was Sergeant Williams. Then we drove to the camp where the Mauritian troops were causing trouble. We pulled up outside the gates and were ordered down off the trucks and told to fall in by the entrance in two ranks.

We could see what was going on, and it was a matter of some concern. There was a large number of men milling around outside the HQ office, and it would be fair to say they were in an ugly mood. They had large pieces of wood in their hands, and bricks were being thrown at the office. No time was wasted, our officer told the sergeant to give the order, 'Port arms' and instructed us to 'put a live round up the spout, and safety catches on.' This had us a trifle confused, as we had not been given any ammunition. When this was explained our officer looked a bit put out, and said, 'All right, give the command to fix bayonets.'

This we carried out as if on parade, and were beginning to get worried. The bayonets we had been issued were the nine-inch variety that looked rather like a screwdriver, and whereas I am sure you would not like one stuffed in you, they did not have the same effect, psychologically, as the old-style sword bayonets glinting in the sun. We were getting just a bit apprehensive at this stage – we had twelve men armed with empty rifles and bayonets and a lieutenant and sergeant armed with revolvers (whether they had any ammunition or not had not been disclosed). If we were about to try to put down this particular riot, then we were outnumbered by at least thirty to one. Maybe I was a coward, but if it was going to be hand-to-hand combat, I personally would have liked the odds to be the other way round.

Fortunately, we then spotted a number of vehicles coming up the road towards us. These trucks disembarked about one hundred plus men, kitted out the same as us but hopefully with ammunition. They formed up outside the camp, and a jeep, which contained the provost marshal and some redcaps drove just into the entrance of the camp area. A burst of machine-gun fire was put over the heads of the crowd, and the provost marshal shouted instructions with a loud hailer to put down any weapons and line up across the area. This they did, without any problems, and the crisis was over. We discovered later that these men had been away from their homes for a ridiculous amount of time, and they were fed up with no notice being taken of their problems. This could, of course, have had serious consequences, as it could well have been classified as mutiny. Fortunately, due to the unreasonable situation they had been placed in, token punishment was meted out to the ringleaders only, and within a month they were shipped back to Mauritius.

Before I came home to be demobilised, I did manage to get ten days' leave in Nairobi. When I knew I was going, I asked around to see if I could borrow any civvies, and a chap called McCallum was good enough to lend me his. What worried me was it was a tweed suit, and I thought I would never be able to wear it because of the temperature. He told me not to worry, when I got to Nairobi I would need it. The journey was made by train. I boarded it at Mackinnon Road in the early evening and did it in style. There was an evening meal and I had a sleeper compartment. It was in the early morning when I awoke, and I then began to see what McCallum meant. We were by now up on the plateau and the temperature had dropped down to less than eighty, which was more than a fifteen-degree drop from what I was used to. When one looked out of the window of the train, there were plenty of animals to be seen – elephant, giraffe, wildebeest, and impala. It was very impressive and all without even leaving the train.

When I got to Nairobi, I made my way to a RASC camp on the outskirts, which was at a place called 'Thika'. The reason for this was the same as usual – money. I needed all I had for the leave, and that way the army paid for my meals and accommodation. This was in 1949 and the city was really quite small and some of the buildings looked impressive from the front but, when you went round to the back, corrugated iron was much in evidence (I have seen programmes on television about Nairobi recently and was amazed at the differences that have taken place). I had a good look round the city and managed to look up a friend who was stationed there. His period of service had been very different to mine. Although only a private, he had servants to keep his kit up to scratch and his room clean. When he was not on duty, he used to play tennis and have a drink in the New Stanley Hotel. It was a different world, but funnily enough, even then, I would not have wished to change places with him.

Chapter Nineteen
Farewell to Kenya

When I got back to Mackinnon Road, the news was that
early in the new year we would be going home for release.
This did not go quite according to plan, as when the
troopship that was going to take us arrived, it was pinched .
to use for evacuating personnel from a trouble spot. This
meant that when the time came for us to go, it was April,
1950. There were a few worries. I was leant on to sign a
short-service agreement, which had the carrot of promotion
to the rank of staff sergeant, but by now I was looking
forward to getting back home and on with my life. The
other worry was medical. I was concerned because the
event I mentioned earlier, when Weary Willie tried to put
me in orbit, had recently occurred, and I had also just had
the misfortune of being got at by a charming creature we
used to call the 'Nairobi Fly'. I have no idea what its proper
name was, but I do remember what they did to you. They
would tunnel under your skin, go for a wander about, lay a
load of their eggs under there, and then clear off! You knew
you had been got at a few days later when the irritation hit
you, and you could see what looked like a scratch. This
then burst open and turned quite nasty, and had to be
treated with Some antiseptic cream to get rid of the
infection. The one I had got started at the top of my chest
and went up my neck and on to my face. My concern was,
knowing the army and its obsession with medical

inspections, that they would decide I was not fit to go. In fact, this was not the case but I lost count of the number of times they would look at my face (which looked like I was just about to go on as the 'Phantom of the Opera'), and then look lower down at the chaffed private parts and say, 'My God, what have you done to yourself?' This I thought to be rather a silly question, unless they thought I was the worst case of masochism yet known to medical science.

The great day came and it was back to Nyali transit camp, but this time, only for a few days and then it was onto trucks and down to Mombasa Harbour to board ship. As we drove down to the harbour we looked at the ships there and laughed and joked, 'That's probably ours, the one at an angle of forty-five degrees that looks like it's sinking' – and it was! The ship was called the *Empire Ken*, she was a bit smaller than the one we came out on, about 9500 tons. We found out that the angle was caused by a design fault. The water tanks were one side and the fuel tanks were on the other. As they were not used up at the same rate, the boat would list according to the difference in their weight. The boat had been refitted as a troopship, and we noticed that she had been built by Blohm and Voss of Hamburg, and the ship's bell had the name 'Iben' written on it.

The return journey was very similar to the outward one, except that we did not have the job of sweeping the decks and the ship was no longer 'dry.' When we had made our trip out, the wartime rule that troopships did not sell alcohol was still in force. The ban had now apparently been lifted. They were still careful about the sales, though; they obviously did not want any trouble caused by overindulgence. We used to queue all round the ship's deck with our mugs (no glasses), and when you were served, you went round and got on the end of the queue again. This way you would get three to four pint mugs during the night at most, and it worked quite well. The price was one of the added attractions – it was only fourpence a pint.

We had a speedier return journey, as we did not damage the boat in the Suez Canal or have to make a detour to Cyprus. We had an afternoon stop at Aden and only a brief wait at Port Sudan, before we went through the Suez. Then there was one day's stop at Port Said, where we were able to get ashore for a while, and a call at Malta without going ashore.

When we got through the Straits of Gibraltar, we encountered heavy weather. There had been warnings that it would be rough, and they were right. This ship did not have the mess deck system, it had a canteen service which was very good. The only drawback we found with this was that the meals were served to you on a pressed-steel tray, which had compartments that the different courses were put in. This was fine until the bad weather hit us, and then we found that the depressions in the tray (that separated the courses) were not all that deep, so you had the problems of custard running into your meat pie and greens or, conversely, gravy on your syrup pud! It was still an improvement on the mess deck system and skidding about with great big buckets of food slurping about, if only in scale.

As before, I found that I had been blessed by nature with the fact that I was not susceptible to seasickness, but will own up to feeling decidedly queasy one night. The problem was that, as so many men were laid low by the bad weather, there was no queue for the beer, so a few of us 'fortunate' people had a seat and table in the lounge and overdid it with the fourpenny pints!

We made the return journey in a mere twenty-nine days, and it passed quite quickly. It was a really good sight to see the coast of England again very early in the morning on the 1st May, 1950. What did come as a shock was that there was snow on the ground. We had all thought the timing would be just right and we would come back to summer temperatures, before we had to get used to the cold again. This, happily, was only a bit of freak weather, the snow had gone by the middle of the day, and it did become an excellent summer.

The situation was the familiar one, the early breakfast, so that we all sat around on the decks for hours. We were back in our crumpled battledresses, which had just been pulled out of kitbags, where they had been for two years. Smart we were not! The ship docked at Southampton, and the disembarkation was another example of the services' strange logic. Announcements kept coming over the Tannoy. 'Personnel who are proceeding to the UK for a course on "Owl stuffing" report to the companionway' and two bods with their kit would leave the ship. 'Commandos who are taking a course on embroidery – report to the companionway,' and three more got off. These sort of announcements went on for more than two hours before finally came 'Personnel proceeding to the UK on release report to the companionway.' As that was ninety per cent of all those on board, it was then pandemonium. We had to go back down below to get our kit on, and then back up to get to the companionway. As everyone wanted to get off as soon as possible, it was a stampede. The chaos of hundreds of men with their kit, trying to get out up those stairs, when only in a good-natured hurry, and not in a panic for survival, again made me think what it must have been like when a troopship was torpedoed or sunk by a mine. It must have been horrendous.

Our kitbags had been unloaded all along the quay side, and the 'find the kitbag routine' was gone through. We were then marched the short distance to the station and boarded the train to take us to Aldershot. There we were met by troop transporter lorries, which took us to the demobilisation centre. The days of being issued with demob suits had passed, and all we had to do was hand in our kit and receive our pay due, and have our release documented. This was done at a great speed I just could not believe it. Before I knew where I was, I was back at Aldershot station with my rail pass, still in uniform but a civilian again – just like that!

It is funny that 'The Homecoming' was one of those things you dreamt of. How great it was going to be. The suntan, the bush hat (with RASC puggaree), the crossed-pangas, East Africa Command flashes on your sleeves, and kitbag on your shoulder – what an occasion! I got off the bus at Kingsbury Green, walked all the way to Burgess Avenue, and who did I see on the way home? Not one single person I knew! The first person I saw was my mother, when she opened the door to me, but then it was great. I had grown a moustache while away and the first thing my mother said to me was, 'What did you have to grow that for?'

My father came home from work shortly after and we had a chat and a cup of tea. I went up to my room and washed, shaved off the moustache (as I thought it would please my mother), and changed into civvies.

When I came down for my dinner, Mum said, 'What did you shave that off for, it suited you!'

Well, you can't win them all. That night I went out to The George with Dad, Keith, and some of my friends for a few beers and a yarn. 'Perfick' – I was home!

Top: The author's parents during the 1940's.
Bottom: Apprenticeship years.

Top: The Eastern Prince.
Middle: Tent lines, Central Camp, Mackinnon Road.
Bottom: The tent survives the second long rains.

Top left: Ready to go on 'Night duty clerk'.
Top right: On board the Kilifi river ferry.
Bottom: The Kilifi river ferry.

Top: The new supply depot.
Bottom left: 'Ready to go on a sortie'.
Bottom right: June, Malcolm and the author, outside
the 'Ongley Arms', Eyeworth, Beds., 1950.

Top: 'The Bomb" at speed.
Middle: HPF99 BSA Scout, summer 1953.
Bottom: The *Iolanthe,* 1956 - Jack and quant
pole in evidence.

Top: Tying the knot, 1952.
Bottom: The author, Margaret and Bernard Battley,
and June, taken at the 'Retirement Thrash', June 1995.

Chapter Twenty
Back to Civvy Street

I took the first two or three weeks after I got back as leave or holidays to get my bearings. Then I went into the works to let them know that I was back and to get a starting date. I found that while I had been away in the forces the company had been in dispute with the union and had been taken off the 'Fair List'. This worried me, so I contacted the union for advice, and was told that my apprenticeship indentures were with the company and that I had to honour that agreement. They also said that the fact that I had commenced my apprenticeship with a union firm would be recorded, and on completion of my apprenticeship, I should contact them and they would issue me with a union card.

When I started back, my employer was pleased to get me back, as he was having to do all the comping himself. It would clear him of that work and he could get out on the road to get more sales. There had been some staff changes in my absence, no doubt due to the row when the firm had been kicked out of the union. As far as I was concerned that was a case of *fait accompli* so I just knuckled down to the job. What really surprised me was how soon everything was back to normal. When I was away I often wondered if things would ever be the same, and after a surprisingly short period of time it was just as if I had not been away.

The firm now being non union meant that I was asked to help out wherever the need was. This did not do me any harm as it widened my experience. In addition to doing the composing, I was also running one of the printing machines when required, and cutting work on the guillotine. The Health and Safety executive was not in existence then; it was the Factory Inspectorate. We did not see them very often, and if they had inspected the guillotine, they would have had a fit. The brake and clutch were not in too good an order, and on occasions the blade would come down for a second strike. It meant you had to keep a sharp eye on it and not get your hands anywhere near it, until you were sure it had stopped. It did have a safety guard on it of a design that was in operation for years. A steel barrier would shoot forward, fractionally before the blade came down. This meant that, unless you had unusually long arms, your hands should be safe but the thump the guard gave you would leave you with either a nasty bruise or break a couple of ribs.

One of the changes that I noticed immediately in the works was that the old shafting, which used to supply the power to all the machines from one large motor, had now gone, and each machine had its own source of power. The other noticeable improvements were hot water to wash in and a cooker to warm up food and make tea – luxury indeed! While the boss was out selling I used to take all customers' calls. If they were new orders, I would keep them as enquiries until they were okayed, but if they were straight repeat orders, I would put them in hand.

During the summer I enrolled for the next session at the London College of Printing at Stamford Street, to take a course as a Linotype operator. This was intended to be looking to my future as this had a higher rate of pay, and if, by any chance, I wanted to get on the newspapers it could be a help.

The friends who were older than me were out of the forces and in circulation, so it was soon back to the old routine. Malcolm, who was younger, was still away in the RAF, but not that far away, as he was stationed at Bushey Park and we saw a fair bit of him. I am afraid that at that time of our lives we probably tended to drink a bit too much, but having said that I would hope that we were not a nuisance to anyone and, as none of us had a vehicle at that time, there were no problems with driving under the influence. Possibly the odd bus conductor or two might have shown a little concern, with 'Are you sure he's going to be all right?' but it was a matter of principle that you were.

One of the things that made my eyes light up when I got home was to see a Jaguar in my father's garage. I wasted no time in applying for my provisional driving licence, and asked Dad if he would help me. I explained that I had driven the odd three-ton truck about on camp sites and knew the rudiments, but would need some tuition and road experience to help me pass the test. He said that was all right, and he would do the necessary, when I got my licence. When it arrived I asked him when we could start and he said the next week – great! My mouth was watering at the thought of getting behind the wheel of that Jag. On the Saturday, I came home for lunch and my mother said, 'Have you seen Dad's new car in the garage?'

I dashed straight out there and looked in. Standing there was a sedate looking Austin 12 hp estate wagon – Blast!

When he came home I asked, 'What's with the Austin, Dad?' and he answered, 'It would not have made sense for you to learn in a Jag, and anyway your mother did not like it – it frightened her to death, so I've changed it.'

I think I managed to say, 'Thanks, Dad.'

The lessons started that week and my father was a good tutor. As soon as I got the provisional licence I applied for my test as there was quite a waiting list at the time. I went through all the usual routines, and used to start the car up in the garage and just move it backwards and forwards a few inches to get the clutch control. My father was the only one to give me actual tuition – which made sense, what you don't want when you are learning is two people giving you different advice. To help out with driving experience, my brother also used to go with me as the necessary qualified driver. This was very successful as on the day of my test it all went smoothly and I passed.

When we got home I asked my father if I could just take the car for a spin round the block on my own and he gave me the okay. On my way round I came down a turning with a milk cart coming in the opposite direction. I thought, 'That's all right. Plenty of room to go by' and held my breath as I went through. My God, it was tight!

On my way back down my own road, I saw my sister-in-law pushing my niece in her pram, pulled over to give her the good news – and put two wheels up on the kerb.

I said, 'I've passed my test,' and got a withering look back. She said, 'It looks like it!'

The car went straight back in the garage, I thought best not to rush things, I will leave it at that. It is a fact that the first month or so when you have got your licence is probably the most dangerous time. My father was right when he said, 'I have got you to pass your test, now you have got to learn how to drive!'

There were several pieces of advice that he gave me in those days that have always stayed in my mind. One was, 'Always consider the other driver an idiot, until he proves otherwise.' Another was, 'Only take notice of indicators when the vehicle's actions confirm that is what the driver is actually going to do.' And, as general advice, 'I was in the right is all very well, but you do not want it as an inscription on your gravestone!'

The Austin 12 had been converted into a station wagon and Dad said its rear springs were not strong enough for the weight of the body. This meant it had some nasty habits, for instance, if you took a corner too quickly, it wallowed around and was difficult to hold on a line. One weekend we jacked the car up and dropped the rear springs off. Dad took them into an engineer's, to have an additional leaf put in the springs, and we refitted them. It was some days later when I was walking down the road and saw the car go by. It was doing a good impersonation of a crab! I told Dad when I got in and drove up the road so he could see for himself. We had to drop the springs off again and, when we checked, they were slightly longer from the centre to the back than the front and we had one on one way and one the other way.

In the August Malcolm had some leave from the RAF and on the Saturday night I went with him to a 'do' up at the mess in Hallum Street. This night was not a great success, largely because Malcolm got involved in the 'Cardinal Poof' routine, which involved consuming a large amount of alcohol in a very short time. I was trying to get him home before nine o'clock that evening and he was as drunk 'as a newt'. We got on a Metropolitan line train, which had the separate 'slam door' carriages, heading for Wembley Park. In the carriage were two dear little old ladies; they were most concerned.

'Is he all right?' they asked.

I did my best to allay their fears by lying and saying, 'It must have been something he ate.' I was relieved when they did not say, 'It smells like it had a lot of rum in it.' I was just grateful that he was not ill before we got out at Wembley.

This all started a strange series of events. The next morning I was expecting to see Malcolm and he had not shown up by midday. Dad was doing some job that he decided required some wood glue, and asked me to go round and see if George, Malcolm's father, would lend him his glue-pot. When I got round to Malcolm's there was, shall we say, an air. It was pretty obvious he was in the bad books for the night before, and I was not sure that some of the blame wasn't coming in my direction. Anyway he walked back round with me and told me he had received the riot act from his parents that morning, when he had returned to the land of the living. He said we would have to slow down on our efforts at trying to get the brewers working nights to keep up with us, and he had agreed to go up and visit his aunt and uncle in Biggleswade, Beds. He wondered whether I would I like to go with him for the day. I had known Malcolm ever since I started school and knew of most of his relatives. There was a picture of this family on the top of the piano in his house and there were two daughters.

'How old would the girls be now?' I asked, and got the answer, 'The eldest would be twenty!' Given this incentive I agreed to go with him. It is strange that on such chance happenings so much of your life's destiny depends. The next day I went with Malcolm and met his cousin June, whom I married two years later.

Two evenings a week I travelled up to Stamford Street for the Linotype course. On Tuesdays we had theory, which consisted of a chat and copious notes to be taken, and, on the Friday, it was practical, when we used to operate the machines. The machine itself was originally produced in the 1800s and I am given to understand that it was used by the national daily papers, to set the news of Queen Victoria's coronation. It is also said that one national daily printed a report the next day with an error that had not been spotted (or purposely overlooked). On the Linotype keyboard the key for the character 'i' is below the character 'a', and the wrong key being struck resulted in the article stating that 'during the coronation procession,

Queen Victoria pissed over Blackfriars Bridge.' The machine was a superb example of how the one source of power (a rotating shaft) could produce so many diverse operations. The advantage was that you could stand behind the machine and see how the cams, cam followers, and levers achieved this. There were two Model One machines, one with electric and one with gas-heated metal pots. A number of Model Fours, and the very latest (at that time) Model 48 Mixer. There were also the competitor's (Intertype) equivalent models, with their flagship, the Model F Mixer. The mixer models gave the facility of two banks of magazines, which meant that the matrices could be used from either bank of magazines, giving greater flexibility. These were very sizeable and impressive machines, and when anyone who had only worked the smaller older models was put on them, nervousness would creep in.

At that time the company that I worked for did not even have a Linotype machine, so when I came in one evening and found my name on the instructors list, down to do a full measure and type change, apprehensive is the word that comes to mind. There were a considerable number of alterations and adjustments to be made to complete this task. I can't remember now how many, but when they were all complete, you cast a blank slug to make sure everything was okay. I checked that I had done everything required, and then came the moment of truth. I pulled the lever to cast and heard the most nerve-shattering noise. For a brief moment I was thunderstruck, but then saw the correct slug had been ejected by the machine, and heard the laughter. A couple of the lads could see how worried I was, and working on their philosophy, 'Never give a sucker an even break!' they had sneaked round to the back of the machine with a galley full of old lino slugs and a metal waste bin, waited until I pulled the lever to cast, and then thrown them into the bin. With mates like that who needs enemies!

Another night we were all standing around the Instructor by one of the machines, and he was demonstrating all the safety stops. As with all machines there were areas where if misused they could be dangerous. One of these areas was the metal pot, which was situated at about the level of the top of your chest to your left. When a slug was cast a plunger in the pot forced the molten lead through the mouth and into the mould. The top of the mould was sealed by the matrices of the line of type set locked into the vice jaws above the mould. The instructor was about to prove to us that, if the matrices were not lowered into position and correctly locked, the machine would not attempt to cast – giving the operator a 'hot foot' in the ear. To demonstrate this he held a previously cast slug between the second elevator and the vice cap as it descended. What he did not know was that the slug he had chosen was a faulty one and hollow. Looking at us, he held the slug between his thumb and forefinger, to create the situation where the safety stop would come into play. The slug collapsed and his fingers were trapped between the vice and the elevator. The starting and stopping handle was pushed in straight away, and he said (quite calmly, I thought, in the circumstances) 'Phone for an ambulance.'

At work, I had just over two years left to do of my seven-year apprenticeship. I had completed the first three years of the City and Guilds course at the London College of Printing, but was now unable to carry on the course, as my employer was not prepared to lose me for one day a week on day release. The Linotype course I was attending was in the evenings and paid for by myself. There was no clash of responsibilities for, as there was never any overtime, I could always get away in the evenings. The learning of my trade was now largely a matter of finding out by doing it, with my employer able to help if he was on the premises, but by now, I was well capable of carrying out the work that was required by the company.

We used to be paid a bonus on the amount of CC41 tickets that we produced. These were the 'utility labels' that were sewn into garments and were printed on linen. We used to print them on an automatic platen machine called a British Thompson which was the equivalent of the German Heidelberg. The problem with running these on the machine at any speed was, that the gripper bar that fed the sheet into position used to return from the delivery, and catch the tail of the sheet it had just delivered, on its return to pick up the next sheet. This was caused by the momentum, at any reasonable speed, causing the tail to curl forward. Having worked out the problem, I bought some rubber tubing and a few gas fittings and rigged up a modification on the machine, to use when running these labels. This was done by redirecting an air blast, used for another function, and calibrating it so that it blew the tail of the sheet flat at the right moment to prevent it being caught up in the delivery bar. This I kept to myself and the fact that I could run the machine far faster provided me with 'a nice little earner' for some time. The secrecy was brought about by the fact that previously I had approached my employer with a proposition regarding the punching of swing tickets, which we used to have done by outwork. I offered to do them at half the price we were paying. After a few months, he asked me how I was doing them and I said I had made a machine to do the job at home. He was not satisfied with getting them at half the price, and made me an offer to buy the machine off me and pay me a royalty of so much per thousand. This I agreed to, but at the end of the first month with other people in the works using the machine, we produced far more than he thought we would. He halved the bonus and said that I was mistaken about the original figure, and being naïve, I had nothing in writing, so I had to put up with getting only half the sum I was due. This was the reason that I kept quiet about this latest gadget – to avoid a similar stitch-up!

My leisure time was being spent with two nights at night school and three nights out with my friends. What we did depended on the time of the year. In the summer, cricket took up one night with nets and an evening match if we had one. It was a period of my life that made me appreciate the *Likely Lads* series when it was shown. The programme was based on the north of the country, but proved that the divide was not as great as some people thought. The problem of trying to have a night in being almost an impossibility. Your friends would descend upon you with the 'Let's pop out for a swift half.' A contradiction in terms and wrong on both counts; it never was a half nor was it swift!

One Sunday morning at our local, we were chatting to one of the lads we knew from our school days. By a coincidence he was also an apprentice compositor and therefore short of the 'readies'. He showed us some business cards he had printed for himself (what is known in the trade as a 'foreigner').

These, we were amazed to see, were advertising him as a vocalist. 'Denny Brown – Sweet and Low.' The mind boggled! He told us that he was singing at a local hotel at the weekend and would see us there if we went. This we agreed to do and, I am ashamed to say, with just a touch of 'malice aforethought'. If Den had a problem, and he did, it was his fondness for the amber liquid. We met him in the bar at the dance and treated him to a more than reasonable amount of his favourite tipple. He was just seeing off his latest, when he was given the word that he was wanted to do a couple of numbers with the band. He straightened his bow tie and went to join the band. The way he handled the microphone quite surprised us, he looked very professional. The band played the intro to his number, but Den blew it, so they played it again; this time he did start to sing. The fact that he was not in tune with the band was a bit of a problem, but the bigger one was he could not remember the words either. The band was in dead trouble and ground yet again to a halt. Den turned to them, and not realising that he had not switched off the microphone, announced to the band and everyone in the dance hall 'I'm sorry, chaps – I'm afraid I'm pissed!' As far as we know, after that the bookings either thinned out, or he went well away from the area to try and carry on with his vocalising career.

Throughout this period I was seeing June most weekends, one weekend it would be at my parents in Kingsbury, and the other weekend it would be at June's in Biggleswade. I had no car in those days and the journey meant three changes of buses. An 83 or 183 from Kingsbury Green, a fairly long run on the 716 Green Line from Golders Green to Hitchin, and a United Counties bus from there to Biggleswade. This was a bit of a drag and caused a couple of occasions that stay in my memory. There was the time when, spending a few minutes too long in a hostelry in Hitchin with June, I missed the last Green Line. This was a bit surprising because it was only just after nine o'clock in the evening. I caught a bus to Welwyn thinking I could get another bus from there – but I was wrong – there wasn't one! At about 10.30 p.m. I started to walk from The Bull, Welwyn (no – I had not been in there!). The idea was that I would be able to thumb a lift from there on the A1. This was where I made my second mistake. I did get a lift eventually when almost into Mill Hill. This was from a chap in a Jaguar. The engine was missing badly, and it was jerking along at a not much faster pace than I was walking. He either picked me up because it would take him so long to get by me, that he would have been embarrassed, or he thought the car was going so badly he might need a push. As the saying goes, 'beggars cannot be choosers', so I got in. That lift took me as far as the Burroughs Pond, Hendon, and then I was back to my hiking. I got in at just after three o'clock in the morning. I had left Hitchin at 10.30 p.m. and I must have walked a good twenty miles. It had crossed my mind to ring my father and ask him to come and get me in his car, but then I looked at my watch. Dad was pretty reasonable in most things, but he started work early and he did like his sleep. I decided the walk would be less of a problem! I had a nice sleep until my father woke me up to go to work at about 6.30 a.m. – Great!

When it got round to the summer of '51 we had a glorious spell of weather, and I had a brain wave. I popped round to Malcolm's and asked him if I could borrow his racing bike for the weekend. I proposed to cycle up to Biggleswade as the weather was so good. Being a good chap he agreed to this and parted with the machine. It was a very good one, an Ace of Spades Vitesse and a joy to ride, with one exception – the saddle! It was like sitting on a razor blade. Now Malcolm knew that I was no stranger to doing distances on cycles, he remembered my racing and touring days, and, not having been out of the services for long, I should have been fairly fit, and my thoughts were along the same lines. I carefully folded up my suit and put it into a haversack, as June and I were going to a dance that night. I slipped into my shorts and was off. I soon settled into the old rhythm, the bike was super, the morning's weather was wonderful, and I was on top of the world. I belted through Hatfield, making very good time, and then saw in front of me on the right a pub called The Roebuck, just outside Woolmer Green on the old A1. What a good idea having a pub in just the right spot for a break. I rode into the car park and went in. The first pint went down without me noticing it, so I had another one to taste. I did enjoy it but had to be on my way. Back onto the A1 the old legs went like pistons, until eventually I came to Stevenage. Here there was an excellent Hotel called The Crown, and the pangs of hunger were gnawing at 'me vitals'. I leant the bike against the wall and went in. Roast chicken and three veg and a couple of Worthingtons, and 'What have you for sweet?' I asked. The waitress had two or three choices, and one of them was bread and butter pudding. Now, if I have a weakness (and I have quite a few) one of them is bread and butter pudding. Not only did I have the pudding, but as it was late and I was probably the last customer to be served, I was given all that they had left! Out of The Crown, onto the old velocipede, and away, but not all that far away. When I reached Baldock, a rest seemed an excellent idea. I rode into a field, put the pack under my head – and woke up at about four-thirty in the afternoon. I got back on the Super Vitesse, and made Biggleswade by about 5.30 p.m.

It would be fair to say that the next day the old legs were in pretty poor shape. Not only had there been the forty-five mile ride but I had been dancing with June until midnight. The only thing I used any energy on, during the Sunday, was borrowing a different saddle. I would be a liar if I said I was not concerned at the prospect of the return journey, for I was! That evening I said my farewells at around seven o'clock and got on the bike and set off back. There was one thing I had learnt on the Saturday and that was that the ale and roast dinners were not advisable for mid-journey stops, and I was determined that, when I got off that bike the next time, I would be outside my house in Kingsbury. It was and I was surprised to find that it was just after 9.30 p.m., a very acceptable time for someone who was knackered before he even got on the bike.

With my apprentice's wages being so low, I was constantly looking for ways to supplement my income. There were two sources at around that period, one of which was helping Malcolm and his father, who had a small building business. When they had a job on, which was going to require some assistance, such as laying concrete bases for garages and similar projects, they used to offer me some weekend work, which gave me some extra cash and kept me fit. Mixing cement or concrete by hand using shovels, and wheeling barrows of the stuff to where it was required was not light work.

Another area was helping my father, who, at the time, had just invented a machine for laying thermoplastic white lines. He had the machines made at two different companies, with a third one assembling the complete machine. In the past he had had other inventions, one of which he had received a royalty for, from the engineering firm who produced and marketed it. This had not gone well for a number of years, and when the company offered a sum to buy the rights out, he accepted. I think it would be fair to say that from that time on their fortune changed, they sold in large quantities and could be seen throughout the country. So this time he had decided to go it alone and proposed doing some work with the machines to get them noticed, and then offer them for sale or hire. He would then plough the profits back into financing the production of further machines for sale.

My brother, Keith, and I had some great times working on some of those early projects with our father. There was the fact that the early machines were prototypes, and it was only by using them that we could identify any problems. There was the additional snag that, once the markings were laid down with the molten plastic, they were down for three years. As soon as they had set, the only way to get them up, was with a cold chisel and hammer, and the surface they were laid on usually came up with them! One of the early problems we had was with the mouth of the delivery chute. It would get a stone or piece of the road surface in it and jam open. Out would pour the molten plastic, much to everyone's consternation. This happened to us for the first time when we were lining the car park of a restaurant, on the outskirts of Radlett. The first thing we knew was that the plastic was pouring out, and we could not shut it off. This resulted in a large white blob, of about a yard in diameter, in the middle of the car park, and by the time we got it up, a fair quantity of the car park's surface had come up with it. When the job was done, Dad went in to get paid for the job, and we were in the car park with the engine running, ready to beat a hasty retreat and killing ourselves laughing at the row we could hear Dad having with the customer.

From then on we had a flat tray to hand, so that, when the same thing happened, we could quickly get the tray under the chute to limit the problem. One of the things we used to pull Dad's leg about was his estimating. If he said to us, 'We've got a little job on for Saturday,' we knew we could write off Sunday as well – he always underestimated the time required. We did a job one weekend that entailed lining the workshops and parking areas at a large Godfrey Davis garage. On this occasion we encountered difficulty in the thickness of the lines we were putting down. We knew they were thicker than they should be, but as Dad said, 'They have got nothing to moan about, they'll last for years!'

Later in the day, one of the chaps who worked there came over to us and said, 'Are you the blokes who are putting those little walls all over the place?'

The machines were steadily improved upon and went on to be quite successful, but by that time it was becoming a job to leave to the professionals. The work had to be carried out at the weekends as we all had our own jobs to do during the week, and it was taking up a lot of our free time for a very small amount of remuneration. It was fun while it lasted and it was a time that I enjoyed, even the occasion when the machine broke down and I laid all the lines, including the lettering, with a handgun that was topped up from the main machine. It was a bitterly cold afternoon, which I had to spend doubled over, to do the marking by hand. I spent the next week walking about looking like a croquet hoop!

The next thing to provide me with my main source of interest and entertainment, was becoming the proud owner of a vehicle. My brother, Keith, had bought a 1930 Austin Seven saloon the previous year and was now moving onwards and upwards to a 1936 Standard Nine. He offered the Austin to me for the 'king's ransom' of twenty-five pounds. The offer was too good to miss and I blew the majority of my savings on it. The car had already gone through a period of improvement in his hands – it now went! It had stood at the bottom of someone's garden all through the war, and their dog had slept on the roof until it had collapsed. A lot of work had to be carried out to make good the ravages caused by the rain getting in for about four years! As I said, it was a means of getting from A to B (even if it was by way of C and Z). It was quite probable that my brother's decision to change the car might have been influenced by his journey from Kingsbury to Birchington, in Kent. This trip, to go on a summer holiday, with his wife, daughter and mother-in-law in the back, took from about nine o'clock in the morning until about four-thirty in the afternoon – not exactly trouble free! He spent a considerable time doing up the Standard. All of the floor had to be replaced and a lot of work had to be done repairing and making good the bodywork. This was something he was well able to carry out as his trade at the time was a panel beater.

I can remember getting up to see him set off for a holiday in the Standard, with his wife and daughter, one

Saturday morning. It was probably the car's maiden voyage, and it would not start. It was in the days of the starting handle, a mixed blessing as they encouraged you to drive about in cars with dodgy batteries. He swung the handle time and again, with no luck, and finally, it must be said, with a touch of bad temper. I would go as far as to say that the handle was turned so vigorously by him that, if the car had come off the handle, we would have had great difficulty in finding it! It still showed no sign of life. At, this point the passenger window was wound down by his wife, who put her head out of the window to give him a little encouragement, by saying, 'I said you shouldn't have bought it in the first place!' Yes, you can always rely on the ladies to come up with the finishing touch at times like these.

With help from my father, more work was carried out on my Austin Seven on the mechanical side, and I spent considerable time getting the interior as near as I could to how it should be (I even had the metal dashboard grained to look like wood). The brass work was cleaned and polished and a brass tube fitted across the front to support the wings, which had a tendency to sag. The bodywork was coach-painted in black and maroon, and for the finishing touch the name was discreetly painted on the bonnet – The Bomb. The window of the driver's door was broken, and I said to the blokes at work that I had to get a new one and mentioned the price. A guillotine operator, called Bob Johnson, said, 'Don't pay all that, bring it in on Friday and I will get you one fitted for half that price!'

This I did, and on the Saturday evening I proudly drove to Golders Green bus station to meet June off the Green Line bus. Let's face it, I was proud of that car; I was only twenty years old and a vehicle owner, and there were not many of them of my age about at that time. I got out of the car, with an air of what I hoped to be nonchalance, and flung the car door shut, at the same time as I started to cross the road. I heard a crash and looked back to see, to my horror, that the new window was now a heap of broken glass lying in the road. I returned to the car and kicked the broken bits underneath it, doing my best to look inconspicuous. I then met June and said that I hoped she did not mind the icy blast coming into the car as there had been a slight accident with the window. Another lesson in life had been learnt, if someone offers you something for half-price – watch it!

June was very good over 'The Bomb' – it was not the most reliable of cars and she became quite accomplished in the art of pushing it, when required. Her sister Rene's husband had a 1928 Morris Minor and we had lots of good times with them. This was at the time when, if we could not maintain and repair our own cars, then we were off the road, for there was no way we could afford garage bills. One weekend we took both cars to visit a couple of June's aunts and uncles who lived in Huntington. They were very lively couples, and we did not leave their house until after twelve that night. When we set off, I thought, I must keep Jack's rear light in view (in those days, not much more than a cigarette end) or I won't know where the hell I am. He thundered off, and I could not believe the trouble I was having, keeping up with him. The two cars had different performance strengths. My Austin had the advantage on acceleration and pulling up hills, and his Morris had the advantage on long straights without too much of a gradient. This usually evened itself out on a run, but this night I was having a struggle – the car was just not running right. We managed it back to June's home in the end, to my great relief. The next morning I went out to check the car. I was worried by what was wrong, for I had the run back to London that night. As soon as I looked in the car, I could see what the problem was. I had a rubber connection piece off an electric iron's flex, which was split, so that it would fit over the choke control, to stop the choke opening before I wanted it to. When the car had warmed up, I just used to slip it off the control and it would allow the choke to open. I had forgotten that this gadget was on and had driven all the way back with the choke closed. It was a miracle that the car had not flooded and packed up!

Another time when the car did not endear itself to June was when I drove too fast through Sutton Splash, and as the handbrake just went through a slot in the floor, the water shot into the car just like a whale spurting out water and we were both drenched! A problem with the Austin Sevens was that they had cable brakes and half rear springs that bolted into the chassis, which ended just under the front two seats. If, when you had two people in the car, your brakes worked well, then, when four people were in it, the weight depressed your rear springs, which stretched the cable to the point where your brakes were binding. Conversely, if the brakes were okay with four in the car, then you had virtually no brakes with two in it. This meant that you had to compromise and you had lousy brakes all the time!

In those days there were lots of problem areas which would have proved lethal in today's traffic conditions. One of the biggest assets for motorists has been the introduction of the car heater, which also heats your windscreen, keeping it free from ice. We used to try all sorts of things to stop the screen from freezing and to maintain visibility of the road and traffic. One method was to rub a raw potato over the screen, another was to keep a bottle of glycerine and smear this over the screen. The trouble with that was trying to see through the rainbow effect it caused. There were windscreen heaters that worked off your battery, which would give you a slit of about one and a half inches to look through if the weather was not too severe. All right, as long as you did not expect the car to start in the morning – because the battery would be flat due to the heater!

Windscreen wipers were not considered necessary to enable the passenger to see out of the windscreen, and only one was provided for the driver. I am not sure if this was good for nervous passengers or made them worse. Most wipers were of the vacuum type that worked off the carburettor. These worked fine if your engine was not being asked to do too much, but as soon as you had to put your foot down on the accelerator to climb a hill they stopped. I used to say, 'These wipers are great, they start going when your car hits something, so that you can see what it was!' They fitted a storage tank later, to improve them, and this meant you were okay on short hills. Effective electrics eventually provided the excellent wipers we have today, and the twelve-volt systems are a great improvement on the old six-volt ones that gave you headlights that you could just about see your bumpers by!

Chapter Twenty-One

Tying the Knot

Life settled into a routine, albeit a pleasant one with work, the college, and the alternate weekends to Biggleswade to see June. The winter was a pretty foul one, and there were times when the journeys back and forth to Biggleswade were troublesome. In the February, when June was down at my place, I decided to put a proposition to her. It was, of course, extremely romantic. I think it went along the lines of 'I don't know about you, but I think all this travelling back and forwards is a pain in the neck, especially in the winter. How about getting married and we will find furnished accommodation, until we can save a deposit for a house?' June agreed and we went into Harrow to buy an engagement ring. It was soon settled that we would get married in the July.

I have had to make numerous decisions during my life, especially later when I was in responsible management positions. The number of times that I could honestly say, 'That was a good decision that I would not alter in any way' were nowhere near as frequent as I would have liked. There were more when it would have been be fair to say, 'I could not have made a better decision, in those given circumstances.' With regards to my marriage, I can safely say, 'It was not only the right decision, it was also the most successful one!' There are still times when I think that taking into account the 'lottery' that marriage can be, what good fortune I had with my choice and June's acceptance.

We were married in the July of 1952. I was still on apprentices' money, as I had started my indentures late. When couples get married now, it is usually a case of jetting off to somewhere exotic, and coming back two or three weeks later to a well-furnished flat or house. This was not quite the case with us. The wedding was fine, with all the trimmings, and we went off to Ilfracombe for a week in a guesthouse. Now, I am not having a go at Ilfracombe, it's a nice place, but let's face it, it's not the Bahamas. We had a great time and could not stop laughing. We had seen the film *Genevieve*, where they had the room with the church clock opposite – well that was us! It chimed every quarter of an hour and when it struck the hour it even rattled the vases on the mantelpiece. Another little thing that tickled us was a couple who were on the 'Capstone' one morning. We were safe in assuming that they were newlyweds, and the husband wanted to get a nice souvenir snap of his bride. He took an eternity getting her pose just right and fiddled for ages with the camera settings. Finally he was satisfied all was as he wanted it. She smiled, and just as he took the snap, a seagull, the size of an ostrich, got a direct hit on her head!

As soon as we got back, we moved into our part-furnished rooms, the furniture was all in the dining room/lounge, and the bedroom had to be furnished by us. This was a bit of luck, as it enabled us to start getting things of our own. The house was in Church Drive, with the possible advantage of being not more than a mile from my relatives and near friends. June quickly got herself a job in the offices of a company called Fischer Foils in the Wembley Stadium grounds and we started our married life. The idea was that we could start saving for a place of our own, and we were together, which was what we wanted.

We were not under any pressure, and it must be said that we did concentrate just a bit on having a good time. We went to the theatre, concerts and dances and generally had a most enjoyable period. There was the odd fracas, like the time when for some reason there was scrambled egg on toast on the dining room carpet, and we were having a 'Mexican stand-off' as to who was going to pick it up! My parents were about to pay us a visit, and with seconds to spare, we hit on the face-saving formula of sliding a sheet of paper under it, so that we could both pick it up at the same time! There was also the occasion very early on, when I got back from seeing my cricketing associates, one Sunday morning in The George, a trifle late. When I sat down for my dinner, June said, 'What time do you call this? I had your dinner ready an hour ago.' My flip answer of 'Well, that was silly of you' was hardly out of my mouth before my dinner was on my head! These things were invariably taken in good spirit and usually ended in the pair of us having a good laugh. One night we had been to see a particularly creepy horror film at the cinema. When we went up to bed I said to June, 'Take a good look at me!' and not surprisingly got a strange look from her. I turned off the light, quietly got into bed and asked, 'Are you sure I'm the same person?'

The weeks and months flew by and I had completed my apprenticeship. I contacted the union for my card, but was told that they would get in touch as soon as they had no unemployed on the books. A good year later I received the letter asking me to go and see Mr Isaacs, at the London Society of Compositors, at St Bride Street, at 10.30 a.m. on a Wednesday. This I did and was there outside his office about three minutes before the appointment. I knocked on his door, looked in, and said, 'Mr Issacs, I have an appointment with you at ten thirty' and his answer was 'Well, that's when I suggest you come into my office.' It was almost a case of losing my ticket before I got it. To say I was not happy with that reply would be an understatement, but I took it. I had a living to earn and was not prepared to let bad manners interfere with that. I was given a probation card, as the firm I was at was non-union, and a call card for an interview at a firm in Tottenham Court Road. The union told me that the firm I was with would not be prepared to continue employing me with a union card, so I should try this company which had a vacancy. When I got to the company, the interview went well and they asked me if I minded doing stonehand's work as well being on the frame, and my answer was that, in fact, I would like the variety. It was agreed there and then I could have the job, and I was to ring them and let them know when I could start.

I went back to my firm, and by this time it was gone twelve. When I saw my employer he asked me why I was so late, and I told him that I had been up to 'the House' to get my union card. He then informed me that I could not work there with a union card and I should know that! I said I was sorry but I had my future to think of, and was told to get my things together and leave the premises, and he would have my money sent on to me. Now it would be untrue to say this did not upset me. I knew what the end result had to be, but I had worked for him for more than nine years (including the two years in the army) and not to even get my coat off, before collecting my tools and overalls and getting off the premises, I thought harsh.

As soon as I got out of the works I made a phone call to the other company, and asked them when they wanted me to start. They asked if I could get there the next morning at eight o'clock. I said that I could, and it was agreed. I had a bit to eat and went off to meet June out of work. When she came out she was surprised to see me and looked at my case with my tools in and the dust coat I was carrying and said,

'What's happened?' I told her that I had been fired and she asked me if I thought I would be able to get another job, with some concern in her voice. I put her mind at rest and told her I had already got one. It was at a much better rate of pay and I was to start in the morning.

Chapter Twenty-Two

Print in the Fifties

My job at the first printing firm that I joined after completing my apprenticeship was quite an experience. It was a far bigger company and the work was totally different. I had a lot to learn and the experience I got there was invaluable. My apprenticeship had taught me the fundamental aspects of the trade, but this was another world, and to start with I had to learn the jargon. I did not get off to a good start on my first morning, I walked past a bench and got my dust coat caught on the handle of a rule and lead cutter, which pulled off onto the floor and broke into three pieces. So it was into the composing room manager's office with the 'You know that rule cutter you used to have' bit.

One of the problems I discovered was finding where things were, only having worked in a small company, where if something existed you knew where it was. In the bigger companies there used to be strange practices of hiding materials for your own use. This was known as 'slumming'. As an example, one-point lead was scarce and much valued. As soon as you knew it had been cast you went to get some, and it had already disappeared. It would be hidden around the department at the back of type cases, or personal drawers, in different 'comps' frames (the racks that you used to work at). I well remember one day searching for a ten-point Old Style acute 'e', and someone said to me, 'Ask

Alf O'Neil.' I did, he looked around furtively and took one out of his waistcoat pocket. He gave it to me with an air of 'Whatever you do – don't tell anyone I gave it to you.' This sort of thing was not unusual, I am sure lots of time was lost by men looking for items to work with, which, if only they had not been slummed, would have been plentiful.

There were also all the rituals related to overtime, the language of which had to be understood for a start. The FoC (father of the chapel, the union official in other trades referred to as a shop steward) would appear by your side and enquire, 'Are you on for a dark'en tonight?' In English this would be, 'Do you want to work four hours overtime tonight?' Or 'Are you on for an all-rounder tonight?' This was doing a further eight or ten hours work, carrying on after an hour's cut (break), through the night and having the next day off! These overtime situations were usually caused by a job getting well behind on a schedule that had to be met, either due to unexpected delays (like the customer not getting copy or corrected proofs to you) or disasters like the dreaded printer's pie, typeset matter that had been knocked over or upset, so that the characters had got mixed and out of alignment. This was something that was a compositor's nightmare. I have seen heavy machinery being moved, in a very precarious fashion, past an imposing stone, with two 'comps', who would have been flattened if it had toppled, much more concerned that the job on the stone was not pied than for their own safety.

There were union rules to watch out for, again not so strict in small companies and non-existent in non-union ones. Most had a sound foundation at some point in time in the past, but some were downright stupid, and there were areas which definitely speeded up the transition from letterpress to litho-printing. There were, for instance, corrections to be carried out on the bed of the printing machine, which were rightly to be carried out by a compositor. There were also times when you trudged off to the machine room, to simply loosen the quoins that locked up the forme and transfer one piece of lead! So many things had come about through the understandable lack of trust between management and workforce. Even to this day, when things are far more realistic, there still tends to be a fear that whoever has the balance of power will abuse it. I would like to say that this is now an unnecessary fear, but with situations like 'the Maxwell pension scheme', it is difficult to say that those fears are groundless. The biggest problems are restrictive practices that are carried out to maintain earning capacity, which realistically are only putting everyone's livelihood in peril. Such things as running machines at agreed outputs, well under their capability, to ensure overtime. It is only fair to take into consideration, before you plunge into your condemnation, the facts that in the past men had to suffer such charming practices as being laid off work every summer just before their holidays and re-engaged in the autumn. One comp that I worked with swore he had been fired and re-engaged thirty times by one company! The situation now is far better and, hopefully, a more enlightened view is being taken by both ends of the spectrum. There are, unfortunately, and always will be, backwoodsmen to be contended with, by both management and labour. Trying to resolve this is no easy task and you can take that from someone who spent a considerable time at that particular sharp end!

It is often said by people in the trade that you do not get the characters in the industry that you used to. That is quite possibly a case of nostalgia striking again, but I know what they mean. We surely had our fair share at that company. The works' manager had been quite a successful all-in wrestler, before being wounded at Dunkirk. We had a bindery overseer who sang in the chorus at Covent Garden

Opera at night, and three men whose gambling exploits were legend. There was another man who could carry out his job perfectly satisfactorily, in spite of the fact that, if he had drunk only half as much, he would still have been an alcoholic. A lad in the machine room, who, even if you were kind, you would still refer to as an 'oik', who was into Nelson Eddy and Jeanette Macdonald musicals, and sang songs (in a superb voice) from them all day as he worked, and those are only a small sample.

We had a trophy that we used to award every week, which was a large 'cup' made out of lead. This was known as the 'Gobbler's Trophy' and it went to the employee who knocked up the most overtime in any one week. It was usually won by a Monotype keyboard operator called Bill Sandal. The story went that, if you left a window open, Bill would be in! The keyboard operators had a small department, there were four of them and Bill worked on nights. At the end of the alley that led through to the works was a London Kiosks' tobacconist's; he would call in there when he came on shift and purchase twenty Capstan full strength cigarettes and an ounce of Condor Flake for his pipe. All of this would be smoked during the night, and he would call in and purchase more on his way out. As soon as the day shift came on, whatever the weather they would open all the windows and the door, to get air in there – and they were all smokers!

The works' manager had a clerk in his office, and it was well known that his treatment of him was not good (in fact, it was dreadful). One afternoon there was a sudden commotion, and Mr Lilley, the opera singer, came tearing through the comp room. He was in a real state and was shouting out, 'Mr Timms is murdering Jim [the Clerk]!' The next thing we knew was Mr Timms made an entrance and chased Mr Lilley round the works shouting, 'If you don't mind your own business – I'll bloody well murder you!' It all quietened down and things returned to normal. We then got the 'gen' – apparently Mr Timms was on the phone and asked Jim a question, he did not like the answer he got and said something most unpleasant to Jim. At this, we were amazed to hear, Jim came completely out of his downtrodden character, and did no more than punch Mr Timms on the nose – not the wisest of things to do to a man of short temper and wrestling background. Timms ended his phone call abruptly and started to settle scores with Jim. When it reached the point where he had him in a head lock and was ramming his face into the filing cabinet, Mr Lilley passed by the open door and went into his 'Murder' routine. Funnily enough, after this event, the two of them got on far better. The day after the event Jim Flowers walked through the composing room; his face had been well rearranged and was a 'four-colour' job! The boys then started.

'Is that right you had a fight with Mr Timms, Jim? Who won?'

My Austin Seven had been sold to assist in raising money for the wedding, and making purchases of furniture for our rooms. This sale was unique in being the only time, in all the buying and selling of cars that I have been involved in, that I have made a profit. I purchased it for twenty-five pounds and sold it for seventy-five. Even then, when you take into consideration the money and time spent on its improvement, it did not constitute a profit in real terms.

A couple of doors down the road from my parents, a friend of the family (a Mrs Pike) had a chap stopping with her as a lodger. I heard on the grapevine that he had been married, was in the throes of divorce, and was selling his sports car to raise some capital. My first reaction to this was that it would be expensive, it looked a little beauty! When I heard the price it was going at, my interest was immediately aroused. I said to June that I would go and have a look at it, just out of curiosity. The owner took me out in it, and let me drive it. The impact on me was much the same as when Mr Toad in *Wind in the Willows* had a similar experience. Fortunately June was of the same mind, my earnings had improved with the better wage I was getting, plus the extra overtime, and she was also at work. We decided, and I think rightly, that we were only twenty-two – so let's live a little! Within a couple of weeks 'HPF 99' was ours, and for the enjoyment we got from it, it was worth every penny. It is true that, in many ways, sports cars, with the dreaded hood and sidescreens, are not very practical in the English climate. There is no question, though, that the exhilarating experience of driving or riding in one is hard to equal. The only things I have found to challenge it are riding a motorcycle, and dinghy sailing (when the wind is lively!). Driving along in that car with the hood down on a summer evening did me a power of good psychologically, if not physically. It was a case of goodbye cares and hello rheumatism!

The company in Tottenham Court Road was all letterpress, which was not unusual at that time, as the lithographic process had not yet made the impact that it was destined to. The higher machine outputs, costs of origination and quality, were not yet at the point where they would eventually dominate the trade. As I mentioned earlier, some of the practices on the letterpress side were also going to be a big factor. I spent a couple of weeks doing all the overtime I was prepared to do, working on HMSO (Her Majesty's Stationery Office) work for example. We were producing booklets for all the British islands and protectorates. Each cover was exactly the same, with the exception of the names. I had preset the titles on the Ludlow machine and, at this point, all I was doing was sitting up by the Heidelberg Platen that was running the job, and changing the titles for each book as it was printed. This was a job which the machine operator should surely have been able to carry out, thereby reducing the cost by at least forty per cent.

Machine corrections used to be a very unpopular job for compositors, especially when they were on the larger flat-bed printing machines. This used to entail taking the type corrections and material to the machine and clambering under the feeder, to get to the forme you were to correct. The machine minder would hopefully have wiped the type matter over with white spirit, to save you being too smothered up with ink. You then lay on your stomach to do the type or positional changes that were marked on the proof. These could be very involved and take hours to complete. When you crawled out from under the delivery, it used to take you a while to stand up straight. On one occasion I had been working like this for several hours, got a pull off the machine to check, and it appeared to be a total disaster. I took it to the overseer, who had one look at it and started to make marks all over it again. This horrified me, so I asked him if the original marks he had made would have meant the sheet would be correct, and he said that they would. I then explained to him that I had carried out all those marks correctly, and he was welcome to come and look at the forme to check that. I was not prepared to start making further corrections, until the reasons that it was not now correct were established. Fortunately, before the conversation became too acrimonious, the machine minder appeared with another sheet in his hand, explaining that the lay-band had broken on the machine and we were looking at a 'bad' pull.

There were times when the letterpress process meant that changes could be made more easily and quickly than litho. There were also times when trouble meant an even bigger disaster. Things like halftone plates that would come unpinned and go across the whole forme smashing the type matter. This could take hours to put right, even to the point of having to get the type recast. This happened one night to a programme we were producing for a motor race meeting at Silverstone, and we were called out in the early hours to put it right. These programmes were bound and delivered while still extremely wet and in the state known as 'a dog's breakfast'.

One of the enjoyable outings we used to have with the firm was an annual cricket match with the editorial staff of a magazine we produced called *The Bakers' Review*. This match was held at the 'Distillers' Ground' at East Molesey, and, as I recall, it was a light-hearted occasion. The first half of the match was played very seriously, but we would then break for lunch, which was a very generous affair. After the break, the match was won by the team who could see straightest and whose batsman picked the right one of the two balls they could see, to hit! One year we were short of players and were going round the works trying to get enough men for the team. One of the compositors finally agreed to play, although, as he said, he was not a regular player.

I had agreed to take three men to the match in my car. This was a trifle ambitious, as three men, plus my wife and myself, made five, and the car was classed as a two-seater. Now this was not quite as bad as it sounds, as the seat was a bench seat, and the car was a front-wheel drive and had no gear shift on the floor. It came out of the dashboard, looked rather like a walking stick handle, and had an unfortunate habit of becoming disengaged, thus leaving you in whatever gear you were in at the time when it came apart! So the game plan was, three in the front and two sitting on the floor behind the front seat, where there was a gap of about two foot wide.

It was a fine day when we set out and we finally arrived at what we thought was the ground. It was, however, the 'East Molesey' and not the 'Distillers'. The Australian test team were playing one of their warm-up matches there, before the start of the test series. This meant that officials materialised very speedily and told us politely to clear off!

We found the right ground and took the field, batting first, having won the toss. Experienced men who were aware of the after-lunch syndrome, made that decision. Battle was enjoined and we were in a good position when the lunch break arrived. Eventually we retook the field and shortly declared. It would be true to say the standard of play at this point had deteriorated somewhat. We were short of bowlers, and after we had had a reasonable number of overs, were looking decidedly jaded. Our captain cast around for volunteers to bowl, and accepted the offer of Les, the comp who had agreed to play, but had warned us he was not a regular player.

When Les came on to bowl he gave his cap to the umpire, who asked him something a bit technical – 'Are you bowling over, or round the wicket?' Les wrestled with this for a bit, but came up with an answer, with which he knew he had a fifty per cent chance of being right. He was then handed the marker, and this really threw him; he looked at it totally bemused, took one pace back from the stumps at an angle, and firmly inserted the marker in the ground. This took everyone aback. Were we about to witness the shortest run-up in cricketing history? Further confusion reigned when Les trudged off into the distance with the ball, the only query being was he going to stop before he reached the pavilion, or was he going, round behind it! Les made his approach, the speed of the run-in varying from time to time (he had indulged in the liquid refreshments and was looking decidedly dodgy). The run-in suddenly slowed right down, round about where the bowling marker had been placed, as it happened, and he made his delivery. The batsman was greatly confused by all this; he had obviously wondered what the hell was going on and had rightly come to the conclusion that the bowler did not know what he was doing. The actual delivery was quite unique, the action and result would not have been out of place on a grenade-throwing practice range. The ball would have been more accurately described as having altitude rather than flight. As it descended, the batsman's eyes lit up, this one was going for a six! He swung at it with such force, it undoubtedly would have done, if he had struck the ball. The shot was made too early, and the bat whizzed round, the batsman spinning with the impetus. On the second spin he was horrified to see that the ball's first bounce was only impeded by the stumps getting in the way, and he was out! This was the last wicket to fall and gave 'Les, the demon bowler,' a bowling average of one wicket with one delivery – what price skill?

On the return journey my problems with my passengers were increased by our being lumbered with the cricket bag. Things were definitely becoming a bit of a squeeze. When it started to rain on the way back, I pulled over and had to get the hood up. This was only achieved by pushing and shoving the odd bumps that were showing in the hood, until I could lock it into position. When I finally dropped the passengers off, they thanked me for the lift, and one said that he knew that you had creases in your trousers, but this was the first time he had seen them in his shoes, but I was not to worry, he would probably be able to walk normally again in time!

When I purchased the BSA Scout 6A, I had been surprised to find that I was having a job getting it insured. I did not worry about this too much, as insurers were not over-fond of sports cars, seeing them as a bad risk anyway. In fact, I was finally very relieved to get it insured. The broker I used was assisting with the insurance form, with little tips like, 'Don't call it a sports car, call it a tourer, that sounds better.' I had bought the car during the summer and while the weather was good, all seemed fine. There were little things, like the time when the gear shift came apart, just as the traffic lights changed to green during the rush hour at the Swiss Cottage junction. The car being out of gear, I had to lift the bonnet up and take the spanners to the problem, and this did nothing for my popularity with the other road users. It was not until the weather deteriorated that I discovered what the insurance companies knew and I did not – the car was prone to front-wheel skids.

The first occasion that it happened was when I was driving with some friends in the car, two in the back and one alongside. It began to rain heavily when I was on the North Circular Road and I was doing a little over forty miles an hour. I came over the brow of a hill and saw a set of traffic lights change to red and applied my brakes. I felt the steering wheel go loose in my hands, the car taking no notice of it, and I took the brakes off to try to get the steering back. Whilst I was doing this, the car had decided to mount the pavement, go past the traffic signals on the pavement, and back onto the road the other side. The steering came back and I continued on the other side of the junction. The amazing thing was that we hit no one – or thing. I looked round at my friends and they were very pale and visibly shaken. Malcolm said to me, 'What the hell did you do that for?' To which I replied, 'I did nothing, ask the car.'

I am pleased to say that I did not have an accident whilst I had that car but I did have a number of similar front-wheel skids. They were never an enjoyable experience, as for a few moments you just did not have control of the car. At this time the only other front-wheel drive car that I was aware of was the old Citroën and I was never able to find out if they had a similar problem. Whatever the fault was caused by, it had been designed out by the next generation of front-wheel drive cars. They now are most reliable and, having driven one for years, I would be very reluctant to revert to a rear-wheel drive!

Having completed my union probation period with my company, and also got my certificate as a Linotype operator, I decided to move on and see if I could get onto the Linotype machine. This did not go all that smoothly. I was delayed for a few months, as, twice, when I approached the overseer and said I wanted to give my notice, he did not accept it and gave me a healthy increase in my wages. This meant about six months' delay, until in the end I made it quite clear that my motive was to get on the Linotype and, as that company did not have any, I would have to leave.

The company I then went to was a tradesetters at Wembley, not all that far from the stadium. The agreement I had there was that I would work on the frame but take the place of any Linotype operator who was either sick or on holiday, and this I agreed to do. This was only a small set-up with four Model Four Linotypes. The owner of the company was the spitting image of the actor, Sydney Greenstreet, and every bit as overpowering. When he called you into his office it was pretty nerve-racking, the war of nerves being added to by the fact that his desk was on a raised platform, which he would look down at you from, and, with a voice that matched the actor's, would boom, 'Yes?' He would query any items that had to be purchased, even as trivial as page-cord, as if the purchase of it would jeopardise his ability to feed his children!

This was a union house and after a few weeks there, there was a chapel meeting, at which I was informed that we all took turns to be father of the chapel, and this month it was my turn. They did not have to tell me, I knew I was being 'stitched-up'. This made me uneasy, as I had just finished my probation period with the union, and at this company things were going on that were worrying, to put it mildly. There was a member of another union, NATSOPA (National Society of Operative Printers Assistants) doing a compositor's work for a start, and twice a week, a man came in on casual employment to remelt the old metal to make new ingots. When I asked to see his union card he gave me one for the NUR (National Union of Railwayworkers). Not wanting to jeopardise my new union membership and being the official, even if only for a month on a rota, I rang the house and told them of the situation. To my amazement they said that they knew about the NATSOPA member, but it had taken them long enough to get the firm to recognise the union, so I should overlook it. As for the chap working in the foundry – well at least he was a union member, if not one of ours!

I had only been able to spend very little time on the machines and was getting a bit bored and worried about the situation when I was called in to the boss's office. He said that he was installing a Ludlow and Elrod unit and he would like me to operate it for him. He offered an increase in my money which was already good, being a tradesetters. The principle with most tradesetters was to pay good money, in return for which they expected a high output, and you had to be able to handle whatever was thrown at you. Tradesetters had to cover a lot of work which the company who gave it to you thought was too troublesome to do themselves, and you had to be able to cope with it. I agreed to do this and went on a course to Martin Slattery's in Grays Inn Road. This also covered the use of a new system the Ludlow company had brought out called 'ruleform'. This added the ability to produce ruled and tabular work of a high standard as well as the display setting that it was already known for and which I had operated at my previous company.

The equipment was installed and was up and running, and the work came in for the machines immediately. The display work on the Ludlow was a piece of cake, but the 'ruleform' had to be carefully worked out and could be tricky, to the point of verging on nightmarish. The Elrod machine, which cast strip materials such as spacing and rules, was no trouble, with the exception of running the dreaded one point lead, and that, to put not too fine a point on it, was a swine! The Elrod machine worked on a very strange principal. The moulds were held in the mouth of the metal pot by virtue of the solidified lead, which was brought about by the temperature controls. The metal strips were pulled through the mould by mechanical wedges. You would feed the strips into the mould, and when the temperatures were solidifying the material at just the right point, start to pull the strips through with the mechanical wedges. These could Gradually be adjusted, until you were pulling the maximum amount each time. This all had to be done with some care and attention to detail, as I soon found out. On one of my early attempts, I had just changed the mould, watched all the temperature gauges, and switched on the pulling mechanism. The only trouble was that I had forgotten to zero the wedges when I finished the last run. Within seconds the machine had pulled the whole mould out of the throat, leaving an aperture of about one and a half inches by two inches, with a zonking great piston pumping the molten lead through.

By the time I struggled back to the end where the controls were, to pull the pin out of the plunger to seal the mouth, I looked more as if I was wearing chain mail rather than a dust coat. I looked at the machine in horror, it looked like an ice-cream cornet where all the controls and mechanism were, only it was lead! As it was a brand-new machine, I was lucky. I was able to quickly pull the lead off the switches and controls as they were covered in grease, but the area around the mouth and the puller mechanism was a different story. There was a plumber a couple of doors away, and I nipped in there and scrounged a blowlamp. The room was full of smoke, and there I was beavering away with a blowlamp, screwdriver and chisel, covered in lead and looking more like one of the knights of the round table than a compositor, when the door opened and I heard the owner say, 'Here is our new installation.' A pause, and then, 'There seems to be a bit of a problem. We'll come back later!' My thoughts at the time were, 'Make it about a week's time and you will probably meet the new operator!'

To be fair 'Sydney' took it all in good part, accepting that it was just one of those things, and as it was all up and running without serious damage, let it go at that. He was a strange man, and when in the mood, would talk about his experiences in the 1914–1918 war, when he was in the army, and the 1939–1945 war, when he was a liaison officer with the French resistance. This was due to the fact that he had owned and ran a printing factory in France between the wars, and had excellent knowledge of the area he was operating in plus his ability to speak fluent French.

There was plenty of overtime available with the company – if anything, the pressure to work was more than you wanted, but the money was very welcome. The 'ruleform' work took a fair bit of working out and, if you got it wrong, a lot of time was wasted. We were getting a lot of setting for a new magazine that had just come out called *The Weekly Motor Advertiser*. The printers, who were doing this job, were putting the setting out to more than one tradesetter, and in its early days, the magazine had editorial matter which we were setting. That there was always pressure on the turnaround time was the bad news, the good news was they used to tip very generously. They used to appear at any hour, often late at night, and when they picked up their typematter, they would often hand you a couple of pounds as a thank-you for a quick turnaround. It was also intended, no doubt, to make sure you did not hang around when the next work came in.

June and I had settled into a nice routine and were enjoying a good social life. The only problem was the unpredictable overtime factor. We were all set for a couple of weeks' summer holiday, and we intended to spend at least the first week with June's people in Biggleswade. I actually got home on the Friday night to start our holiday, when the bombshell landed. The people we rented the furnished rooms from told us they needed the accommodation we were renting and gave us a month's notice to leave. Although we had some of our own furniture, it was still classed as furnished accommodation, and that was it. We had to go! This threw us into a spin and we went up to Biggleswade in no frame of mind to enjoy a holiday. We had decided to have the week anyway and then start worrying about it.

While we were there, June's parents were good enough to make us the kind offer that we could live there with them, until we could sort something out, and the father-in-law came up with an appointment to see the works manager of a local printer for me. When I went for that interview, he asked me what I was earning in my present job and visibly paled when I told him. He told me he could not offer anything like that amount, but when he knew I was also a Linotype operator, he made a phone call and got me an interview for the next day with *The Bedfordshire Times*. The interview was a success. I would have to take a nasty cut in my wages, but not too drastic, as I would get the Linotype rate. It also meant that at last I would be working on the machine I had taken the course for.

Our decision was also helped by the fact that the firm June used to work for heard by the native drums that she was coming back to the area and they immediately offered her her old job back. So it all seemed to be working out for the best. Our earning capacity was down, but looking on the bright side, the price of property in Bedfordshire at that time was much less than in the London area, and we wanted to buy our own place. The wheels were set in motion, and when we returned from our holiday, we had to give our notices in and get organised for the move. I do not think June had a lot of problems giving in her notice, but I was worried about mine. 'Sydney Greenstreet' was a strange cove, and the fact that I had only worked there for about six months was a worry, especially as I had received the training on the new equipment, but the nettle had to be grasped. I went in on the Monday with no small amount of trepidation, and the situation was not improved when 'Sydney' was in a friendly talkative mood. This was the morning when he chose to tell me a little reminiscence, of the time when he had killed a German soldier with an entrenching tool in the 1914–1918 war. It was along the lines of, it was either him or me and it had to be done, but it had played on his mind. It was playing on mine, but like a lot of these things, once you take the plunge and face it, it is seldom as bad as you feared.

I had got the move cleared with my union, which was then the London Society of Compositors, and there were no problems, as long as I took out a dual card with the Typographical Association, and this I did (not knowing at the time how fortuitous it would prove later). When my friend, Malcolm, knew I was moving, he came up with the suggestion that some friends of his who had a van, would do the move for us at a reasonable price. They were circus performers and things were a bit quiet for them at that time. Their act involved a mechanical contraption, which consisted of a tower with a powered turntable at the top. This spun round with one of them dangling from it and the other one supported by him holding a strap in his teeth. The problem was that during the last performance they had given (fortunately at a hospital fête) the turntable was spinning a bit too enthusiastically and the one holding on by his teeth had come off. He was now out of hospital, but they were working out a new routine, as part of his injuries had been losing his teeth!

The day of our move arrived and we had all our things like dinner and tea services and so forth packed in orange boxes, and the lighter things in old tea chests. I was assisting with the move, helping to load the van, and returned up the stairs just in time to spot the one who had the 'fang' shortage stooping to pick up two of the orange boxes at the same time. I was about to shout a warning about how much they weighed, for I had moved them and they were really heavy, but I need not have bothered, he picked them up as if they were nothing!

There was one small snag about the removal. When I saw the van pull up outside, I noticed that it had painted on each side superb pictures of trapeze artistes swinging on their trapezes in glorious Technicolor, and a large sign announcing, 'The Flying Cobinas'.

I can remember thinking, 'This will make a few curtains twitch when we pull up outside the mother-in-law's – and it did! I had no fears about how the in-laws would take it, they were a great couple, and I knew the only effect it would have on them would be to amuse them. The performers (two men and a girl) were really very accomplished and had been used in the making of the film *Trapeze*, starring Burt Lancaster.

Chapter Twenty-Three

Biggleswade

The move to Biggleswade was not moving into the unknown. June came from there and I had been visiting the area frequently over the past few years. The fact that we had friends and relations in the area was also a factor in settling . in quickly. The town was much less cosmopolitan than it is now, and far more rural, the majority of people at that time still earning their living working in, or connected to, agriculture. There were a couple of engineering companies in the area and the usual trades to support a community which at that time numbered around twelve to fifteen thousand. Although in its day Kingsbury was quite rural, it had by then become suburbia, and as it was in close proximity to London, I was more used to the town than country.

On my first morning at *The Bedfordshire Times*, I drove past fields with men crawl-hoeing in them. I could not believe it, the thought of getting down on your hands and knees and setting out to weed a vast field of cabbage or lettuce, row by row, made my mind boggle! When I arrived at the factory I could not find a car park, so I left the car outside the works and went in and found the composing room manager. When I asked him where to park my car, this was a conversation stopper. The staff were, for the most part, local and either walked, bussed or came in on their bicycles. I got a strong feeling of disapproval that I should actually own a car (at that time a Y model Ford Eight) and was told to park it in the yard. This was only small and housed the paper's Jowett van. Nearly every night I had to ask for it to be moved to get out, and again every morning to get in. This was usually accompanied by bad temper and muttering, and you felt that the problems you were causing were obviously resented.

As usual nothing was straightforward. I was asked to work on the frame, setting adverts, as the Linotype machine I was going to work had been dropped from the second floor when it was being moved into the new building. I found time to have a word with the engineers who were working on it, and when I told them I was going to be operating it, they said, 'Good Luck.' They had never seen a machine with so many welded parts. When I finally got on the machine, I found it quite nerve-racking. With most types of machinery you get used to the sounds and way they work. Not this one, for the very good reason that it never made the same sound twice. Parts would suddenly move so slowly that you stopped and watched to see if it was actually going to work, and the very next minute things would become virtually supersonic, with the bangs to match. It was not a machine for the nervous. Because of the misalignment of the v-bar on the disser mechanism, some matrices would jam and stop the machine. You got to know which these characters were, so, as the line went away to cast, you would stroll round to the back, wait for them to arrive, and unhook them as a matter of routine.

Bedford was very much the county town – you could not move for hacking jackets and cavalry twills. Sit-up-and-beg cycles were thick on the ground with wicker baskets on the front, and the ladies had strings covering their back wheels, to prevent their skirts from catching in the spokes. The buses were used as a form of delivery service. On the occasions when I went on the buses, I could not get over the way that, when they came to stops in the villages, the conductor would enquire, 'Where's Mrs Pepper today? Better give her a knock and see if she's coming.' Which was quite a change from the London approach of 'If I hadn't been quick with the bell – they would have been on!'

It was definitely a more relaxed and laid-back approach to life than I had been used to in London. The difference between the areas has noticeably narrowed over the years – house prices have shot up, due to the motorways making it even possible to commute to London – not that I would wish to. The market gardening industry is still a big factor in the area, but the influx and growth of other industries have had a considerable impact on the labour forces, much reducing the proportion of people now employed on the land. One of the things that caught me by surprise shortly after I started at *The Bedfordshire Times* was that, when the fire alarm was sounded in the town, half the staff turned off their machines and ran from the works. The reason for this turned out not to be blind panic, but the fact that the fire brigade was a part-time organisation and a lot of our staff doubled as firemen. The first winter after we moved up to Bedfordshire was a bitterly cold one, with heavy falls of snow giving me some hairy drives backwards and forwards to Bedford in my old Ford Eight. One night on my way home in the snow along unlit country lanes, I pushed the dipswitch for the headlights and every light bulb in the car blew, due to a short. When that particular car was built, Ford apparently thought that fuses were a luxury and did not fit them for the lights. I was more than a little concerned at driving along in the dark without lights, and was relieved to find out that I did have one light left. This was the interior light, as it had not been switched on at the time of the short. Fortunately, as it was late and the weather foul, I made it home without even being stopped and only saw a few cars on the way.

The copy that I used to get to set at *The Bedfordshire Times* seemed to be, for the most part, less than exciting, consisting mainly of reports of funerals and weddings. These comprised endless lists of mourners or guests with the same family name. The hazard was that, if you were not careful, you could miss one set of initials out and be in trouble. I used to look forward to getting a report with one of those mistakes in it, like the often quoted 'At the funeral one of the mourners dropped dead at the graveside, casting a gloom over the proceedings', but no such luck. There was a review of a concert which came close, when a reporter managed to get the words cacophony, bowdlerisation, and tintinnabulation all in one sentence. This amused me, and with the mistaken belief that my galleys of setting would be seen by one of our readers, I added some copy of my own to cause some amusement. Unfortunately, it was getting late on a press night, and the readers were being helped out by the editor, who did not share my sense of humour or appreciate the descriptive prowess of the reporter. We both received 'rockets' over the matter, and that particular reporter's attitude to me noticeably cooled.

That same Christmas quite an amusing gaffe occurred in one of the papers. We were surprised to see a report of a nativity play produced by Goldington Kindergarten. This was accompanied by a photograph of a group of sandalled characters, about six foot tall, with beards and hairy legs, wearing very authentic-looking costumes, albeit of the wrong period. Further on there was another strange article, captioned 'Bedford School's production of *King Lear*'. This included a picture showing a group of four- to five-year-olds, with very amateurish costumes, standing around a manger. When the pages had been moulded for the rotary press, the foundryman had lifted the halftone plates off, to plane the forme down, and put them back in the wrong order.

After a few months of working on the Linotype machine I realised that it was not the job for me. At first I was interested in getting my speed of setting up to scratch and with only a reasonable percentage of errors, but, once I had achieved this, it was boringly repetitive. I found that I began to look forward to the machine breaking down, so that I could repair it. As I was operating the machine that had been dropped from the second floor, it did provide me with a higher than normal proportion of breakdowns. It was not surprising, therefore, that I spotted an advert of interest to me in one of the local papers stating that compositors were required by the Garden City Press at Letchworth. The advert stated that housing would also be available, and I applied for the job. I was informed that the housing would not be available for some time, as it was still being built and details were not yet known. I decided to take the job, as I preferred the variety in the work of a compositor to being a Linotype operator, and there was bags of overtime available. There had not been any overtime on the paper, so the change of job, the availability of overtime, and the possibility of a house, was good enough for me!

The Garden City Press was a large concern, and the staff in the composing room alone was more than the total staff in any company I had worked for before. It was a big factory with a large extension that would be completed soon after I arrived on the scene. In the grounds were some hutments that had been built to house troops in the 1914–1918 war. These were being used as type stores, and there were a couple of compositors working in them who had been in there for so long we were not too sure that the management knew they were still there!

As far as the composing department was concerned, there was a manager over the whole department and three sections each with their own overseer. One section was producing book work, one periodicals, and one general jobbing work. The periodical side was much the largest, and groups of magazines were run by a number of 'clickers' (chargehands being the nearest equivalent in other industries). I started on the jobbing ship and was involved in a large job that nearly sent me crazy, which was called *The First Ten Years of the National Coal Board*. The first six weeks I spent correcting six-point Monotype galleys by hand, and this took me into levels of monotony that it would be hard to surpass. Since then, if ever I had a job that was unbelievably boring, I would just think back to that time, and what I was currently doing would then seem to be almost exciting in comparison.

When we were imposing the formes of this job, all the illustrations had been mounted on solid metal base and there were complaints that they were too heavy to lift down off the imposing stones. Two comps used to lift them down and wheel them to storage racks. To check this, we took a couple of formes into the foundry and weighed them and we found that they weighed approximately four-and-a-half hundredweight! After a few months I was moved on to the periodicals side, and later was made the 'clicker' in charge of several magazines with about six to eight men to produce them. There was not a great deal of time spent on management training in those days. I was called into the manager's office, and told that as from the Monday I was in charge of three magazines – *Amateur Cine World*, *Cycling* and *Vanity Fair*. I was told who the regular staff were and that, if I needed more men, to see him about it, and that was all. I then had to chat to the other 'clickers' to find out how they were running their magazines and what records needed to be kept and suchlike. More jobs were added later, and more staff, but by and large that was to be my work for the next four-and-a-half years.

When the firm's houses began to be allocated, I changed my mind about having one. Two major points influenced my decision. Firstly, the houses were all next door to each other and not spread about among different firms, so that you could well be living next door to the person you worked with all day, and secondly, I calculated the cost of the rent was only just under what you would have to pay to buy a house of your own. June and I started to look around and found some new places being built in Biggleswade and decided to go for a bungalow, which was for sale at the now unbelievable price of one thousand, seven hundred and fifty pounds. Even at that price it was not easy to get the mortgage. The building societies at that time took neither your wife's earnings nor any overtime into their calculations. Your monthly repayments were also not allowed to be more than twenty-five per cent of your earnings. We sorted everything out, but at the eleventh hour I ran into difficulties with raising the deposit. I had relied on selling my car and as yet did not have a buyer. I told one of the comps I worked with about this in the morning, and after lunch, he slipped an envelope into my hand, with the amount that I was short in it. He said, 'That will get you out of trouble, let me have it back when you have sold your car!' I thanked him and asked him if I should give him a receipt, but he just answered that, if he had not trusted me, he would not have lent it to me in the first place. His name was Geoffrey Cooling and I have never forgotten his unsolicited kindness.

Without the car I was having to catch a bus to get to Letchworth and this was a real pain in the neck. The bus I used to catch went straight down the A1 to Baldock, and then through to Letchworth. It catered for the people who worked in Letchworth and was the only one. If I missed it, by the time I got to where you caught the other service bus (which went all round the villages and took twice as long) it would have gone, and I would be stranded. This then meant a train to Hitchin, a bus to Letchworth, and about a mile walk. This 'Round Britain' tour meant that I did not appear on the scene at the works until 10.30 a.m. which was not appreciated by the management.

I used to cycle down to the market square and leave my bike in 'Whitemans' yard, as did many others who were going to Letchworth, Hitchin, or Bedford. The charge for this was one shilling and sixpence a week. You would hurl your bike down, then dash off to catch your bus in the morning, and when you came back at night, it took you ages to find it again among the tangled heap of bikes. I had to catch the 7.15 a.m. bus in the morning and, if I was getting pushed for time, I would cut the bus off at 'Bygraves' corner, lean my bike against a garage's wall, and hope it would still be there in the evening. It was, though one night one of the mechanics saw me and said, 'We were wondering who kept leaving that bike there' but when I explained he said it was okay to carry on leaving it there.

I then had a brush with the inflexible attitude of the union. I got to work every morning ten minutes late due to the bus times and had to wait every night for half-an-hour before I could catch a bus home. This meant I lost a quarter of an hour's pay every day. I explained the situation to the firm and they agreed that I could do the quarter of an hour after hours, to make up the lost time and not lose any money. The union said this was 'balancing time' and was against the rules. This arrangement would not have thrown anyone out of work as a result, and it meant I was going to lose an hour and a quarter's pay every week. I was not pleased with this bureaucratic approach and I considered it to be a misuse of the rule.

One of the compositors who worked at the firm was a dedicated trade unionist, served on the Co-operative Society's management board, and was on the Joint Industrial Council. His name was William (Bill) Hobbs – a very well-read and intelligent man. He held strong views regarding the 'closed shop', which he was totally against, contrary to most trade unionists, and also had an ongoing dispute with union rules over working overtime at weekends. The official line was that you should not work overtime on the weekend preceding or following your annual holidays. Bill's argument was that there were not three weekends in two weeks, and, if he was taking two weeks' holiday and wanted to work overtime on either the weekend before or after the holiday, he would. This dispute eventually got to national level and he lost the argument. I still think that he was right, once you took into consideration that you cannot be made to do overtime and it can't be forced upon you.

The bus journeys were getting me down after about a year and I came up with the idea that I would get a motorbike for the journey. One of the machine minders had an old Ariel 350cc motorbike, which he offered to me for twenty-five pounds. It was ancient and covered in muck, but it was there every day in the rack, and I had never known him late. I put the idea to June and she was less than enthralled. She was not keen on me having a motorbike in the first place, as she thought they were dangerous, and secondly she felt that buying such an old bike would be nothing but trouble. In the end she gave in on the idea of the motorbike, but thought I should get a new one, which would be cheaper in the long run. When I started to bring home brochures of different bikes, I could not convince her that the bigger motorbikes would be the safer ones. In the end I had to settle for a small bike – an Excelsior (125ccs of uncontrolled fury). The first morning I went to work on it, as I came round the corner just near where June's parents lived, I 'ran out of road,' hit the kerb, and came off. I got back on (red-faced) hoping that no one saw me, as I would never have heard the end of it if they had.

Right from the beginning that bike was trouble – it would do about three miles and then pack up. I would remove the sparking plug, find that it had whiskered up (a small piece of carbon formed between the plug and the electrode). You removed this 'whisker', replaced the plug, and off you would go again. The favourite place for this to happen to me was as I was passing a desolate cemetery near Stotfold, usually after dark, on a windy night when it was pouring with rain. If it was really cold you could almost enjoy burning yourself on the hot sparking plug as you juggled with it in the dark. That winter was a bad one, the roads were covered in snow and ice for weeks on end and it was freezing on that bike. After a few miles you could even tell where the buttonholes were on your coat. In those days not many people had the Sidcot suits or leathers, other than scramble riders and professionals. I had a riding coat, which had straps on to keep it round your legs, waterproof trousers and motorcycle boots (an essential in the winter, as, if you were wearing shoes, you felt like your feet had been amputated at the ankles after a few miles in the cold). Sometimes I had to go straight down the A1 to Baldock and keep to the main roads to Letchworth, as the B-roads were too bad to ride on. That winter all sorts of road grading and surfacing equipment was being delivered from the Euclid factory, where it was made, along the A1 to the docks for shipment to Brazil. The equipment was being supplied for the work on the roads to the new capital city that was under construction and had 'Brasilia' painted on the sides. These were huge pieces of equipment and the wheels towered above you, let alone the actual vehicle. There was many a morning when I found one of these vehicles alongside me on my 125cc bike and had to go straight on, when I should have turned right, as I dared not turn in case I skidded or slipped. I purchased a windshield and fitted it onto the bike to get a bit more comfort, but with that size of engine it was better than the brakes on a windy day. My cap blew off one morning and every time I tried to leave the bike by the side of the road, to go and get it back from the hedge, the wind would blow my bike over. In the end I had to ride the bike over the verge to the hedge to get it.

The problems with the bike got steadily worse, it was now not simply a matter of cleaning the plug – it would just pack in and refuse to go. I pushed that bike further than I rode it in the finish. When I got to work I would find they were having a sweep on what time I would get there, and always in the bike rack would be 'the old Ariel' (I could swear it was smiling at me). It looked even dirtier and older – but it was there! I had taken my bike back countless times to the motorcycle shop where I had bought it. They always checked it, said they could find nothing wrong with it, and it would break down again the next day. One night I was pushing the bike along the A1, when a large flat-bed lorry pulled over and asked me where I was going. I told him I was heading for Biggleswade, and he said he would give me a lift. We heaved the bike up onto the back of the lorry and decided I would have to sit there with it, to keep it upright on the lorry, because of the petrol. Thus started what I can only describe as one of my most nightmarish experiences. The lorry hurtled off, and as it bumped along I was gradually shaken along the length of the flat back until I was at the far end, and only stayed on by virtue of my heels pressing against the edge of angle iron, not more than two inches high. The driver was completely impervious to my shouts and hooter blowing behind him. Once he was back in his cab, the fact that he had the motorbike and myself on the back had obviously been erased from his memory. To make matters even worse, not only was I anticipating flying off the back, complete with motorcycle, at the next large bump in the road, but we had by now sailed through Biggleswade and out the other side and were heading for

Sandy. To my relief he eventually remembered me, pulled up and came round to help me down off the back. I told him he shouldn't have bothered – one more good bump would have saved him the trouble. As he had at least meant well, I refrained from telling him that I now had just as far to push the bike back in the opposite direction.

One Friday night I came to the end of my tether and pushed the inanimate bike into the shop's garage. I explained that I was not a happy person and still thought that it was the magneto. They assured me that thirty-year-old motorbikes were thrown on the rubbish heap and the only part that was still okay was their magneto. As I had had such a lot of trouble, their generous nature prevailed upon them to loan me the use of a motor bike for a couple of days, so I could get to work. I thought this good of them until I saw what they were prepared to loan me. It was not a motorbike but an autocycle called a Mobylette. It had pedals to assist if necessary and they showed me the knob you slid over to bring them into use (I should have smelt a rat – but I didn't). Apart from riding the machine home, I did not bother with it, until I set out for work on the Monday morning. It dawned on me fairly quickly that this was not a 'mean machine', and the 45cc engine ensured that there were no frightening surges of power. I soon realised this when I was laying on the petrol tank, to reduce drag, with the throttle wide open, and a three-year-old overtook me pulling a plastic duck on wheels! It took me about ten to fifteen minutes longer than usual to do the journey to Letchworth, and at lunch time some of the motorbike fraternity at work gathered round for a laugh and to see if they could soup the bike up a bit for the return journey.

I got about two thirds of the way home that night, before the bike began to lose what small amount of power it had. I reached for the knob to bring in the pedals and this helped for about a mile, but then the engine packed in completely. I did a mile on the pedals only, and had to carry it for the last half mile. The fact that I was not best pleased was fairly apparent when I carried the bike into the shop, and they mistakenly thought that it would please me when they told me that they had found the source of the trouble on my own bike, which was a faulty magneto. It did not occur to them that I might be a tidge put out by the fact that I had been suggesting that this was the source of the trouble for the past three months. This did get through to them though before I left their premises, when I informed them that I hoped the problems with the bike had been resolved, for their sake, as, if it let me down again, I would throw it through their bloody shop window! In fairness, this did resolve the main problem, its reliability was greatly improved, and it was my source of transport for about another fifteen months until I was able to get back on four wheels.

June and I had agreed to join forces with her sister, Rene, and husband, Jack, that year to tour Scotland for our holiday. We were going to share the costs of petrol and the driving, but it was not to be. There was the altercation with Egypt and Nasser over the Suez Canal. This was an action which I was wholly against and that earned me the title at work of 'the firm's most unpatriotic man'. I am quite happy that the historians, for the most part, support the view I took at the time, and it is generally accepted as an ill-judged blunder! As far as we were concerned, it meant that petrol was rationed and we had to cancel our Scottish tour. The good side of these events was that we decided to have a cabin cruiser on the Cam instead, and it started us off on a type of holiday which was to give us considerable pleasure for a number of years to come.

We hired a 4-berth cabin cruiser from Banhams in Cambridge and with it we had a fourteen-foot sailing dinghy. The rivers available for you to cruise were the

Cam, the Old West, and the New Bedford, and this meant that you had more miles of river to cruise than you could cover, certainly in one week. Banhams were the boat builders that used to provide Cambridge University's boats and they were extremely good. As well as cruisers they put a two-berth sailing boat on the market called the *Silhouette*, which sold quite well. The main difference from 'the Broads' was that here there were only rivers, no expanses of water for easier sailing – and locks, lots of locks. Cruisers on these rivers at that time were even less well known than on the Broads, so, like on the canals, it was very peaceful and ideal to get away from all the rush and tear of everyday life. In addition to this you were welcome for your trade, wherever you went, by the riverside pubs and village shops, and it was an ideal holiday.

This did not mean that there was no excitement, especially in the early days when you were less familiar with the rules of the river and how to handle the boats. An early lesson that you learn is that, leisurely as they might seem, when things start to go wrong, you quickly realise that boats need time to react, and most people who have used them know that feeling of unavoidable impending disaster. For the most part, certainly then, people were reasonably behaved and did not belt along rivers like bats out of hell, collecting fishing rods and swamping knee-waders. I have never been a great enthusiast of fishing and used to wonder where a lot of its appeal came from, so it amused me to come to stretches of river where you could see dozens of rods with the attendant tackle by the side of the river and nobody with them. A little further along, you would come across the answer, a riverside inn that was open!

As you leave Cambridge the last of the manned locks with a lock keeper is Bottisham Lock. The keeper was paid by the number of boats through his lock, and his approach had definite shades of piecework about it. It made me think of the episode in *Three Men in a Boat* where the man kept being told to watch his nose. The keeper would pack in the unsuspecting boats like sardines and then let the water level drop at an alarming rate, causing chaos. I have seen old ladies, who were holding the chains that hang down the side of the lock, cling onto them when the boat dropped and be left dangling from the wall! Once through that lock you have two choices, you can moor up at each lock and go in search of the keys, or you can hire your own keys and keep them on your boat for convenience. This faith in people who have lock keys being of a responsible nature is quite horrifying. Unfortunately my experiences with the public at large would make me think twice about turning them loose with anything that had so much scope for creating disaster.

The boat we had was called *The Iolanthe*. It was sturdily built, had a reliable engine, and some other good points going for it. What was its major problem was its steerage. It 'yawed', so, with the wheel kept perfectly still in one position, it would make its way down the river nudging alternate river banks. This meant you had to attempt to correct this with the wheel, but it was an art form in itself. It had much the same feel as trying to drive a car with about six inches of play in the steering (what we used to refer to as a kerb inspector). About two or three days into the holiday we felt that we were pretty well at home with the boat, including its idiosyncrasies. We used to check our river map and plan what we were going to do the next day, checking the book of the river and map for potential hazards. We had seen the horror on holidaymakers' faces as they stormed round a bend in the river and saw a bridge in front of them, under which they could not pass without dropping the canopy of the boat. This would mean the 'bloody hell' approach; they would try to drop the canopy in a world-record time, or slam the boat into hard astern –

with all they could get on the throttle. It was even quite likely that they would try a combination of both and fail, so they would steer into the river bank and pay for the resultant breakages. Breakfast or dinner time are particularly good times to choose for this, if you want to achieve the best results.

We had planned to go through a lock at Brownshill Staunch, there was an informative little map that showed you just what you had to do. You kept to the left of the river (excuse the layman's terms) to avoid a shallow area that was roughly indicated, then you swung the boat out to the centre of the river, to line the boat up for entering the lock. Here things got a bit trickier, as you had to judge carefully how much way you had on, to ensure that it was enough to counter the pull from the weir on your right, but not too much for entering the lock – simple! I had drawn the short straw on this occasion and was piloting the boat. It had occurred to me that this particular boat's self-willed approach to steering was not going to be an asset with this little number, but I was not quite prepared for the impending fiasco! The shallows I managed, but as I swung the boat to line up with the lock, the boat's delayed response to the steering, combined with the pull of the weir, worried me. I gave the boat a bit more throttle and then noticed that this particular lock was one of the scuttle variety, where the gates lifted instead of swinging open. The last person through had been a lazy canoeist I am sure, who had lifted the gate just far enough to miss his head, but there was nowhere near enough clearance for a cruiser. Panic reigned, the top of the boat was dropped in record-breaking time. I had throttled back only to find that the weir was pulling us, so I had to give the boat more throttle. One of life's interesting little quirks came into play at this point – the boat's hooter was carefully positioned so that, when you opened and closed the throttle drastically, you could not avoid sounding the horn, and this in its own way added to the situation. Meanwhile there were people in the lock who had spotted, as well as heard, our predicament, and they were busily trying to lift the gate for us. *Iolanthe* – game to the last – refused to go where I was steering it and was heading with great purpose for the side entrance of the lock. Jack, who had been involved in canopy dropping, dashing about on the deck and giving instructions to anyone who was interested, spotted our latest problem, and quick as a flash he picked up the quant pole. This was about twelve to fourteen foot long and weighed a fair bit. Jack, who is closer to five foot than six, dashed to the prow, armed with the quant pole to fend off the side of the lock. It was a brave act and undoubtedly helped. I thought how much he resembled 'Don Quixote' at the time. Unfortunately, as he lurched back along the deck from the impact on the quant pole and just at the point where he was looking forward to enjoying his success, he was laid out by being struck on his head by the lock gate, which had been opened enough by that time for us to pass under it, but did not allow for someone standing on the deck with a quant pole. We had made it into the lock, although we still had the problem of losing way. This was soon resolved by striking the stern of a boat that was already in the lock.

The boat we had struck had some American servicemen and their wives on board. They took it all in their stride and thought it hilarious, they did not seem to mind having their gin spilt, and we were on our way. That night we were in a riverside inn and we heard American accents and laughter from one of the bars. Our victims were recounting the exploits of earlier in the day to everyone's enjoyment. We joined their company for the evening, and met them several times during the holiday. We actually met them on quite a few occasions over the next few years and had some great times in their company.

The sailing dinghy that we had hired with the cruiser was well worth the extra cost, as it could be rowed to spots which were too shallow to take the cruiser, and we found the sailing to be great fun. I know that it is commonly said that the one thing you do not want when sailing a dinghy is a book on sailing dinghies. This I accept as very true, for things happen quickly and require immediate action, and there is certainly no time for 'See if you can find Chinese Jibe in the index.' This really means that you should get a fair idea of the rudiments of what you are going to attempt, before you actually jump in the boat. As far as we were concerned it was the opposite approach – 'I think that is how the sails should be,' 'Good God, there's a hole in the bottom of the boat! Oh no, that is where the keel drops down' (This is daggerboard in more modern dinghy parlance). We were lucky to survive the learning process which was based on trial and error – 'What happens if I put the rudder to the left?' or 'Shall I let out more sail or pull it in?' The advantage of sailing small boats like dinghies is that they react so quickly to what you do, so that, if you survive for a short while, you begin to get the idea. We also found that other sailing types were usually only too pleased to help out with advice, most of it genuine. Simple concepts like, when in doubt let everything go and the boat will do the right thing, it's you interfering that causes most of the trouble. An oversimplification, but not far off the mark, and helpful to remember if panic sets in – which it will. I have always likened sailing to riding a motorbike – just when you think you have got it all weighed up the boat or bike just lets you know you haven't. Both sports are excellent means of inducing occasional moments of blind terror.

The cabin cruisers are much more sedate and less alarming, or should I say, alarming on fewer occasions. There are moments, though, and it is amazing how many common little accidents occur, which obviously shouldn't, such as 'catching a short rope'. You are so engrossed in catching the rope, you do not notice that it is falling short of the bank and step into the river to catch it. The hazardous 'coiling your ropes or raising a fender out of the water' – you bend down to perform the operation, hit your backside on the cabin and do a swallow dive into the river. The 'I will be helpful, throw me your rope' gambit – the person in trouble is obviously an amateur to get into this situation in the first place, but you thought he would untie the rond anchor before he threw it to you (this can require hospitalisation). 'I will just push the boat off the shallows with the quant pole.' Just is the word to worry about, so just make sure you stay on the boat you are pushing off – many do not. 'That's moored her up okay for the night – what is the tide like here?' The boat looks silly hanging on the bank of the river above the water. These, of course, are just a sample, there are so many more but that is what makes it so much fun. We found after a number of years we were getting too proficient and the laughs were getting much fewer; we even entertained the thought of putting to sea instead of being on inland waters – just think of the scope that would give you!

At the Garden City Press I had been asked by the chapel if I would be prepared to do the father of the chapel duties, and I agreed. In my own way I have always been an idealist and did not see that the fact that I was in a supervisory position with the company should make any difference. Over the years I have carried out duties that were representing both union and management. I always felt that what I was trying to do was no more than to be fair, which in my view should upset neither faction, but I am afraid this is idealism. Nobody is held to be unbiased, and the events I was about to be involved in would begin to bring that fact home to me.

What was about to happen was a national trade dispute over pay and conditions, which would result in a national strike in the printing industry that lasted six weeks. It was also the last national strike to take place in the industry. Although there have been several negotiations which have gone to the brink, until now the 1957 dispute has been the last occasion when national strike action has been used.

There were endless problems and meetings before the strike action was taken, with difficult situations to try to control like 'working to rule'. It was not an easy time and, as was to be expected, more than a little acrimony was felt on both sides of the dispute. When it came to the crunch and the strike was called, I was worried about the loss of earnings, with a mortgage to pay and hire-purchase commitments. A friend of mine, Walter Hesse, was a painter and decorator, and he offered me work with him, painting a large farmhouse at Broom, which I gratefully accepted.

When the first payout from the union to the men on strike took place, I queued up for mine and when I got to the table they said to me, 'Oh, you are a dual card holder, aren't you? You get paid by both the TA (Typographical Association) and the LTS (London Typographical Society).' What a relief – with those payments and what I was getting for the painting work, I was doing quite nicely.

The thing about this dispute that was a first was that we were told when the strike ended over the television. Our instructions were to return to work on the Monday, and a ballot would be held to ratify the agreement when we were back at work. This obviously had the proviso that, if it was not ratified by the membership, then the strike would be back on. There were quite a number of members who were unhappy at things being done that way round but, in fairness, the union felt it had as good an agreement as they could get and were recommending its acceptance by the membership.

It took weeks for the ballot to take place and that period was another difficult one for me. Management were pushing for cooperation on works' committees and productivity talks, and a lot of my members were most unwilling to take part in anything that they considered helpful to management, certainly not until the agreement was ratified. I pushed the chapel on these items and said that in the long run it was in our own interests to cooperate in these areas with the understanding that all we would be doing was setting up the means to take part in these areas once an agreement was in place. This was a struggle and it came to the point where I resigned my office as FoC, as a matter of principle, because I was being censured by the chapel for being pro-management. Within two days I was asked to take back my resignation and carry on in the office with chapel support and I agreed.

The result of the ballot was announced as accepted by the membership and immediately the union officials in the company were called to a management meeting in the boardroom (at that time there were about eight different unions involved). The management gave out a list of items that they were going to put in hand immediately, and having checked them I was far from happy. I called a meeting that night and asked the chapel to back me in withdrawing all the cooperation we had agreed to, so far, unless a number of the items that we strongly objected to (as not being in the spirit of the agreement) were removed from the list. I got unanimous support from the chapel, and several days' negotiating took place, with the items finally removed from the list. I had stressed to the chapel that the reason I could negotiate was that by giving me the authority to give cooperation to the management on items like works' committees and so forth, they had given me something to negotiate with.

When things got back to normal after the dispute, I resigned the office of FoC and there were a number of repercussions. The composing room manager retired and one of the overseers took over his position. I had been given to understand that when this occurred I would replace the overseer. This was not the case – not only that, but the position of 'clicker' was removed from me. I was most annoyed at this and asked to see the MD. At this meeting I asked why this had happened and to be told where I had not been carrying out my duties satisfactorily, but he refused to give me an answer and just said that it was a management decision. I went to the composing room manager and gave him my notice straight away. His words to me were, 'Don't be silly, it is only a slap on the wrist for being a naughty boy and doing the FoC's job. Leave it, and you will be reinstated within a couple of months!'

This did not go down well with me as I said earlier, I had carried out the office as fairly as it could have been done, and it rankled.

Before I actually left, union officials came to the company, as a victimisation charge had been made by the chapel on my behalf (without my knowledge). I was called into the meeting and all the ground was gone over. The result of it all was that the union had to accept the management's decision, which was that the reason for my demotion was that I was not psychologically suited to management. The union officials told me afterwards that, when you take on a union office and you are in a management position, you are in trouble, and they could not resolve the problem by contesting the reason given. I accepted this, for to be fair I would not have stayed then, even if I had been reinstated. I wondered how many people had been in my situation – there cannot be that many who get accused by the union membership of being too pro-management and demoted for being a union troublemaker within the space of a few weeks. I have come across the term 'psychologically unsuited' over the years, business consultants rather like it. The reason being that it is almost impossible to counter and comes down in the end to a person or person's opinion. I will say in my defence that the management positions I held over the next nearly forty years, up to and including general manager, and a directorship on the management board of a company should go some way in disproving that 'psychologically unsuited' theory!

After eighteen months of using the motorbike as my source of transport I had decided to see if I could get back on four wheels. There was a definite drawback to the motorbike, and that was that it only provided transport for me. There was no way June was prepared to go on it, so the need was there but the finance was more than a little limited, so there was only one kind of car we could have – a cheap one! I had been scouring the local papers for the garages selling second-hand cars, and for some reason had decided to go over to a garage at Toddington when I finished work in the evening. I was going to leave a bit earlier than usual, as the journey was about twelve to fifteen miles each way.

I set off, and things were going quite well until the daylight started to fade and I had to switch on my lights. This was just the other side of Ampthill, and to my alarm no lights came on. There was a torch battery in the headlight and that provided a backup to the head and rear lights when the dynamo was not working. I pulled into the side of the road and had a look but could not see what was wrong with it. This meant that I had just a dim light from the headlight and nothing at the rear. It was now approaching 5.30 p.m. and, as soon as I saw a small garage that was still open, I pulled in to get help. The mechanic had a look at it for a while, but could not find the cause of the problem and the garage was about to shut. To get me out of bother he fitted a cycle rear light with a battery in it and said that was the best he could do. It would at least mean that I was not breaking the law, so off I went, still heading for the garage at Toddington. By now it was really dark and I soon found that on the unlit roads I could not see much further than my front wheel, so I decided that discretion was the better part of valour and turned for home. It was a struggle, I was having to creep along and the journey was going to take ages. After some miles I could see the lights of Shefford ahead of me, and the main road that I was on was now lit. This was great news, and as soon as I could see where I was going, I opened the throttle to push the speed up, but not for long. The bike suddenly hit a rough bit of road with a nasty hole in it, the bike was jarred very badly, and my headlight disintegrated all over the road. I pulled up and searched for the bits of my light. I was able to find the broken front glass and the reflector (complete with broken bulb), but the chrome band that should have held it all together had disappeared off the face of the Earth. No doubt it was somewhere in the ditch or the fields by the side of the road. To find it in the dark, not knowing exactly where it flew off, was going to be impossible, so I gave up the search and rode into Shefford. The only shop open that I could find was a newsagent's, so I went in to see what I could get. They did not sell bicycle lamps or torches, but having heard of my plight he offered to lend me his torch, as long as I promised to give it to him back by the weekend. I thanked him and set off again, this time armed with a torch for my front light. A couple of things soon became apparent to me – one was the fact that a normal hand torch just does not give a good enough beam of light to see where you are going at twenty to thirty miles per hour. The other was that holding a torch in your hand and directing its beam to see where you were going, while at the same time steering a bike and operating either a throttle or clutch, was damn nearly impossible. The gods must have thought that I was having it far too easy, so they threw in a peasouper fog for good measure. This was so thick that at one time I found myself riding on grass, which concerned me, and I was relieved to see a finger post, which was helpful, I was in the middle of a triangle at a road junction.

I rode into our drive at about nine o'clock that night. June emerged from the front door and asked if I had seen anything that I thought was worth buying and was surprised to learn that I had not even reached the garage. A fact that was just a bit irksome, as it had taken me five hours and I was freezing. I did reach the garage that weekend on the bike with the lights repaired and working, and bought a Ford 10, of 1938 vintage. It was the model after the 'Y' model, and had the spare wheel on the back of the car, covered with a metal cover like a dustbin lid.

I knew that it was only a means to an end because of the price that I had paid, so at least I was not disappointed when I found out what a shambles it was. It was not the worst car I ever had, but that was only because it was beaten by a short head by a 1936 Standard 9. The main difference between the two being, terrible as the Ford was, it at least went, whereas the Standard confounded all as to why it would not go. Experts were reduced to tears by that Standard. By the time we finished it was getting like 'Wallace's axe', which has had three new blades and five new handles. Carburettors were reconditioned, a new condenser and coil were fitted, holes were drilled in the petrol tank (to prevent a vacuum), and the petrol feed pipe was replaced in a different position to get it further from the engine block (as they thought the petrol was evaporating before it got to the carburettor). Even after all

that, once you had driven it a distance of five or six miles –
look out! It would suddenly stop and that was it. If you
were not anywhere problematical when it stopped and time
was not of the essence, you could just go for a stroll and
smoke a pipeful of tobacco, and when you got back, it
would start and sound lovely, good for at least another five
miles. People just would not believe you, including the
policeman that found it pushed up onto the pavement in
front of some shops, on the main road near Haringey
Stadium. We had abandoned it there one night when we
had tickets for a 'car rodeo' at the stadium – it nearly got us
there. As I explained to the officer that night, 'You are not
going to believe this, we had to push it onto the pavement
when it broke down to avoid a traffic jam, and I know that
when I turn the ignition key, it will start without any
trouble – it always does.' He must have thought that our
story was so improbable it had to be true, so he took no
action.

The newly acquired Ford 8 did have some minor
irritants; the brakes did not work and the steering was so
bad that the car would nudge alternate kerbs without you
moving the steering wheel. The bodywork was in the
category commonly known by the term 'a rust bucket', and
the lights had to be seen to be believed (and even on a dark
night, that was not easy to do). A couple of friends walked
over and tapped on my window one night in a cinema car
park. I wound down the window and they said, 'Where can
you get those electric fires you have got on your
mudguards? They are unusual!' They did not seem all that
convinced when I told them they were headlights. They
just walked away shaking their heads and laughing.

During the process of trying to make the car something
you could sit in without getting nervous every time a
policeman walked by, I found that the vehicle had been
rewired several times. I tore out enough wire to prove it – I

removed yards and yards of it, and nothing went out or refused to work, that was not already in that state. The engine had been ticking over at an alarming rate, on my way back from the garage, and, as the engine warmed up, it ticked over faster and faster. By the time I reached home it was hard to tell whether you had your foot on the accelerator or not. I lifted the bonnet and screwed both the slow runner and the mixture screws completely in and out, without it having any effect on the tick-over. A replacement carburettor was obviously going to be high on the list of priorities.

Our new bungalow was our pride and joy. The description *bijou* could be applied without any fear of the Trades Description Act giving you any trouble. It had a nice big lounge – a feature, and the kitchen was not at all bad. After that it did have little snags, like the gull-wing door that led into the lounge (it was not intended to be gull-wing, it was just the way they had fitted the door). The bedroom was extremely small, but the toilet and bathroom did have the advantage that, if you leaned forward a little on the toilet, you could open the front door. Not a facility one would use very often – but possible!

We decorated the place throughout and it really did look quite nice. Being our first place the décor had the advantage of all being purchased at the same time, and editions of *Ideal Home* had been studied for ideas. The hall I had decorated with white skirting boards and doorframes, a predominately light-grey wallpaper and for the *pièce de résistance* the doors were going to be 'harlequin'. An idea snitched from *Ideal Home*. Each door in a different matching colour in pastel shades. I remember going into a shop in Letchworth to buy the pots of paint. As I chose them, I ranged them up along the counter (the elderly lady serving me looked on in an interested manner). I had green, yellow, red and blue pots on the counter and I was trying to get a fifth one that would blend. The lady said, 'Can I help?' So I explained that I was trying to get one more colour that went with the others, as I was painting the hall doors, one in each colour. I don't think she was into *Ideal Home* because she reeled back and said, 'Jesus Christ.' I chose lilac as the last colour. I would stress that these were delicate pastel shades and not the 'pillar-box red and hooker green' type of colours. Just in case you are still not convinced they looked very nice and we were complimented on the décor (genuinely) by a number of people.

To start with we had a series of duff second-hand televisions that were prone to break down frequently, and you kept having the embarrassment of having to ask people how the play ended the night before, or who won. To solve this we decided to rent a set, which we did from a company in Bedford. Now, at that time, not many booster aerials were around, and ITV just reached the area on a good night (if you did not mind watching it through a snowstorm). The one thing you had to have was a good aerial, and for this you had to purchase a massive contraption that was fitted to your wall or as in our case, on your chimney stack.

The first winter we were in the bungalow was a winter of gales, and Bedfordshire being very flat in that area, the gales were quite something. We were awakened one night by an alarming crash that took me back to the Blitz. I got up and, when I opened the door to the lounge, there was a nice view of the stars through the ceiling, and our aerial plus a large amount of chimney stack was in the middle of our carpet. The next-door neighbour had heard the din and was good enough to come round and give me a hand getting a tarpaulin over the roof where the damage was – not an easy task in that wind. We were lucky, as the builders were still on the site, building other houses, and they made good the damage for us without charge, on the condition that the aerial was not put back on the chimney. The problem had been due to the combination of a thumping great aerial, a small chimney that had not long been built, and exceptional winds.

I telephoned the television rental company the next day and said that they had better supply me with a garden mast, and they agreed that they would. I was amazed to get home and find in the garden something resembling a telegraph pole bolted to a railway sleeper embedded in the garden – and was not best pleased. Shortly after this the winds got up again, and my neighbour gave me a shout and said the new aerial was looking like it was going to do even more damage than the last one. This time we were into tree climbing and had to lash the aerial to a tree, to ensure that it did not come down on the bungalow again. I rang the television people and told them they must come and take down the monstrosity they had erected, and quickly, for, if it damaged my house, I would sue them for damages. It was gone when I got home that night. The funny end to this sequence of events was that we had never had a very good picture and, when I walked out into the garden and just stuck the aerial straight into the ground, we achieved the best reception we had ever had!

While I was at the Garden City Press I was involved in cricket again and played for the works' team. This was in the local works' league and was most enjoyable. The works' team had a number of good players, one had had a trial for Essex, and several others played in local leagues, with their exploits enthusiastically recorded in the local press. For some strange reason, when we played as a team, the result was almost invariably an unmitigated disaster. On paper we should have been local champions, but on the field – to call us clowns would have been unfair to clowns. John Stanford and myself used to open the bowling and if one of us was a better batsman than the other it was John, so my place as number eleven was secure. It was therefore worrying to arrive a couple of minutes late for a match and be told to get your pads on! But not unusual. We were to share in the best partnership of the match on one occasion, twenty-one runs between us (John scored twelve of them). In spite of this, it was all good fun, we had the sort of matches that Michael Green of *Coarse Rugby* fame would have written about. I am pretty sure he did not do a book on cricket, probably for a similar reason to that of Stephen Potter who did not cover it in his gamesmanship books either. His excuse was that he wrote about gamesmanship in sport, and ruled cricket out as being all gamesmanship!

We had some disputed umpiring decisions that could only occur in works' league matches. The best of these was when a batsman objected to being given out by the umpire, for being dismissed by a catch on the boundary. His complaint was, 'How did I know that he was a fielder taking part in the match, and not a spectator?' This was because it was raining fairly heavily and the fielder had put on a plastic mackintosh and a check cap to keep dry! The decision stood. Another dispute was how high over your head did a bowler's delivery have to be to be classed as a wide (the player who was involved in this dispute was one of ours). He was often used when we were not getting the wickets, as a bowler. He specialised in the hand grenade, short delivery. This could be very successful, with the batsman hurtling down the pitch to smash him out of the ground and missing. This often resulted in a stumping, or being caught, as, when the mighty blow did make contact, it frequently achieved height but not distance. He, unfortunately, had a rather short fuse and was banned from the game in the local leagues for trying to throw an umpire in the duck pond.

Around this period I was feeling somewhat restless, and consequently got involved in a couple of things for added interest. I was looking at the adverts in the daily newspapers, with a view to a change of job, and came very close to moving into a sales career. A friend of mine worked for a national company that sold soup as its main line. Now the thought of being a soup salesman did not inspire me as such, but what I did find interesting was that he had a firm's car, was still at home when I left in the morning, and was always back at home long before me at night. Add to this the fact that he appeared to be quite affluent and you get the general picture. He informed me that he had been promoted and was taking over as area manager in the Channel Islands, and would I like to apply for his job. I decided that I would, and did, and furthermore I was successful. At this time I was only on a weekly contract with my company and, therefore, had no need to give in my notice until two weeks before I was going to leave. This turned out to be fortunate, as, before I gave in my notice, the soup company contacted me to say that they would honour the offer to me as far as pay and conditions were concerned but the position had changed. This turned out to be that the sales representatives worked in groups of three for an area, two covered retail and one covered wholesale. The job I had applied for was the wholesale one, which was the better job, and the two existing representatives, who had been covering the retail, thought that one of them should be offered the wholesale position, and not a new applicant. The firm saw the fairness of this and changed their offer to me to that of a retail representative. This was definitely less appealing – sticking your foot in small grocer's shop doors, trying to get orders, was not what I had in mind. I was very lucky that I was not committed and could change my mind. In fairness this was not a decision that I have ever regretted.

The other interest came about by getting involved in the general election. The Liberal party was having a revamp and doing quite well, and at that time I was very sympathetic to their views and decided to do something about it. The Mid-Beds Member of Parliament at the time was Lennox-Boyd and the constituency had been Tory-controlled since way back. The Liberal candidate was a local man, George Matthews, and a very good campaign was run by an excellent agent called Pratap Chitnis (now Lord Chitnis). At the end of the campaign the Tory candidate, Lennox-Boyd, held the seat but with a much reduced majority, and the size of the Liberal vote was very encouraging.

This was exciting stuff and caused quite a stir in the political world. At that time I was the press officer for the constituency and spent one night chauffeuring Joe Grimond from meeting to meeting. I found him to be a very likeable person, strangely enough, for all his academic background, a very down-to-earth man with no noticeable airs and graces. He certainly was very amiable and interesting and showed no signs of being at all concerned with having to clamber into my little two-door Standard 8 to be driven about from meeting to meeting. These experiences were an eye-opener to me as far as politics were concerned. I was at the meeting when the candidate was selected for the general election. It was not a difficult decision to make as the list of prospective candidates was a short one. The other people on it were unknown and George Matthews was a local man, who had put in a lot of work on the party's behalf over the years, and the choice made itself!

A by-election was called only a brief period after the general election, and the fact that we had done so well, plus the resurgence of Liberal support made a considerable difference to the prospective candidates list that we now received. It was not only a long one, but also included people who were well-known names nationally. We stuck by our local candidate, it seemed only right, but there is a chance that we went with sentiment and that a celebrity may have just thrown the balance to give us success. At that time, although I did not agree with all the policies of the Liberal Party, it certainly was closer to my beliefs than any other political party. I got a bit excited later when the Social Democrats split from the Labour Party. I nursed the idea that there would be an unselfish coming together of the parties of the centre, but I was wrong. The strange diversity of the Liberal party's support, which swings from fairly loony idealism in some areas, to extreme ideas in others that could frankly frighten both the Conservative party, and the Labour party, proved troublesome. The other main reason for the lack of success was, in my view, that the personal ambition of some individuals took priority, rather than a preparedness to serve a common cause. As far as my own allegiances are concerned now, they are such that I could not be described as a 'don't know', for I do know. I know that none of them have sufficient policies that I agree with, to enable me to give them my support!

After my upset at the Garden City Press, I moved to a printer's in Bedford. They were interested in me because of my background on periodical work, which they were moving into, and I was interested in them as the firm was operating on a work-measurement bonus scheme. I had heard about these schemes that were coming into the industry, and was intrigued to see what they were like. The change was for the best, although I was no longer in a supervisory position. With the bonus that I was earning and overtime, I was better off financially.

Over the years the different companies I have worked at have been fairly similar, regarding what is euphemistically referred to as 'goings-on', complying with the norm I should imagine. Not this one, this was the exception, it certainly appeared to me that nearly everyone was at it. The Managing Director was a public school man and had a rather bad stammer and always sounded to me as if he was the person Terry-Thomas had modelled his character on. On one occasion the composing room overseer was reputed to have dashed into his office during the lunch hour to report that one of the compositors was making love to one of the secretaries in the building's foyer.

In answer to him the MD asked, 'T-T-Tell me, are they c-c-c-copulating?'

The overseer answered, 'No!'

'Well,' said the MD, 'There's b-b-b-bugger all I can do about it!

One of our drivers set out after having his lunch and got nearly as far as Rushden before he noticed a lot of noise coming from the back of his van. He pulled up, went round the back and unlocked the van doors to find a woman from the canteen and a warehouseman in there. They had obviously nipped in there for some out-of-sight hanky-panky and had the misfortune of finding themselves whizzing off up the road. They were duly returned, somewhat red-faced, to the works.

One of the compositors, who was well over the age for retirement, decided to call it a day and was presented with a radio when he left the company. Before a year had passed he came back and asked if we could find him a job as he was bored and wanted to get from under his wife's feet. He said he did not mind what the job was, and the firm gave him a part-time position in the composing room stores. Some time later the MD was walking round the department with the overseer, when he stopped and stared into the stores. 'Isn't that Jones?' he asked the overseer.

'Yes,' said the overseer. 'We have given him a part-time job in the stores!'

The MD said, 'Didn't we give him a radio when he left?'

'We did,' answered the overseer.

'Well, what's he c-c-come b-back for – a b-b-bloody television!'

The company, though not a very big one (approximately one hundred employees), had a thriving sports and social club. The club fielded three football teams, although a large number of the players were not employed by the company. A Christmas draw the club held was also on an unbelievable scale and well-known in the town. The man who ran the club used to obtain extremely good support from the local businesses and traders, and its fame was only rivalled by our pre-Christmas celebrations in the firm. As a large part of the company's work was seasonal it usually meant that by the Christmas closure date we were just going through the motions. I was most surprised on my first Christmas there to find, when I arrived at eight o'clock, the shift work staff had been knocking back the home-made wine for some time. There were plenty of varieties of home-made wine on offer, and, if someone uncorked a bottle and smoke didn't come out of it, you knew it was all right! After the lunch break, I was talking to someone who was dancing with a girl from the bindery, who said how great it was, and that he came every year – and he didn't even work there!

One of the characters there used to cause a great deal of fun; he was one of those people who had to be different. If everyone thought it was cold, he would say he thought it was hot. One of my workmates and I decided to put him to the test when he got back from his holidays. He went in to see him first and said he was sorry that he had had such bad weather, with all that rain, and Charlie answered that he had had wonderful weather, with hardly a drop of rain. About an hour afterwards I went in and said to him that I was glad that he had such superb weather, and he said that it was the worst he had known and it poured down both weeks. He was reputed to have come to work on his bike one winter's morning, in an open-necked shirt, when everyone else was in balaclava helmets and mittens, and said it was a lovely sunny morning. Then he had to take two weeks off, with frost-bitten ears. One winter we had some real peasouper fogs. Charlie said that his big old car stood so high off the road that he had much better visibility than we had, with our more modern models, and he had no trouble at all in fog. On our way in to work the next morning we saw his car stranded in the middle of a field of Brussels sprouts. He had fortunately driven off the road just where there was an entrance for the tractors, or he would have gone into a deep ditch. The car sank in the mud up to its axles, and the chaps he was giving a lift to had come to the conclusion that he was a dangerous bastard and walked off, refusing to help push it out of the field.

It was in one of those fogs that I rode home on my motorbike up the A1 from Baldock, with a string of traffic behind me following my rear light. It was a fact that you could see much better on a motorbike than you could in a car, looking through a windscreen. When I got home and pulled into my drive, I looked round and saw, to my horror, that the lorries and traffic had followed me into the side roads. I had to go out to them and tell them how to get back onto the A1.

Chapter Twenty-Four

Work-Study and Work-Measurement

Having worked for the company in Bedford for about eighteen months on a work measurement bonus scheme, I found the scheme to have its idiosyncrasies but, by and large, it was quite workable. There were without doubt areas of work where the values were more generous than others, but with a mix of work, if you put the effort in, you could make a reasonable bonus. If you accepted that the evaluation was bound to vary to an extent and were prepared to accept that the bonus was paid on how effectively you worked and not on how hard you worked, then the system could, and did function reasonably.

In fairness, you had to take into account that the people who were doing the time studies and the evaluation had to combat the working man (bless him) whose prime object was to take the study man to the cleaners. Pulling the wool over the study man's eyes to get unrealistic values was considered to be fair game. It was roughly in the same category as tax evasion. One of the areas that was always troublesome was controlling quality, and another was the penalties for spoilt work, which were a minefield.

One evening I was working late on overtime when the chapel officials, having just left a meeting, approached me with a proposition. They had discussed having a union representative in the bonus office with the management. It had been agreed that this would be a good idea and should be helpful in smoothing out problems and mistrust. The representative would receive training on work-study and work-measurement techniques, and so be qualified to ensure that things were fair, accurate, and above board. The chapel had discussed this, and it had been agreed to approach me to see if I would be prepared to do the job. I said to them that I was worried about taking an official union position again so soon, as my back had not yet healed from the last one. They gave me the weekend to think it over. I did so, and it did appear to be an interesting number, and, for someone with as low a boredom threshold as myself, any challenge like that was bound to be a temptation. On the Monday I told them that I would take it on, totally unaware of how much that decision would eventually affect my working life.

Within a couple of weeks I was moved into the bonus office and started my training. This was to cover work-study and work-measurement, right through from time studies with a stopwatch to logging the studies and analysing them to produce time standards. In addition to this I was engaged in calculating bonus payments from the dockets. The training would enable me to assist in producing standards for the bonus scheme and liaise between the shop floor and the management on the union's behalf. Once trained, I would be in the position to check values and safeguard against a biased approach. I found all this to be most interesting, but a far from easy position. As soon as I had a stopwatch and clipboard in my hands, I found myself once again in that unenviable position of trying to sit on the fence. There was no difficulty on my part in trying to be honest with what I was doing, but the problems arose in trying to get others to accept that fact. For a start, as soon as you began to take time studies with a stopwatch, you ceased to be the union representative and were perceived as the enemy! People wanted me to say it was all a 'take-on' whether I thought it was or not. There were areas within the scheme that I was not happy with, dare I say from both sides, but I can only say that for the most part the setting of values and evaluation was done fairly.

It was generally believed that some jobs were much better bonus earners than others, but it appeared to me that, in general, the person who made a good bonus, if moved from one job to another, still made a good bonus. The same went for someone who did not. Of course, occasionally, there were bad values that had been set. This was not surprising, as the men did their utmost to mislead you and they were very skilful at it. One of the problems that arose was that the consultants, who were installing these schemes, were all well-educated men and not fools, but the consultancy had this strange notion that they should not have their judgement clouded by prior knowledge of the trades they were working in. It is therefore not surprising that some very strange values were set. Sticking my neck out, the general view of the shop floor was, if it was in their favour, that was one they had won and don't let the cat out of the bag. If it was tight in the other direction then kick up a stink and try to get this totally iniquitous thing changed.

Many a time I had the moral dilemma of watching a study man being taken to the cleaners by the people I was representing. I felt I could only take the line of seeing that my studies reflected reality and that they would balance the situation, and if the management study men wondered why the result was different it was up to them to check why. If you think that these situations have no ethical problems, then you should try it!

During the time that I was working for the company at Bedford, I was involved in a difficult period of adjustment.

I lost my father, who died after a short illness, and I felt his loss deeply. In recent years I have read so many accounts of people's lives where a considerable time is spent denigrating one or both of their parents. I am pleased to say for the record that I could not have wished for better ones, and the loss of my father was probably felt more by me largely because he died when only sixty-three years of age and we had become accustomed to his having good health. He had been a large influence on me and had imparted lessons of good sense and advice that have served me in good stead throughout my life. My mother outlived him by just over twenty years, which was one of life's ironies, as she had suffered bad health for most of her life. It is always a blow to lose someone who is close to you, but you are certainly more prepared for it when they reach an age like eighty-four. When Dad died, June and I sold our bungalow and bought a large house to be able to accommodate my mother, whose house my brother and I had sold. This was due to the fact that she did not wish to stay there alone, and the money invested would help to provide a reasonable income for her.

Our new house was great, although a lot of work had to be done on it. June had taken one look at the kitchen and said, 'The rest of the house I like, but until that kitchen is sorted out I am not moving in!' I could not understand this, I thought it had a certain 'old-world charm', with the dark green and brown paintwork (which was peeling nicely here and there), the earthenware 'butler' sink, which stood on two brick piers and had the two taps fixed to the wall (one about eighteen inches higher than the other – to effect just the right splash factor). This work was achieved in record time with help from my friend, Walter, only days after the purchase went through. Units were fitted and the kitchen was decorated and tiled.

The house had been constructed in 1916 by a builder for his own use, and was, by and large, very sound. It had the largest garden I have ever had, with a lawn and flower garden, an area where I used to grow chrysanthemums (about four rows), an area for soft fruit (five or six rows of raspberry canes), a salad and vegetable area, and a large orchard with pear, apple and damson trees. The soil in that area of Bedfordshire was so good that I have had much smaller gardens and have had to work far harder to look after them. At the time when the house was built rates were assessed on your frontage onto the road. The house had been designed accordingly – it was half a house wide and two houses long. This accounted for its unusual layout of rooms and passages. My predecessor had written under the light switch covers in each room how much wallpaper was required to decorate the room. When I was about to do the entrance hall, stairs, landing and passages, I was horrified to read twenty-seven rolls!

One of the things we used to enjoy when we had company was for the visitor to ask where the toilet was. We would keep a straight face and say, 'Outside the lounge turn left, go up the stairs to the landing, pass the first two bedroom doors and turn left, at the end of the passage turn left, and it's on your right.' We would get a variety of answers to this – the contents varying in both their amusement and vulgarity.

My brother had purchased a house in Ealing, of similar age and size, a couple of years before mine, and it had cost him virtually twice the price. Some of the features of this house caused us some amusement. It had a bell system for servants which had been operated by a complicated wire and pulley mechanism. This accounted for strange spooky noises heard throughout the house. The previous owner had also spent a considerable amount of time carrying out 'improvements', which achieved a level of ghastliness and incompetence, which I don't think either of us have seen equalled, before or since. We used the man's name from that time on as a means of describing anything of extreme bad taste or bad workmanship. In a dictionary the entry would read either, 'the essence of bodge' or 'naffer than naff!'

June and I paid Keith, Betty and Judy a visit the weekend that they moved in, to see how they were getting on. So did quite a number of their friends. The excuse was to give them a hand moving in, but I am afraid when we got there it had already turned into a 'let's all sit around and have a good laugh and a drink party'. Standing in the middle of the lounge was a large oak sea chest. It was a heirloom of Betty's family – the Buchans – and had been handed down for generations, the last two or three of which had used it as a children's' toy cupboard. It was very heavy and had a large brass plate on it inscribed, 'Captain Carnac Bart. RNVR (Royal Naval Volunteer Reserve)'. Keith wanted to get it down to the cellar and this required a number of friends' assistance. Three of us to carry it, two at the bottom end where the weight would be, one at the top to steady and help take the weight, someone to hold doors open and switch on lights and several to give advice, which you would ignore, if you had any sense, and the rest to barrack! Everyone was enjoying this task, the type of laughter and its causes perhaps betraying the fact that a reasonable quantity of the 'lunatics' broth' had been put away before the task was attempted. When we were no more than a step or two away from reaching the foot of the stairs leading down to the cellar, the stairs collapsed and Keith and I plus Captain Carnac Bart's chest were deposited on the floor in a heap.

About a year after we had moved into our new house my daughter Karen was born. We had suddenly realised that we were already the wrong side of thirty, and, if we intended having children, we had got to start thinking about it. In those days it was quite usual to have your children at home and only go into hospital if there were complications. No problems were envisaged in June's case and everything was planned for her to have the baby at home. This as it turned out was not trouble-free. Firstly there were a number of false alarms. I would get a telephone message that the midwife had rung and I was to get home straight away. This I would do, only to find that when I got home June would be in the kitchen getting our evening meal. When it actually happened it was nerve-racking; it went on for about two days, and when it got to the evening of the second day, I was getting worried and June looked dreadful. It got to about seven o'clock and the midwife said to me, 'Call an ambulance. I want to get her into hospital as quickly as we can.'

I did this, but time passed and still no ambulance appeared. The midwife then asked June if she would be okay in my car and she said she would, so we set off for Bedford General Hospital. As soon as we got there, there was a panic, although, in fairness, she did get immediate attention. They checked her and gave her an injection to knock her out, as she needed rest badly. The doctor then asked me to sign to give them permission to operate if necessary, and I had to fill in some forms. I was then told to clear off, as there was nothing more I could do and they would not be doing anything until June had got some rest. So I was to ring them at nine o'clock in the morning to find out how things were going. I must admit that I managed to get some sleep, aided by a large Scotch provided by my brother-in-law. I had not had much sleep in the last few nights and it had been a hectic day. It was the usual situation, you do not realise how tired you are until you stop, and then it hits you. The next morning I rang the hospital and was told to ring them again at 12.30 a.m. When

I rang this time I was told that I had a daughter, and her weight, and that June was just coming out of the operating theatre. The visiting times were much stricter then and I was told that I could see them that evening, but only me, and normal visiting could start on the Sunday. What a relief! By the end of the night before, I had been my usual calm and collected self, apart from a few elementary mistakes like getting my wife's names wrong on the form that I had filled in. June was a bit miffed to find herself being called Pamela by the nurses and the name tag on her wrist also saying Pamela. I had written her two names the wrong way round on the form. She was very good about it, I don't think she has mentioned it for several years now!

June had left work to have Karen; it was now only my salary coming in and this indirectly brought about my next move at work. Since I had been the union representative on the bonus scheme, I had not had an hour's overtime and was living on my flat rate. Not to put too fine a point on it, I could not manage financially and said so to the manager. His answer to me was that there was no reason why I should not be able to do overtime in the composing department and they could do with it as they were very busy. It obviously would not be practical to do the odd hour, but half-nights and Saturday overtime was acceptable. Armed with this information I went to the father of the chapel and asked him to put me back on the overtime rota. The chapel had a meeting and I was told that they would not allow me do this. Strangely enough, this got right up my nose and I told them so. I had taken the job at their request, to represent them, and they expected me to do it with a reduction in my pay by preventing me from working at my trade. That weekend I was fuming, and, when reading the paper on the Saturday, saw an advert for a company who required a work-study officer to work on a similar scheme to the one we were using, at a firm in Essex.

I wrote off an application straight away. I felt I had been badly treated, and if I was going to be regarded as management by the men I was representing, then I might just as well be employed in that capacity and receive the full benefits from doing the job. My application was answered, and I had to go to Southend for an interview on the Thursday morning. I drove down with June and Karen, complete with baby bottles, nappies and food.

I went into the factory for the interview leaving the car and family parked nearby. I was met by one of the consultants, who was in charge of implementing the scheme and would be carrying out the interview. I had a reasonably short grilling on the work-study and bonus scheme side and then was taken to a room where I was given a series of intelligence tests. These were fairly nerve-racking. They were printed, four, six and eight-page tests, and each time the consultant would run through what was required and set a timer going for the period that you were allowed. This would be whirring away, adding to the pressure, with the needle steadily moving round towards completion time. When this was all completed I was introduced to the work-study manager of the printing firm, who, to my surprise, I knew and had worked with before. He had a chat with me and that was that; I dashed back to the car where June was sitting, wondering where the hell I had been for all that time.

The next day, which was Friday, I went in to work as normal and, when I got home in the evening, June informed me that a telegram had arrived and I had to ring the firm at Southend. When I rang them they informed me that they would like to see me the next morning at ten o'clock to finalise their decision on the appointment. The MD was flying to Holland and wanted to resolve the situation before he went. So the next morning I made an early start and it was down to Southend again. I had a short successful interview with the MD and the job was mine. They wanted me to start as soon as possible, and said they would arrange accommodation for me in Southend for three months, so that I could arrange moving home.

The next Monday I gave in my notice to the firm at Bedford. I only needed to give two weeks' notice but I made it a month to give them a chance to replace me. Once again it was one of those situations, the chapel asked me to stay on and they would give their approval on the vexed overtime issue, but, as with my last experience, I decided there was no going back. Apart from anything else the position I had been offered was a staff appointment. The pay was better and the intention was that the work-measurement bonus schemes were to be installed throughout the group. The present work-study manager would move on to oversee the introduction into the other firms in the group, and I would take over his position at the Southend factory, with an uplift in salary to cover the position.

The night before I was to start my job at Southend I set the alarm clock for some ungodly hour, as it would take me about two and a half hours to drive down and I had to be there for eight o'clock in the morning. This started a chain of events which I have found to be par for the course over the years. The new job had created a bit of euphoria, the company I was joining had done a good job of selling it to me. I was on a high; this was to be the move I had been waiting for, words like executive had been used, and the fact that they were paying for three months' accommodation for me added to the feeling of achievement. At about three o'clock in the morning the rot started – the bedroom ceiling fell down on us with a crash. There was dust and plaster everywhere and, frighteningly, one large piece was dangling over the cot our daughter was asleep in. This meant I had to move furniture about and clear up the mess and did not get a chance to get back to sleep before I left for Southend. I asked June to get in touch with our friend, Walter, who, I hoped, would be able to arrange the work on the ceiling in my absence and I would be back on the Friday night.

I got to the factory at Southend on time and was shown up to the work-study department. There everyone was dashing about, but eventually someone was found to show me where I had been booked in. It could be referred to as a guesthouse, but it looked remarkably like what used to be known as 'digs', and that I was either the lodger or paying guest. Not to worry, it looked pretty reasonable. Back to the works to find that my executive status had not qualified me for a desk. Either it had slipped someone's mind to arrange for one, or the piece of chipboard balanced across between two other desks and a rickety chair was what was given to newly appointed executives in this company. I began to have some feelings of foreboding. I was shown around the works and introduced to everyone and had lunch in the canteen which was very reasonable. During the afternoon I was informed that they were doing a proof study in the Linotype department and they would like me to cover the period between 10 p.m. until 2 a.m. that night. I went off a bit early to my digs and had my evening meal and then back to the factory for the proof study. I did not enjoy my first taste of being an executive; for some reason the euphoria was difficult to maintain. A four-hour proof study with a fly-back stopwatch at that time of night, when I had been up since about half-past three, was just a 'tidge' trying, in fact.

During the three months I was working away from home I had a problem with boils and that certainly did not help. I had been through a similar period when I was at Letchworth, when I was plagued with the cursed things. You do have these spells in your life, when, for some reason or other, your body seems to think that the time is ripe for your health to play up in general. I could only have been in my mid-twenties when I had one of those spells. It started when I slipped whilst carrying a large heavy page of type matter on a galley, grabbed at the nearest rack to save myself and felt a bit of a wrench. Over the weekend I was getting pains in the abdomen and, being a sensible chap, thought the best cure for it would be to mow the lawn and drag a bloody great garden roller over it for a few hours. This, surprisingly, was not a good idea, as it happened, and by the Monday morning I had gone a delicate shade of green and could not sit up in bed without help. My brother-in-law got me down to my doctor's, an old boy around the eighty mark, who had a fixation about malingerers. He checked me over and said that it was a hernia. For this he wrote out a prescription for a truss and told me to go with it to the chemist who would provide and fit it.

'What about time off?' I asked, and he answered, 'No need for that – when you get that truss on, you will be all right.'

If I was all right, then all right is a state that you should avoid being in too often.

My body at this point thought it would be a suitable time to provide me with a plague of boils. I had them on my elbow, the small of my back, and on my backside. I would ease myself into my car in the morning to drive to work and go through the pain barrier with the one on my backside as I sat on it; this would usually make me jerk, so that I could strike the one on my elbow on the door. I would then sit back so the one on the small of my back could get into the act and complete the set!

The truss was very good at stopping your intestine from popping in and out through the wall of your stomach, but did have its drawbacks. In appearance it was like having a

.38 service revolver, in its holster, strapped, in my case, to the lower right side of my stomach and finishing in the groin area. This made you resemble a lopsided male ballet dancer and could be embarrassing. This made me appreciate Spike Milligan's tale of when he was worried that playing his trumpet could give him a hernia and wore a double truss to prevent it from happening. He bought a very long jacket to cover the area and, when he turned up for band practice, the other members of the band were getting at him, with comments like, 'Where did you get that bloody jacket?' To this Spike answered, 'These are all the rage. Cab Calloway wears one!' and got the answer, 'Does he – he must look a right prat!'

The other problem was that, as it was the summer it was not the ideal thing for comfort and succeeded in completing my misery by giving me a sweat rash. This made you want to tear yourself to shreds because of the irritation. It was a period when it would be fair to say I was at a low ebb. I had to look at my birth certificate to reassure myself that I was only twenty-six and things should improve. It was hard to convince myself of this for, with the way my luck was running at the time, if I had to have a zimmer frame it would probably have metal fatigue!

The time at Southend was quite enjoyable, the work was interesting and had its lighter moments. There was a lady who worked in the canteen and was affectionately referred to as the 'Black Hag'. This was a trifle over the top as she only had black hair and a rather swarthy complexion. Her style was a little short of silver service. When I was in the queue for my lunch one day, the chap in front of me was having his dinner served to him canteen-style, and a large spoonful of sprouts were plonked on his plate. He told the 'Black Hag' that he did not want any sprouts, so she said 'okay' and grabbed them off the plate with her hand and put them on mine! If this had been witnessed by a food and hygiene inspector, he would have gone into a dead faint – with the chilling prospect that the kiss of life might have to be administered by the 'Black Hag'!

One of her best moments was the day when she tiptoed into a meeting that was taking place in the boardroom between the MD, management and the consultants who were putting in the bonus scheme. There was a dumbwaiter in the corner of the room, and the tray, loaded with the office teas, used to be sent up in it. She peered round the boardroom door and whispered, 'would it be all right to come through and get the teas?' The MD nodded his approval and she went silently to the dumbwaiter. The meeting carried on until, on reaching the dumbwaiter, she opened the doors and bellowed down to the canteen, 'Fred would like twenty Senior Service but Players will do if you haven't got them. Charlie would like a cheese roll, and have you got a packet of crisps for Margaret?' This, followed by the return dialogue coming up from the canteen, brought the meeting to a standstill, with the MD having an expression of 'I don't believe it' on his face, and everyone else choking with laughter!

On Wednesday afternoons the work-study office used to produce control figures for the group's head office. This was quite a thrash and used to mean working on until the figures were calculated and ready to send off early on the Thursday morning. One of the good things about the system was the wealth of information that it produced. The costs of all areas of the operation were available. Materials, downtime split into specific areas, such as waiting for work, looking for materials, and spoilage. All this was analysed in each departmental area, and with costs per hour of labour. These were available for the week, month, or year to date. This was extremely useful data, and if used sensibly, a great asset in running the business. For the early sixties, which to all intents and purposes was pre-computer, this was good going. A lot of the calculations were done by using a slide rule and meant reading off to the fourth figure accurately, and that was good enough for control uses.

Four of us got into the habit of going off to Westcliff Golf Course as soon as we were finished. We would get nine to eighteen holes played, dependent on the time of the year and the light. The standard was not that great (we were all beginners) but it was most enjoyable. One evening we were playing and got caught in a really bad thunderstorm. We made for the shelter of a wood that ran down the side of the course and, whilst we sheltered, it gradually got darker, now due to the failing light as well as the storm. When the rain began to ease, we started to make our way back (we thought) in the direction of the clubhouse, only to find ourselves lost as it was now pitch dark.

We made our way down a footpath and finally emerged in a side road, which ran along the side of the course but which we did not recognise. It was still pouring with rain. I said to the others, 'Hang on, I will find out where we are, or we will get soaked to the skin.' I walked up the path to the front door of a bungalow and knocked on the door. The door was opened by a man, who looked at me a bit strangely, and I said, 'I'm sorry to bother you but we have lost our way in the dark on the golf course, can you direct us to the clubhouse?' He grinned and gave us the directions, shook his head and said, 'I have heard of golfers losing their ball, but this is the first time I've heard of them losing the clubhouse!'

We enjoyed the Wednesday evenings and the pint after the game so much that, when the nights closed in, we decided to go to a pub in Rochford and have a game of darts and a pint during the winter, in its place. This meant we still had a laugh and joke and became surprisingly adept with the darts.

One night, while we were playing, the landlady came over to me with a raffle book and pint mug with cash in it. She asked us if we would like to have a go in a raffle for an injured motorcyclist. I thought about it for a moment and answered, 'No, thank you, I wouldn't know what to do with him if I won him!'

She stared at me for a while and then said, 'No, he's not the prize, the proceeds go to help him!'

We then said, very seriously, 'Oh well, that's different, we will have some tickets!'

The agreement with the unions was that the bonus scheme would run for a trial period and then a vote would be taken for its approval. By the time all the departments were up and running in the composing room, the six-month period had already elapsed. The machine room and bindery values were set and ready to be applied, but not up and running, when the composing department voted against the scheme. This was strange as the average bonus being earned increased their wages by between twenty and thirty per cent. I think that the main reason was a dislike of working on a work-measurement scheme, with all the detail it gave, and a fear that the extra achieved output would mean a cut in the amount of overtime they would earn. It was explained to them that if the overtime was reduced in the early stages it would only be a temporary condition, as it was obviously in the firm's interest to get as much throughput as possible, but it would mean a time lag while an additional level of work was generated by the company.

As a result of the rejection, union officials with bonus scheme experience looked into the studies taken, the analysis, and the way the values had been set, and gave them a clean bill of health. A major union official visited the factory and saw all the members in the works' canteen. Before he went into the meeting, he said that the scheme was sound and his members would have to accept it. The meeting was a very rowdy one and he was virtually thrown out of it! This brought about a crisis in the company and gave me an insight into big company politics. The first thing I knew was that the work-study manager had been given his notice (apparently as a scapegoat), which was a shock to me. I drove him home that night, as even his company car had been withdrawn – just like that! In all fairness, very little of the blame could be laid at his door; he was extremely conscientious and I was worried about the effect it would have on him.

When I got into the office on the Monday, I was quickly called in to the MD's office. He told me what had occurred and said that they would be promoting me to take over his position as work-study manager. A new person would be arriving from the consultancy company, and it would be his responsibility to see that the scheme met the requirements of the unions and was successfully implemented throughout the company. My answer to him was that I was, not in a position to do anything other than accept the offer but that I thought the man I was replacing was in no way at fault, and I thought he had been treated extremely badly. He thanked me for accepting and reassured me that time would prove that he had not been treated as badly as I might think. This became clearer when I saw him the next weekend to find that the consultants had offered him a choice of a couple of higher positions with other companies at a better salary.

In spite of all the work that was put in over the next twelve months the bonus scheme was doomed never to become fully operational. After a further trial period and more revisions, it was again rejected and this time abandoned by the group. This gave me concern about my future with the company, but I was pleased to be informed that they wanted to retain my services. They were going to send me on a Method Study course for six weeks, and after it was completed, I would be used as a trouble-shooter within the group. I was given an office which I shared with the works' engineer, who was a great character, and I got on with him very well.

The course was made up of a mixture of very interesting areas and totally boring ones all mixed together. Overall it was both useful and very informative. It covered such areas as method study, production control, factory layouts, industrial psychology and the Factory Acts. This all took place in a good hotel, with first-class accommodation and food and with a very convivial group of people. The one snag with the course was that the people who ran it thought that you had to put in long hours to cover what was required. On several nights, when we were still working on projects, we could hear a band playing *God Save the Queen*, which meant that the dance the hotel was holding had finished, it was midnight, and we were still beavering away!

Nearly all of the management and accountancy techniques that I have come across have been based on reasonable principles, with a few glaring exceptions. When things go off the rails, it is usually due to someone's loony interpretation of them. Worrying signs started to appear when I was on this course, when at one of the earlier lectures a hypothetical situation was put to us. A problem with a local council was that waste paper was being discarded and making the place look very unsightly. We were asked for suggestions on how to improve the situation. There were suggestions forthcoming such as, 'A publicity campaign against waste', 'Ensuring that there were plenty of obvious wastepaper bins provided for the public' and so forth, but I started to worry when someone suggested 'issuing flame-throwers to the council to burn it where it was – to avoid collecting it.' When I was asked for my suggestion, I proposed that the men who went around with a spiked stick picking up the paper should hang the wastebag around their neck and be given two spiked sticks, so that they could pick up twice as much in the same time. To my horror, the suggestion was taken seriously, although, in fairness to them, the flame-thrower idea was rejected!

During the course, we were sent in groups to different companies and given the task of looking into some problem areas that had been identified by them. At the end of our investigations we presented our reports to them, and they could act on them or not, as a matter of their own choice. Over a period of time quite a number of the suggestions were put into practice by these companies and with a reasonable amount of success. We also had free rein to make our own recommendations on other areas we saw, where improvements could be made, and these were often the most successful ones. It is often the case that things change over a period of time, and the people close to the situation are so used to the procedures that they do not see that the needs have changed and the methods being used are no longer the best in the new circumstances.

Over the next two to three years I was used in this troubleshooting capacity within the Southend company, and other companies within the group. The assignments were pretty varied and in general I found it quite enjoyable. They covered such things as installing production control systems, factory layouts, stock control systems, and on occasions the whole company system of management and control – quite a nerve-racking job! In the true method study tradition, a lot of the success would depend on your ability to gather sufficient facts and information, to be sure that you knew exactly what was happening. If you did that well enough, the answers were usually staring you in the face.

One of the tasks that I had to do at Southend was to produce a factory layout that would allow for the replacement of a very large piece of bindery equipment to be installed. This had to be achieved without losing any production from the, existing equipment until the new equipment was up and running satisfactorily. As the new machine was over forty foot long, and from six to eleven foot in width, this was quite a task. It entailed dismantling the existing machine and moving it to a site in the factory where it could be operated temporarily until the new machine could take over production. This had to be accomplished during the weekend, so that the periodicals' schedules would not be interfered with. The new machine was delivered in numerous crates, a crane was hired for the offloading, and the engineers and electricians were assembling it, following my plans and layouts. It was brought into the factory, a section at a time, and each one was bolted into the concrete floor as it was assembled. When approximately thirty foot of the machine was installed into position, there was only the last of the main pieces of machinery to be added. This was the gluing and binding carousel, which was about eleven foot in diameter and had a delivery unit coming from it at right angles, which was about seven foot long. I climbed up and looked into the last crates and saw, to my horror, that the delivery unit came out on the opposite side of the machine to the plans I had been working from. I just could not believe it. I rang the suppliers and had a pretty heated exchange with them. They drew my attention to an escape clause in their contract that said they reserved the right to make any modifications or revisions to the machine that they thought necessary, and I drew their attention to the fact that they had supplied these plans for the installation of the machine and it was reasonable to assume this was the machine they were supplying. Some quick revisions had to be made, and by moving a small machine, we were able to get round the problem. This was pretty fortuitous as the last part of the machine only missed a main support girder, that held up the roof, by a matter of inches.

The installation of equipment always has its tricky moments and you have to be aware of the amazing differences that can exist between the sales pitch and the actuality. Prior to the arrival of some moulding presses, I asked the company that was going to do the installation what sort of problems there would be with getting them into position on site, and how long the operation would take. They had checked the factory to see exactly where they would have to be unloaded and the route they would take to get them to the desired site. I was assured that, as long as I had a suitable crane standing by, they would only have to be lifted off the lorry and, once on the ground, they had built-in rollers, so they could easily be pushed into position in a matter of minutes. This was to minimise any inconvenience in the factory, and their electricians and engineers would have them fully operational within twenty-four hours.

The day they were to be delivered I had a crane standing by ready for them at ten o'clock in the morning as requested. It was still standing there at three o'clock in the afternoon. I had made a number of phone calls and had been reassured they were on their way and would be with us at any minute. Shortly after three, I got a call from them, to say that the lorry had gone off the road at Baldock and had hit a cottage. Another lorry was being sent and the presses would now be with us at the same time the next day. I asked for reassurance about our machines and was told that they were not damaged. They also apologised and said that they would reimburse us for the cost of the crane hire. The next day the lorry arrived near enough on time and I went down to the loading bay to keep an eye on things (usually a wise move on these occasions). The offloading went smoothly enough, but the built-in rollers were non-existent. The presses had to be levered round to the site with a pinch bar and steel rollers that had to be slid under the machine and replaced every time the machine had travelled its own length.

The two engineers (to add to the impression of their businesslike efficiency) had a row with each other, which ended in a fight, before they even began to move the machines to their location. There were three presses to be installed and, by two o'clock, the first one had not yet reached its position. You can see how easy it is on these occasions for the unwary to be committed to a schedule that they have not got a prayer of meeting! The suppliers are past masters at invoking the *force majeure* clause, which can leave you paddleless and up the proverbial creek!

It has certainly been my experience that there are several words that are frequently misused, and one of those is 'expert'. I have come across many people of whom that word has been used to describe their capabilities, and only a very few who have deserved it. Crane drivers in my experience are usually deserving of the qualification, certainly if they are in charge of cranes of a respectable size and capacity. It is, after all, an occupation with a magnificent scope for wreaking havoc, if you are not an expert. I have held my breath while twenty-ton machines have swung over factory roofs, seen prefabricated buildings swung high over the top of listed buildings, all without a problem (that is if you overlook the odd tree being knocked over, and I still say that was not our fault!).

There was the occasion when we were having great fun at our site; we had cones and police notices outside the firm. When I was driving in to work I could see the jib of our crane towering into the sky, long before I got there. The crane picked up the prefabricated building we were replacing and swung it up and over the buildings, plonking it onto the back of a low-loader, clean as a whistle. The two replacement buildings were then swung into their position in our yard. They were both approximately thirty foot long by eleven foot wide, and had to be accurately positioned, with only about a six-inch gap from the two neighbouring walls and at exactly the right distance apart for a communicating passage to be fitted between them. All this was done in a matter of just over three hours. I would use the term 'expert' in referring to that man, with confidence that I was not misusing the English language.

I had been with the Southend company for just over four years and was enjoying the troubleshooting and method study work that I had been doing both at Southend and at other companies in the group. The work was interesting, but not necessarily an area to be in if you were seeking popularity. One assignment that I had in central London was a good example. The management's relations with the staff could be summed up best by the occasion, when I arrived at the factory one morning in the pouring rain, and the works manager came in soaked to the skin. He had no raincoat or umbrella and squelched in doing a passable imitation of the last moments of a drowned rat. I asked him why he had not given the firm a ring from the station and asked for one of our vans to pick him up, and he answered, 'I would rather drown than ask those bastards to do me a favour!' In that atmosphere it was only to be expected that a method study consultant (which was my current title) would not be welcomed with open arms or, for that matter, given a great deal of cooperation. Nevertheless, I was a trifle miffed to come into the factory one morning and walk past an effigy of myself hanging from a gallows (even before I had made any recommendations) and get a message later in the day that someone had set light to my briefcase.

One evening, at about seven o'clock, there was a knock on my front door and I was surprised to find the work-study manager whom I had replaced, standing on our doorstep. He had a quick word with me and June and asked if I would like to pop out for a pint and a chat. An offer that I seldom refuse, and this was no exception. He was now the assistant to the managing director of a very large company up in the Stockport area, and asked me if I would like to join him up there as the work-study manager. He also mentioned a figure that he could offer as the going rate for the job, apologising for it being so low (whilst I was sure he knew that it was nearly twice what I was getting). I said that I had the usual Southerner's approach and was not sure of anywhere north of Watford. Another little appetite-whetter he added was the price of the property up there, which meant a far grander house for the same outlay! He arranged for me to drive up to the factory the next week and have a look at both the company and the area. The size of the factory and some of the equipment impressed me, and the areas that he drove me through to look at housing were really very attractive – I was nibbling at the bait!

They agreed to pay for rented furnished accommodation for three months, to enable me to find a house in the area, and would pay for the expenses I incurred in moving. I went back and discussed it with June, and she was all for the move. To be fair, if June thought it was the thing to do, the thought of uprooting home never worried her. In fact, later on, when I was offered a position with a major group, which would have meant spending a number of years in India and South Africa, I was the one who was not prepared to make the move. I am sure that if I had wanted to go – June would have been quite happy!

I gave my three months' notice in at the Southend company and explained the situation. I had some reservations and I think that if they had made me a serious counter offer, I may well have stayed with them. As it happened, they did, but not until one week before I was due to leave, and I was not prepared to break faith with the other company, who had waited three months for me to start, so I stuck to my decision. I had enjoyed my spell with the Southend company and it had been a very good learning experience for me. The company had not been one with outrageous goings-on taking place, but one departmental manager had caused a laugh when he arrived one week on a bicycle and tried to convince us it was for his health. I suppose it was in a way. His wife had found out he was taking a receptionist up to a local wood in the lunch hour for a bit of naughtiness and had impounded the car. Quite effective, it cannot be easy to sell the advantages of passion on a pedal bike. It does appear that wherever you have a mixed group someone is bound to be at it!

At one of my previous firms, I was told that the general manager went in to see the MD and told him that the sales manager had been caught misbehaving himself with a secretary on a table in his office. The MD was furious and said, 'We can't have this sort of thing – fire him!' The general manager agreed to do this, but did enquire whether the MD was aware that he had the best sales record in the company, and had brought in more than £500,000 of sales the previous year. The MD thought about this for a moment and then said, 'All right – get rid of the table!'

Chapter Twenty-Five
Cheshire

Our house at Hockley was put up for sale and we set out for the north-west on the Saturday morning of the Easter weekend, with the car well loaded down with clothes and items like clocks, everyday cooking utensils, and the items . to keep a four-year-old daughter happy. We had a deadline to meet to pick up the keys for the furnished house in Bramhall, and this was not a worry to me until about three o'clock in the afternoon, when we were still a good number of miles short of our destination. I had based my timing on how long it had taken me on my own in an unladen car and had not appreciated the time it would take in an overloaded Ford Prefect grinding over the hills. I had to ring the agent, who agreed to give me a little extra time to get there. We were well pleased with the house when we finally arrived, it was in excellent condition, well-furnished, and in a nice area. In fact, the house that we purchased was to be no more than three-quarters of a mile away from the house that we rented. The owners were obviously much travelled and a number of items in the house were indicators to this fact, including the strangely situated old map of the West Indies, on the wall of the toilet.

During the years that we lived up in that area, we found that the summer temperatures were, by and large, somewhere around eight degrees Fahrenheit below those in the south of England. That weekend was one of the exceptions – we were getting a heatwave that the south was not getting. We had heard all the standard jokes about Manchester's weather and we were not ten miles from there. There is no doubt that the area gets its fair share of rain. The locals claim that the rainfall is not wildly different from anywhere else, but what is fact is that you don't go too long without any! Those lush green fields in Cheshire are not some freak of nature. It is because they get a regular watering. After a while, we got into the habit of getting up on a Sunday morning, looking out of the window and, if it was raining, we would start to plan a picnic for the afternoon and, if the sun was shining, we would not bother – the odds would be that it would be raining later. The local saying was that if you could see the hills, it was going to rain and, if you couldn't see them, it was raining! We loved the area, it had such beautiful scenery which was so varied. Without driving more than a few miles, you were in the soft hills and meadows of Cheshire, or change the direction and you were into the rugged rocky scenery of Derbyshire. We went into Derbyshire for a picnic and to have a look at a scramble meeting one Sunday, and stopped for a drink in a village called Wincle. A film crew were there taking shots for a film, the story of which was set at the turn of the century. The only alterations the film crew had to make were to spray out the white lines on the road and take down two television aerials.

On my first day at the new firm I was taken round and introduced to my own staff and the admin and sales staff. Apart from a couple of cracks from two departmental overseers, who muttered things like, 'Not another bloody Southerner', it all went very well. I hasten to say this was the exception, the people at the works, our neighbours, and people in general bore out the sayings about northern hospitality and friendliness.

Before I had been with the company very long I began to get concerned about its viability. As at the Southend company, my department was producing the control figures for the company, and to put it mildly they were appalling! The whole operation was ill-conceived. Originally the factory was built to produce a series of local papers and at the last minute the plans were changed. Three companies (none of which were making a profit) were all brought together under the one roof, with equipment that existed, rather than which was required. Some equipment was excellent and needed a large turnover to keep it running. There was some duplication of higher management from the amalgamation of the three firms and, most amazing of all, an admin staff had been put together, none of whom, almost without exception, had held the same position before. This is not an intended criticism of the individuals, any of whom, in the right situation and surrounded by people with experience, may well have been successful. The fact remains that an experienced management team would have had an almost impossible task to survive in these circumstances, and an inexperienced one had virtually no chance.

The man who was doing the works' manager's job when I arrived had an engineering background. I was in his office one morning and one of our drivers came in and was told to take the manager's car to the garage for a service. He was then given a little velvet bag, which he stared at askance, until the manager said, 'That goes over my Advanced Motorist's badge, you're not one are you?' The driver muttered that he was not and left the office. The sequel to this came a few months later when the bad weather was upon us, bringing the snow and ice. I was with the same manager and he had wrapped his car up in an accident on the way in to work. The same driver (as luck would have it) was being asked to drive it into the garage for repair. On receiving his instructions he paused for just the right amount of time and, when the manager asked him what he was waiting for, he got the answer, 'What about that little velvet bag?'

The experience of being on the staff of a large company that is a member of an equally large group and having trading difficulties was far from pleasant. There were so many 'Nights of the Long Knives' that we got to the stage where we thought it would be a good idea to have a roll call in the mornings, to see how many of the executives and managers were left. People disappeared from the company – sometimes overnight. One of the worst examples was that of a manager, who was brought in from another company within the group (where he had been successful for about twenty years) and fired on the same day that he and his family were moving into the house they were purchasing in the area.

At one stage I was asked to look into setting up a bonus scheme for the sales department, and on doing a preliminary look into the sales records, found one salesman on a very high salary and running a Jaguar car on the company. The problem with that was he had not secured one job for the company in over twelve months. Some suggestions were made by myself about the sales operation, but it was agreed to go no further with a bonus scheme. Another of the areas that I could not come to terms with was the fact that the group's member companies had to quote for work within the group against outside companies. The work then went to the lowest tender – not necessarily kept within the group. The intention of this was to maintain companies within the group's competitiveness. As I said earlier, the principle was sound, but the application was not. One of the problems was that ludicrous cost rates had been imposed on the company, by ruling that it had to take unsuitable equipment that could not be filled with work. It would have made far more sense to offer their own companies this work at the competitors' prices, which would have at least defrayed the losses that were being made, by covering labour costs and making some contribution! One of the other unbelievable decisions was to put the company on double-day shiftwork (when it was unable to provide enough work to fill a single-day shift). The idea apparently was to reduce the cost rates by putting the company on shifts, to see if it enabled us to be more competitive and secure work. It would appear that no one thought that this exercise could have been done administratively, by just calculating the new rates and applying them to estimates to get the answer without incurring the additional wage costs for shiftwork.

The company was heading for disaster, and crisis meetings were held. At one memorable one, the group executive, who held a meeting with all the management staff to explain how we were to get out of the predicament, fell asleep while he was addressing the meeting, his voice trailing off in mid sentence. We were told that he had jet lag, which may well have been, but it was not too clever on the psychology front. Among the experts that came to us was one who I nicknamed Lloyd George (simply because he looked like him). He was an efficiency 'expert'. We were told to give him top priority and cooperate with him, giving him any information that he required. He walked past my work-study office one morning and tapped on the window. I went out to see him, and he said, 'Are those girls in your office working with slide rules?'

I answered, 'Yes.' He then said, 'My word, we will have to watch our step!'

This was a bit more than I could take seriously, so I replied, 'There is even some talk of them getting the vote!'

He, like Queen Victoria, was not amused. The best was yet to come. After causing chaos for just over a week, he disappeared, and we were told he had come to the wrong company in the group!

It now became obvious that it was not a question of whether the company would survive but one of how long it could last. This was a great shame as so many people would be out of a job through no fault of their own, and I include those who had been promoted to their own level of incompetence. It is, after all, management's responsibility to make the right appointments and ensure that the staff are given the right circumstances to enable them to succeed. As a result of all this, I was back to scanning the adverts again. I was not prepared to move this time, with the ink hardly dry on the signature for the mortgage of our house. The financial losses incurred would be punitive so soon after the purchase. This time I felt that I wanted to get back to a line-management job, as, for a good number of years, I had been in an advisory or consultative capacity. Foolishly, I thought it would then be my decisions which would be paramount in running a company. This, of course, was 'cloud-cuckoo-land'. The closest you can get to that situation is if the company is owned by you, and then it is still amazing how many constraints there still are!

The result of all this was that I applied for the position of works' manager at a company that was near enough to where we lived to avoid a move of house. This was to lead to a period that proved to be quite a challenge and in a lot of ways great fun! My first two interviews were at the owner's house. I had to get through that stage before I was shown the factory.

A father and two sons carried out the interviews, which were quite stringent and nothing like any that I had had before or since. I got through to the factory and was shown round. It was a reasonable size with a staff of about one hundred and twenty employees. Part of the company was a trade bindery, which also carried out the finishing for the printing works, and was all on the same site. My responsibilities were to manage the printing works, which included all of the factory premises, and virtually purchase the binding and finishing from the trade binders unit. The company produced about sixty per cent of its work for book publishers, with some very good accounts that were household names in the publishing world. The remainder was all brought in by one sales representative and was from comparatively local companies. It occurred to me that three sales representatives producing the same kind of turnover could have saved the company I was at!

When I finally saw the works, it came as a bit of a shock as most of the printing equipment was older than me, and in worse condition. It looked an ideal location for an Ealing Studios comedy. At the conclusion of this tour I was told to go to the nearby hotel for lunch, the bill for which I could submit to them for payment, and make my decision. I was then to meet up with them at the owner's house at three o'clock, and, if my answer was yes, we would finalise the details. It was not the easiest of decisions to make, while eating my lunch. In the finish (round about the time that I was consuming the golden syrup pudding), I decided to take it. I had several reasons. A: It was a job and the one I was in would not last much longer; B: I would not have to move house; C: It was back in line management. The firm looked in such a state that, if I could not improve on it, I might just as well give up any management aspirations! I returned to the owner's house and started the arm wrestling over pay and conditions. One item I remember well was asking about a pension. The answer I got was, 'We have an arrangement with our employees – We pay good money and they look after themselves!' At the end of the day we reached agreement and a starting date, which included a week with another company they had a close relationship with, before I started with them, to add to my experience (I think this was while they constructed my office).

The previous works' manager was moving over to the publishing side, and there was no resentment; in fact, I got on very well with him and was able to gain a lot from his experience. He had the somewhat cynical approach to work that is hard to avoid after a number of years running a company and dealing with people every day. It does have an effect on you. I was once asked what number of staff do you have to employ before you get labour relations problems. My answer was 'two.' The most difficult problems to resolve are seldom anything to do with work; they are trivial things like, 'He wants the window open and I don't!' Something as simple as that can set loose enough attitudes and inhibitions to keep a psychologist going for life, the wisdom of Solomon being required to resolve such problems without creating resentment from one or other of the parties concerned.

My first week at the company was spent with the works' director, who was also the owner's son. He was going through the systems that were in operation and generally putting me in the picture. The works' order sets were unusual in that they were in four-part sets that separated and went to each general departmental area. This surprised me, as the only information available was that which was deemed to be all that that department had to know. I queried this, and was given the answer, 'There is no point in telling them more than they have to know.' Later, I was to find that there was far more than the normal amount of spoilage. The workforce had responded to this approach by adopting the attitude of 'that is what it said, so that is what I did!' This was largely because they had not got information on what had gone before or what was to happen after they had dealt with the job. You could even say that a certain amount of pleasure was obtained from following wrong instructions without querying them, even more than the usual sort of query like, 'These cutting instructions don't seem to be right, there is an awful lot of waste.' You would answer, 'Thank you for letting me know, how much have you cut?' Only to have the *coup de grace* delivered – 'All of it!'

After a couple of days, the door was flung open by the composing room manager. He looked the works' director straight in the eye and said, 'Once, just bloody once, can't you get something right?' and slammed down a works' order bag onto the desk with such force that it blew all the papers that were lying there all over the place. He then stormed out slamming the door.

The works' director looked at me and without batting an eye said, 'That was Mr McDougall, he is leaving us on Friday!'

The company was a bit of a culture shock; the equipment was for the most part getting past its 'sell-by date' and the premises were pretty unsuited to the 'white-hot technological era' that Harold Wilson was informing us we were about to enter. This company looked like it required a lot more of those 'pounds in your pocket' that he was also making reference to, if it was going to be able to get there. The central heating system would have gladdened the heart of Heath Robinson, who may have been able to equal it, but I am sure he could not have surpassed it. When I arrived on the scene it was run from a coke boiler, and we had a sweeper/cleaner/stoker, a huge Irish chap, to whom the description, 'He was a nice fellow – but he didn't have both his oars in the water' would have applied.

The system had a heat exchanger situated up in the roof of the building, with a huge belt driven fan that blew the hot air through a system of ducting throughout the factory. If you were up in this area (where some offices were situated), when the system was turned on, it was quite frightening, even when you were used to it! If you were an unsuspecting customer in the area for the first time, the experience was really unnerving. The rumbling noise would begin and grow to a crescendo not far below the decibel rating of *Concorde* at takeoff! The whole area would be on the move, with floors creaking and an alarming amount of movement, until the huge fan settled down in balance, and normality returned. If you noticed the customer turning white or heard their knees knocking like castanets, you would explain to them, 'Don't take any notice of that – it's just the central heating.' Funnily enough, they never really believed you.

This was a problem eventually overcome by installing diesel-heated blowers, and these were a definite improvement, as long as you were not standing in close proximity to one when they switched on. A fairly noisy ignition would take place, lifting a flap on the side of the heater, and a tongue of flame would shoot out of it, uncomfortably close to one's ear! The only other hazard being that the engineer, who had installed the ducting, had a perverse sense of humour, which could result in some nasty experiences when you were suddenly struck by a blast of hot air striking some sensitive area. The lady customers did not always appreciate the experience of taking part in what looked like a retake of the Marilyn Monroe scene from *The Seven Year Itch*.

The firm was large enough to employ a maintenance staff which consisted of one engineer, his assistant, and when the work was suitable, 'Paddy the Stoker' would lend a few foot-pounds (not always in the right place). The engineer was a character; he had been a sergeant-pilot and flown *Spitfires* during the war. He was able to turn his hand to most areas, machinery repairs, electrical work, plumbing, vehicle maintenance, you name it he could do it! We did not get off to a good start, as the first Friday that I had taken up my duties as works' manager, I had the machine room overseer dash into my office and tell me that there was boiling water pouring out of one of the heating pipes in the roof and it was landing on one of the printing presses. I dashed into the factory, and he was right. At this precise moment who should be walking through the factory, with his boiler suit under his arms and carrying his tool box, but the maintenance engineer. I said to him, 'Thank goodness you are here, we are in a real spot of bother with the plumbing!' His answer to me was, 'Yes, I can see that, but I'm off, here is the name of a plumber – give him a ring!' and he walked out.

The plumber came fairly quickly and got us out of the problem, but we had to do an emergency act with containers to catch the water and keep emptying them until he got there. I could not find a valve to isolate the pipe that was damaged and was more than a bit put out! That afternoon I had words with the owner, and told him what had happened and said, as far as I was concerned, the maintenance engineer could have his cards. I was warned not to do anything too hasty, as we would never be able to replace him at the rate we were paying him. He often did little jobs (like wiring a house) on the side, and we closed a blind eye to it, and he was happy. I could hardly believe what I was being told but agreed not to rock the boat. To be fair to him, over the years he was worth his weight in gold. The only problem with him was that he was probably the role model that Ernie Bilko tried to emulate, and unfortunately I was to be his Colonel Hall.

The owner of the company used to disappear from the scene when the weather got bad in the winter and slip off to the Canaries for a few months, leaving us to it. When I drove into the factory grounds on the first Monday that he was away, I had to look twice at the car park, for, in the front row of parked vehicles that faced the main road, there was a number of vehicles with 'For Sale' signs and prices on their windscreens. I knew roughly which direction to head in – the maintenance department! Before I even got there I saw the composing room overseer and told him what I had seen. 'Oh yes,' he said, 'that would be Barry and Roy, they always do that when the Boss is away.' This, I am afraid, was 'a bridge too far', even taking the risks into consideration; it was stopped and the prices came off! I still had the uneasy feeling, though, that the deals were still happening, maybe it was because of the number of times I tripped over a gearbox covered with a bit of cloth in the maintenance department, and was that a dismantled clutch that was slid under a work bench when I entered the department – or could it have been my imagination?

After I had been with the company for a month or two, I put a production control system in, with control boards in both the composing department and the machine department. The overseers ran the system with daily check visits from myself to agree and give rulings on any problem areas. It worked quite well, with the only snag being that the bindery was a separate entity, which I had to negotiate with, rather than control. My two overseers were as different as chalk and cheese. The composing department overseer was a typical ex-army NCO and had everyone organised to ensure that he had the minimum amount to do himself. He was quite efficient as long as you were aware that he always underrated and understated his department's problems. The machine department overseer was just the opposite. His approach to a problem was to overstress its difficulties. 'There is no way we can achieve that by Thursday – it's just impossible' meant it would be done by late Wednesday morning! Once you took this into consideration, they were both good reliable men at their jobs.

As the bulk of our throughput was publishers' book work, it meant that we had a large typesetting facility compared to the printing machinery, with the Linotype and Monotype departments both being on day and night shifts, while the machines and hand composing were only on days. The head reader was an excellent man, he would check manuscripts and mark them all up for style and any typing errors, before they were passed to the typesetting departments. The accuracy of his reading and his foresight on any style problems was so good that I have not seen them bettered before or since. His literary and general knowledge over a great range of subjects was astounding. If he queried any quotation or date, you knew he was going to be right. It was therefore surprising that he was so gullible in everyday matters. He was chatting to me one day and said that a young chap in the bindery had asked him if he was interested in buying a brand-new television at a ridiculously cheap price. He told me who had made him the offer, and it was a young Jack-the-lad, who was about as genuine as a seven pound note. He told me that he was suspicious of the price and, when he queried it with the lad, he had winked at him and said, 'Don't worry about that, it fell off the back of a lorry!'

'Well, I wasn't going to buy that,' he said. 'You don't know what condition it could be in after it had fallen off a lorry.'

Paddy, the stoker, began to have some health problems. I got an inkling of this when I found him standing in my office one morning, he had a red bandanna tied round his head and a large shovel in his equally large hand (he could have coped quite easily without the shovel with hands like that). 'There are some people in this works who think that I am daft,' he announced. I hastened to reassure him. 'What gave you that idea, Paddy?' I said. He thought about it for a few moments and then said, 'I have got a certificate to prove that I'm all right, and I bet they haven't!' There was a pause while I struggled for a suitable answer but before I could come up with one, he walked out of the office. Shortly after this he was off work sick. I went to see his wife and asked how he was getting on, she told me that he had had problems of a similar nature before. He was off work for a long period and eventually returned, able to do his job, but, unfortunately, after a short spell back, he was off again and this time he was unable to return.

While I was living up in the Manchester area I used to be amazed at how the shops were able to survive. Everyone seemed to know where things could be bought at cheaper prices from warehouses. Well, Barry, my maintenance man, did for a start. I only had to mention something and he would say, 'Don't pay that for it, come with me on Wednesday and I'll take you to a place where you can get it much cheaper than that,' and he did! Funnily enough it is something that I associate with that area. The work study manager, that came to the Bedford firm, was from Manchester, and when he moved into his house in Bromham, he said to me that he wanted to buy a dining room suite, and asked me about the shops in Bedford. During the lunch hour we popped into the town and went into a shop, which was a very well-known upmarket establishment. He had a look round and finally saw a suite he liked with the price clearly marked on it. When the assistant came over and asked if he was interested in it, he said that he was, and then horrified me by saying, 'I'll give you "so much" for it cash.' The figure was well below the asking price and the assistant was taken aback.

'We do not do business like that here, sir!' he said.

'That's all right,' Ken replied. 'Here's what I am prepared to pay, cash, and there is my phone number if you change your mind,' and we left the shop.

Later that afternoon Ken said to me that they had rung him back and accepted his offer. It was an eye-opener to me, if you think that the company you are dealing with would be prepared to negotiate on price or not, it's always worth making an offer!

We settled in at home very well with the help of good friends and neighbours. The Wards, opposite us, became great friends. They had three children, a boy and two girls, the youngest of whom was the same age as our daughter. Vera Ward was a teacher at a local school, and Colan, a technical representative for a large engineering company in the area. He travelled all over the world with his job. I would often chat with him and find he had been in Turin for most of the day, or had spent the week in India or the Philippines. Customers who were visiting his company would often be entertained at their house, and we had some most enjoyable evenings over there. I well remember one night, which coincided with the festive season, and a bemused Indian gentleman looking at the guests celebrating, shaking his head and saying, 'I thought the English were a quiet, reserved race.' They weren't that night! Colan had played lacrosse at international level, and one night I was his guest at a 'Centurions' dinner held at the House of Commons. It was a most enjoyable evening that included a guided tour round the Houses of Parliament, which was most informative and enjoyable. It was a night in the late summer, and prior to the dinner, we were having gin and tonics, standing on the balcony by the river. While we were chatting a pleasure boat went by and someone said, 'They think we are Members of Parliament – give them a wave.' We did and were most amused when the people on the boat waved two fingers back at us. We laughed and said, 'That proves it – they do!'

Vera is a lovely warm and generous person, who will launch into almost any topic at the drop of a hat, and we have had some great discussions. She could also come out with remarks that Alan Bennet would give his right arm for. The best one that I recall was when my wife, June, inquired how a wedding had gone. Vera's answer was, 'I don't really want to talk about it. I will just say that my mother is eighty-four, and she said it was the worst day of her life!' I don't think I have heard that bettered. On one occasion my Mother and an aunt were staying with us, and I took them out for a drive round some of the local beauty spots in the evening. With us in the car were June, Karen, and Rachel, the Wards' youngest daughter. I stopped at a quaint little pub that was in a nice spot with lovely scenery, and went in to get everyone a drink. Among the drinks I had got schooners of sherry for my mother and Aunt Clare, neither of whom could exactly be described as drinkers! After a while my mother said, 'Why don't you get yourself another drink? We will be ages drinking all this.' I answered, 'No, that's all right, I don't want another.' My mother was suitably impressed by this, to say nothing of surprised, until Rachel piped up, 'He's already had one pint while they were pouring ours out, that is his second.' She had been watching through the window!

One of the things that happened while we were living in Cheshire was that England won the World Cup at football, and I was caught up in the excitement like everyone else. Until then I had not been at all interested in the game. This was probably due to the fact that I had not been allowed to play as a lad due to the doubts about my back. Having tasted the excitement and enjoyed the games so much, it started me off. After the World Cup was over, I thought, 'Here I am, quite near Manchester, with two major clubs, United and City, on my doorstep. I can go and see a few matches!'

When the Saturday came round, I decided to go to see City play Leeds. I had noticed that the chap over the road was often listening to matches on his radio while he cleaned his car. Maybe he would like to go with me, so I strolled over and asked him. He answered, rather coolly I thought, that he didn't. I went on my own and thoroughly enjoyed it; it was a good game and for a bonus the wheels were still on my car after the match! It was some weeks later that I realised his house was painted red and white, and he was a raving United fan. I went to a number of matches while we were up there, at both grounds. When friends or relations visited us, it was usually United they wanted to see, but for some reason I favoured City. After all it was the Francis Lee, Colin Bell and Mike Summerbee team. I used to enjoy the matches, the only thing being that, when they were playing Tottenham or Arsenal in particular, it was best that I kept my mouth shut – with my accent!

While we were living in that area June decided to get herself a driving licence. I arranged for her to have lessons from a driving school, for the sake of our marriage, as I was aware of the pitfalls of teaching a wife to drive. There is something about husbands and wives giving instructions to each other that can play havoc with a relationship. When we used to play doubles matches at badminton, you were always pleased to be opposed by a married couple. The strategy was then to return the shuttle down the middle of the court (this was known as the 'divorce court'). Either they would both leave it for the other one and lose the point, or they would both go to return it and get in each other's way. A few of these returns and you could then watch their relationship deteriorate, giving you the advantage. Unmarried mixed couples, especially if the lady is attractive, are so understanding that you cannot believe it. They make remarks to each other like, 'I'm sorry, I should have left that return to you!' or 'So sorry – I should have covered that!' The answer, accompanied by a pleasant smile, is, 'Don't worry about it!' or 'No, it was my fault entirely!' This is, of course, much less likely to create the wrong atmosphere than the married partners' replies, which are usually made in a somewhat different manner, such as, 'Don't just stand there like a dummy!' or 'How the hell do you expect me to get that?' A few of these remarks and the game is as good as yours!

Let's face it, husbands and wives do not like to take what amounts to being given orders from each other, and that is what instructions tend to be taken as. My decision to let the driving school take the strain was, I am sure, the right one. All I did was back up his work by accompanying June, to give her the hours of driving experience needed. These were not entirely trouble-free; the minefield of 'Well, that is not what my instructor told me to do!' still had to be negotiated. The Austin A60 Cambridge that we had at the time did have a slight snag, the handbrake was between the driver's seat and the door, and not in the usual position between the driver and the passenger seat. I am well aware of how useless a handbrake is to stop a car in an emergency. I had to try it once when the brakes' master cylinder let me down. My survival was much more due to the driving ability of the lorry driver who missed me than the effectiveness of the handbrake, which I was yanking on for all I was worth. Psychologically, though, it still makes you feel better when it is there between you, to grab if necessary!

June's tuition went quite smoothly with the exception of a few minor incidents like her being the only person I know who has achieved getting an Austin Cambridge into reverse with the car still moving forward in gear. During the weeks before her driving test, I had been amazed at her ability to perform the 'hill starts'. She used to achieve this with the absolute minimum of revs required to prevent stalling the engine. The night before her test, we were on a hill in Stockport that was so steep it would have worried Sherpa

Tensing! This was to be the one where she was to get it wrong for the first time. The engine stalled and the car rolled back down the hill, and there were a few nasty moments before she realised what had happened and slammed on the footbrake. The chap in the Triumph Herald which we were whizzing back towards, got over it in time, I am sure. On the day of her test I watched her come up the steep hill out of Stockport, in a line of traffic, moving up a few yards at a time, without any problem. When the examiner got out of the car, I could see her grin from ear to ear and knew she had passed the test. On the way home she said to me, 'Do you know he never gave me a hill start, and I was dreading it!'

I said, 'I don't know what else you did in your test, but you did the equivalent of about twenty hill starts perfectly well, in the last quarter of a mile!'

The fact that June could drive was of immediate benefit to us. I had had trouble with a lump on my foot for some time; in fact, when I was still at Southend, I went to see my doctor about it. He looked at it and, after a short examination, said, 'Ah yes, that is a ganglion. The cure for that is the "family Bible". Put your foot on that chair.'

I did as he said, and was momentarily surprised when he raised the Bible in the air and smashed it down on my foot. At that point I stopped being surprised and decided that hopping around the room was a more suitable reaction (with my eyes watering).

'That's funny,' the doctor said. 'They usually disperse when you do that.'

This had been quite a time before and, as the lump had got larger rather than disappear, I went again to the doctor, this time in Bramhall. I was relieved when he did not opt for the 'family Bible' routine, but sent me to hospital at Stepping Hill. There I was seen by an Indian doctor who was doing a passable impersonation of Peter Sellers in *The*

Millionairess. After he had looked at my foot, the accent changed a bit towards 'Clouseau' and he said, 'That is a lurmp!' I tried to be tactful, and said I wouldn't argue with that. The conversation then took a turn towards a 'Jimmy Wheeler' sketch. He said, 'What do you want us to do about it?'

The whole thing was becoming a bit of a strain on me by now, so with a supreme effort not to let an air of sarcasm creep into my voice, I said, 'Well, this being a hospital, and you being the one with medical training, I was rather hoping you would come up with something.'

He did. I was sent to have an X-ray. Within ten days I had a letter from them and an appointment to go into Stepping Hill Hospital for an operation on the foot. The letter said, 'Do not come in your car, as we will be giving you a general anaesthetic, and it would not be advisable to drive home.'

On the day, I caught a bus to the hospital, for, as far as I knew, it was a ganglion and they were going to remove it, slap a bit of Elastoplast on it, and send me home – no trouble. I said to June, as I walked out of the door, 'I'll see you later, preferably without a parrot on my shoulder!'

When I got there I was put into a gown and given a premed. A delightful nurse then came and gave me an injection in my backside. Shortly after this the men in green came along and wheeled me off to the operating theatre. Now, as far as hospitals and operations are concerned, this is something that pushes me to break new frontiers of cowardice; it is an area where I have all the moral fibre of a jelly that has not set. I was therefore surprised to hear myself say, 'Right oh' (that stuff they put in you has this strange effect). I swear I would have been interested in the surgical instruments, if I had seen them, something I should only be shown normally when there is some sal volatile at hand to bring me round. This was at about midday and I came round at four o'clock in the afternoon. A nurse materialised and asked me if I was okay and did I feel sick. I answered yes to the first and no to the second. She then said, 'Would you like a cup of tea?' and the answer to that was, 'Not more than three or four cups', for I had a mouth like the bottom of a birdcage.

I sat up and drank my tea and noticed that there was no sticking plaster, and I had my foot bandaged up just like the ones old gentlemen in bathchairs have in children's comics.

Later on a nurse came to see me and said, 'I will go and get some crutches for you and we will organise an ambulance to take you home.'

I was given some painkillers for the first couple of nights, some pills, and an appointment for outpatients' in ten days' time. I had no instruction on how to use the crutches. You may well think that their usage is obvious, but do not believe it. When negotiating the two flights of stairs to get down to the ambulance, I came pretty close to receiving major injuries in the process. I got back home at about nine thirty that night and said to June, 'I was nearly right about the parrot!'

The visits to outpatients' and just getting about meant that June being able to drive was a godsend. After a few visits, the doctor gave me an outpatients' appointment card and said that the visits would get longer between, but they would keep an eye on my foot for three years. That surprised me and I said, 'Isn't that a long time for a ganglion?' The answer I got was that it was not a ganglion, but a growth, which they were fairly sure was benign. I am very pleased to say that that is what it turned out to be.

On one occasion we got into a bit of a problem in a multi-storey car park. The spaces allocated were very tight and someone had parked close to our car on one side. June, who was still not that experienced a driver, had several goes at getting out and could not. I said to her, 'Move over and

I'll have a go!' This was easier said than done – the well-bandaged foot was so big that I was not sure which pedal I was putting it on, and it was not beyond the realms of possibility that it could be two! The advantage was that I did not have to use too much pressure, so I got away with it and managed to get the car out eventually.

I was sitting in my office one morning in the summer, when a couple of men walked in, one quite old and one who appeared to be his son. I do not know how they had found their way through to my office, but as it was summer there were lots of doors left open. I asked them what I could do for them, and the younger one said, 'You are the boss, aren't you?' I answered that I was the works manager and what could I do for them. The son then said, 'You are publishers, aren't you?' and, when I said that that was correct, he said to his father, 'Go on, Dad, tell him!' Dad looked at me and said, 'It was a frosty and foggy morning, in October, as I recall. I was working on the railway. I'd been on the railway for more than thirty years. It was bloody cold and I couldn't see my hand in front of my face, when out of the fog...'

I had to interrupt him, as I could not see where all this was leading. I said, 'Look, I'm sorry to interrupt, but what is this all about?' The old boy looked equally surprised and said, 'I'm telling you my story, so that you can print it!'

I had to give them a rough rundown on how it all worked, and said if he would like to write his story and submit the manuscript it could then be considered for publication. They then thanked me for my advice, somewhat grudgingly, I thought, and went out muttering something about it being a lot of 'old toffee.' They obviously thought that any decent firm by now would have the presses thrashing out the memoirs!

This was not always the way that things went. I had a little old chap come in with a large briefcase one day and say to me, 'I would like you to produce a book on weight-driven clocks. I have it all written, and the photographs, illustrations and diagrams that are required.' I thought, 'Oh no, not another one.' This old boy was obviously more knowledgeable than the railway duo, so I was more circumspect with my answer. I informed him that it would be quite costly to produce such a tome, and we would have to look into the matter, to see if we were prepared to take the book up as a publishing venture. The answer that I got put things into a different light. He said, 'Oh, I have not made myself clear, I am quite prepared to finance it myself!' This was a different kettle of fish; I asked him if he would be good enough to wait a few moments while I made some enquiries. I went into the office where the owner's sons were and said, 'There is an old boy in my office who wants us to produce a book on weight-driven clocks.' Without looking up, one answered, 'Tell him to push off!' I said, 'He is willing to pay for it to be produced!' and got the immediate answer, 'That's different, tell him to come in!'

It was different; the volume was produced and was a success, so much so that further volumes were produced. They sold well and were enthused about by the quality national press. Who would have thought it? I am sure if it was not backed by the author's finance it would never have got off the ground. One that went in the opposite direction was when the company was asked if they wanted to produce a series of children's books. They turned the idea down flat and said that the market was flooded with children's books. It was Ladybird Books, which were a thumping success. It was nearly as bad as the record producer who turned down the Beatles as not having any appeal!

About this time, I heard from a paper representative that a nearby local paper had a Nebiolo A1 press for sale. They had purchased it a few years earlier with the intention of producing general printing, but it had never happened. It was virtually brand-new and, he thought, available at a very good price. That was good enough for me – I gave them a ring, and went over to see it with Barry, my engineer. We checked it over and liked the price, so I said we would like to purchase it. The only problem was it was on the second floor and had to be moved across a wooden floor, which I did not like the look of, to where it could be got out. Barry reassured me, 'Don't worry about that, we will move it out over steel plates to spread the weight!' The general manager then slipped us the main snag. He said, 'We finish the print run in the early hours of Friday morning, and you have to have it all clear by 10.30 a.m. for the next run.' The difficult area was that, when we measured up, we found that the press had to pass the 'pony' that cast the rotary machine's plates. This meant disconnecting the last unit of the machine (which was water cooled), and pulling it to one side, to allow the machine we were buying to be got out. When this was completed, it would all have to be reconnected and in running order for the 10.30 a.m. start. Barry checked it all out and said, 'Okay, I can do it!' The arrangement was made for it to be done the next Friday. Barry and one of his chaps would go over on the Thursday afternoon and get the Nebiolo disconnected and stripped ready to move the next day at 7.00 a.m., to get it all clear for the print run.

When the time came, all had gone well on the Thursday and the machine was all ready to move, with the steel plates ready in position. The crane was ordered and the lorry to transport it to us. Barry, with two engineers, set out at about 6.00 a.m. to get there in plenty of time. I did not go with them. Barry was a capable engineer, and the year before had dismantled and moved a Quad Royal Miehle Perfecter out of a firm in Liverpool and installed it in our factory in Cheshire, and that was quite some machine. The

Nebiolo would be moved almost in one piece and should be nothing like as much trouble!

My first phone call was at about 8.00 a.m., it was Barry to say the floor had proved dodgy and a joist had broken giving them a fright, but they had got the machine down to the ground floor. This was good news and all was going roughly according to plan. My next call was from the firm's general manager. It was not all that easy to make out what he was saying, as he appeared to be having some kind of seizure at the time. He was a touch put out – that came through fairly strongly. He was also somewhat critical of my engineer and also myself for turning him loose in their factory. What I found worrying was his reference to the fact that his staff were swimming around in the factory, due to my maniac of an engineer disconnecting a water supply pipe and flooding the place. I did the best I could to soothe him down, reassured him I was on my way over, and asked to speak to my engineer. When Barry came on, he was great; a man who has flown Spitfires in combat is not one to get ruffled by a mere bagatelle like flooding a printing works. He first of all put his side of the picture. He had asked their engineers to show him where the water supply to the machine came from, and checked with them that he had shut off the correct valve. He had then been horrified when he separated a two-and-a-half-inch water pipe to find that the water was not off and God knows how many gallons were gushing out. He then reassured me it was now under control and rang off.

When I arrived on the scene, things had quietened down. The machine was already on our lorry, and the 'pony' was about to be started up again, and the time was just after 11.00 a.m. I had a chat with the general manager, who had now calmed down, and was much more amenable, thanked him for his tolerance (without him blushing) and left.

With this firm it was part of my duties to deal with the trade union officials. The works' director, who was quite young and whose experience was largely confined to his attending university, would discuss with me some amazing stratagems. I would be more than a little worried after only a few sentences. His middle name should have been Complexity or, alternatively, Devious. He would say things like, 'We will tell them "so and so", they will come back to us and say "so and so", we will then say "so and so" and they will have to say "so and so".' This all sounded to me like some of the free kicks football managers work out. Me, I am a simple man, sadly lacking in extrasensory perception, and I like things to be straightforward. In other words, I may be prepared to put my money on a double – never a treble. Call me cautious, I had a bit of the General Montgomery approach. If I started something I was pretty sure how it was going to finish.

The mother of the chapel came in to see me one day to make a complaint about the way one of her girls had been treated. When I asked her for details she mentioned the name of the girl and said that one of the apprentices had upset her by making lewd suggestions to her. This surprised me for a start. Now I know that looks are not everything and I would not wish to be unkind, but the girl mentioned would have been safe in Portsmouth on pay night. If she had asked to play the part of 'Godzilla' she would have been given it without an audition. Attractive she wasn't. I asked the name of the apprentice and was given it. I knew the lad, and he had obviously been thinking that this would amuse his mates, and I knew that some action would have to be taken. To be sure of my ground, I said that this was a difficult area, with the language in general use and the sort of things said on the television. I would have to know the exact words used before I could decide what kind of action should be taken, if any. The young girl looked straight at me and repeated what had been said, without batting an eyelid. It was both totally obscene and physically impossible. I agreed on the spot that this behaviour was not to be tolerated and promised action. I had the guilty lad in and read the riot act to him, for his unkind and loutish behaviour and promised him that if there was any repetition of it, I would break his indentures. There was no recurrence, to the best of my knowledge.

The owner of the company was a shrewd old boy. I remember approaching him on one occasion about the quantity of type metal we had in store. It amounted to tonnes and I asked why we did not turn it into cash as there were plenty of areas that required money to be spent. The answer I got was, 'You leave that alone, there is nowhere you could invest the money that is doing any better than leaving that where it is!' He was right, the price of lead was going up at an unbelievable rate at the time. I hope he realised the cash before it eventually nose-dived.

He could be quite an old scoundrel, but I could not help liking the man. I had brushes with him when my monthly cheques were not forthcoming, but they were always eventually honoured. I spoke to him once about my salary; I was dead straight with him and told him I had been offered another job doing virtually the same as I was doing, but the salary was considerably better than what I was getting. I told him that I was not going to leave the company but I was disturbed with the amount of the differential. He said to me that, if I did not want to work for them, I had better go but, if it was only the money, he would have a look into it for me. I expected a lot of arm wrestling to follow but was surprised to find the matter dealt with in my next salary cheque.

I am not sure how he treated others but he never questioned my decisions and I appreciated the trust. The fact that I found myself on the train down to London with him one morning, for example. Neither of us expected to see the other, we spent the journey together and chatted about any number of things – none of which were work and at no time during the conversation did he ask me why I was making the journey.

After about four and a half years with the company, circumstances made me think seriously of a move. The firm, I hoped, was in a better situation than when I joined it but there were a number of things bothering me. In my opinion there was not the amount of serious reinvestment being made to ensure the long-term security of the firm. It was totally letterpress and the trade was swinging to the litho process, with its obvious economic advantages. The company's outlook was that there was a continuing future in its letterpress operation, an opinion which I did not share. In addition to this, the fact that both June and I had parents who were getting no younger, such a distance away, was becoming a problem. We were belting up and down the motorways at regular intervals and it was not going to get any better. The other deciding factor was our daughter's education, which was reaching the stage where she needed to be settled, and the final, though not paramount, area was health. The area that we were in we loved, but it was not the best of areas for the two ailments that gave me most trouble – rheumatism and bronchitis. During the time that we were living there I had more than I wanted of both!

The decision was made that we would return down south if and when I found something suitable. It did not take too long, as it happened, for, not many months later, the phone rang and it was a firm of Management Consultants that I knew and had been on courses with in the past. It was completely out of the blue – 'Would you be interested in the position of general manager, with a firm in South London?' In their opinion there should be a satisfactory match of needs and requirements.

Arrangements were made, and a week later I went down to London for the interview. The first signs were not auspicious; we drove down, leaving very early in the morning, when my interview was not until something like 2.00 p.m. The idea was to look at property and get a feel for the prices, and this was pretty horrifying. It appeared that to get something not quite as good as the property we had in Cheshire was going to cost us more than twice the price. With this in mind, I went in for the interview with more than a little apprehension. As I got out of the car, June said (to cheer me up), 'Your suit is in a mess and you need a haircut!' My answer was, 'Well, I won't be taking the job anyway, so it doesn't matter!'

These factors could have helped, for I went into the interview nicely relaxed, as I was not too worried about the outcome. In the event I was most impressed with the company; it was certainly totally different to the firm I was with. The team were, with the exception of the sales manager, all younger than myself, in fact, one of the questions at the interview was, 'I see you are forty years old, how do you feel about being able to take this company into the seventies?' They had recognised the swing to the lithographic process and had recently installed their first litho machine. They did a good job of selling me the position, I felt I could fit in with the team and was looking forward to taking the job if offered. It was, and I agreed to start as soon as my three-month contract period was completed with my present company. It was time to start house hunting again, and that was not going to be easy!

Chapter Twenty-Six
The Return South

Finding the right house at a price which we could afford looked as if it was going to be a problem, and it was. We had the disadvantage of the difference in property prices from north to south, made worse by the need for our new home to be reasonably accessible to London. The house in Cheshire was sold with the least trouble I have ever had selling a property. I placed a sign in the lawn of the front garden on a Saturday morning, and by 2.00 p.m. the same day, it was sold. I did not use an estate agent; I had checked carefully on the value of the property and was able to price it competitively due to the fact that no agent's fees were involved. A surgeon dealt with the purchase, on behalf of his mother. She liked the house and its location, and, when he asked me about the price, I told him that I had set a fair price for the property and, as I was not using an estate agent, I had split the agent's fee down the middle. It was a good price and I was not prepared to negotiate on it. He said that he thought that that was fair enough and he would be happy to purchase, a shake of the hand and that was it. If only all my other deals could have been so straightforward and genuine!

During the three months, while I was working out my contract, we were receiving lists of properties from estate agents. By some quirk of fate we had driven down through London, on the day of my interview, and kept going south until we saw an area that we thought we liked. We were natural suburbans, requiring the access and facilities of the town or city, but needing to be in reasonable proximity to the country. When we reached Coulsdon in Surrey, we parked in a side turning, and walked the short distance to the shops, where we called in at the Estate Agent's and made our first enquiries. The house that we finally purchased was not more than five houses away from where we parked on that first day – an amazing coincidence! Nearly every weekend we would drive down from Manchester and, armed with the estate agent's lists, charge round, looking at properties. The routine was that we would go into the agent's and say we would like to look at these properties that you sent us, and be told, 'They are no good, they have all been sold.' It was 1971 and the first of the great gazumping periods, which made a normally difficult transaction even more hazardous than usual.

We were getting quite desperate and running out of time, when we drove down to Biggleswade one weekend for a family wedding. I rang the agent from there on the Saturday, and he told me of a property that he had, which had just come back on the market, as the sale had fallen through. I agreed to view it the next morning, and June and I both tried to think where it was. We both thought it could be in the road that we liked and had parked in, on that first visit, but could not be sure. When we arrived, it was and we were shown over it by the owners, who seemed very nice and were moving due to the husband's firm transferring him to another area. We liked it very much, it was unusual in design and in a nice location, though it did need a fair bit doing to it. We were asked if we were interested and we agreed that we were. The owner then told us that he had another interested buyer and he would have to have an answer by two o'clock. No time for a survey or any shilly-shallying! We drove off to look at one other property and, having seen it, we knew that we would go for the one we had seen earlier and dashed back to close the deal before the two o'clock deadline. It was to be a decision we never regretted, although the surveyor's report had me wobbling. It was full of foreboding – I imagined I could hear the woodworm chomping away, even from Cheshire, but we stuck to our guns and the deal went through.

I started at the new company virtually the first week in December, and spent a week or two with the MD, getting briefed on the company and its methods of operation. The staff seemed to be a good crowd, and I felt that I should not have too much difficulty in settling in. I attended the production and management meetings and during the second week the matter arose of a job that we had got behind with. The customer was doing his pieces and putting no end of pressure on us to get his delivery. The production manager informed us that there was no way we could get the finishing done, due to over-commitment in the works. After the meeting, the MD asked me if I would look into the problem. It was essential that we did not lose the customer, and would I see if I could resolve the matter. I spent a considerable time on the phone, contacting trade binders in the London area, and finally got a company in Tottenham who would get the job out for us, as long as it was with them by lunch time the next day. I agreed to this and went to see the production manager, who said that the folding of the job would be completed that night and he would organise getting the sections palletised and over to Tottenham the next morning. The next morning I arrived at about eight o'clock and, as I parked my car, could see a large furniture van in the drive and a couple of firemen standing around. My curiosity aroused, I went down to the bindery to see what was going on. There I spoke to the production manager who informed me that they used the firemen and a hired van on this sort of occasion. Somewhat reassured, I then went to see how the loading was proceeding. What I then saw was not for people of a nervous disposition. The pallets were stacked about four foot high with printed and folded sections, and were secured (if that is the word) by string. They looked very unstable and had me quite worried, but when I went into the yard to see the loading operation – panic began to set in! We did not have a fork-lift truck at the time, and the method being used to get the work into the truck was with scaffold boards and pallets to achieve the height required. The first board went from ground level up onto a pallet, the second board onto two pallets, the third board onto three pallets (by then things were getting definitely 'hairy'), the fourth board went round the corner of the building onto four pallets, and the last disappeared into the truck. The whole affair would have been perfectly acceptable in the *It's a Knockout* or *The Game with No Frontiers* television shows. I remember thinking at the time, 'The only thing needed here to finish this off is Stuart Hall doing the commentary!' This was before the formation of the Health and Safety Executive, which was just as well, as this *modus operandi* would have been enough to make an inspector swallow his manual!

Having viewed the operation taking place, I hurried back to my office to drink a cup of tea and try to find some Valium to steady my nerves. I was relieved, about three-quarters of an hour later, to see the van drive off out of the yard. The MD was having a Christmas lunch for some of our major customers at his house, which at the time was close by the factory. The sales manager, studio manager and production manager were also with the MD for the occasion. I was not present myself, I assume that, as I had only just joined the company there was no point in introducing someone to your major customers, only to find, a couple of weeks later, that you had to get rid of him due to him being unsatisfactory. I was sitting in my office having a spot of lunch when my phone rang. It was the production manager from the bindery firm in Tottenham. He asked me, 'Are you the firm that has sent us this job in a furniture van driven by a couple of firemen?' I thought, 'There can't be a lot of those, so it must be ours!' I answered that it was and he said, 'I think they must have thought that they heard a fire bell on the way over, all the pallets have gone over and all the sections are all mixed up. I have never seen anything like it!' I said to him, 'Right, I will get a couple of chaps with me and we will drive over to you and sort the mess out!' He said, 'No, you won't, I have sent the van back to you.' I counted up to ten and said, 'Thanks – mate!'

At about two o'clock the van returned into our yard and I went out, climbed up, and looked in the back, to discover that he was not the only one who had never seen anything like it in his life, there were now two of us! Most of our staff were up to their necks in getting programme work out for that night and could not be stopped to deal with the problem, so I got two apprentices to help me sort it out. One was a big lad from the bindery, who was wearing a tartan shirt and jeans that showed the fashionable amount of cleavage, in the gap between them and his shirt, and a pair of Doc Martens. The other was an apprentice compositor, who had long blonde tresses hanging down his back, the 'John Lennon' glasses, and was wearing an old RAF greatcoat (fortunately, he was not wearing his German army steel helmet). We laid pallets in the yard and started sorting the mess out, and it was quite a job. I cannot remember the run of the job but it was a few thousand and there were at least ten sections, so there was a minimum of about fifty thousand to be sorted and being December it was not all that hot out there. I can recall two things going through my mind when I saw the bindery lad bending down, placing the sections on the pallets. One was, 'Has the company got a bike rack?' and the other was, 'That would be a nasty place to get frostbite!'

At about three o'clock I heard voices coming up the yard and, to my horror, it was the MD with some of the customers. One of them was Ken Tynan; he had caused quite a stir on television by using a four-letter word. If he had been with me when I looked in the back of that van – he would have heard another one! The MD introduced me to the customers as the new general manager. I often wonder what they thought, as I had just emerged from something that looked as if it could easily qualify for the 'Fly-tip of the Year Award' and the appearance of the duo I was working with was just a bit unconventional!

A large part of our work was with what we referred to as the arts market and entailed work for the theatre, opera, concert orchestras, and the ballet. This work was very interesting to produce (it definitely had the edge over bingo tickets) and the people we were dealing with, for the most part, were a pleasure to work with. The fact that they could be a bit eccentric on occasions added to the association's interest. When I had only been with the company for a short while, I took a phone call one evening from the literary advisor for one of the theatres. She announced herself and informed me that she had just got her copy of the programme for a new production, and she was so —ing annoyed that she could not tell me what was wrong, and rang off! It turned out to be nothing all that major and it was easily put right, but the mode of complaint and the good lady's language came as something new to me! Most of the queries that arose about the origination (but not necessarily the quality of the work produced) went direct to the studio manager, who was the direct contact for the majority of the 'arts' work. This was a good thing as I often described myself as being an 'aesthetic peasant'. I hope that that description was an exaggeration, but there were times when I must confess that I found it hard to take some complaints and remarks too seriously.

I was called up to one of the theatres, in the studio manager's absence, to look into a problem that was giving some concern. When I got there they had copies of a programme open at a particular page with a solid red on it. These were strewn all over the desk and they were saying to me that the job was ruined. I must confess my problem was that I could not see why and had to play things carefully, until someone would let slip what this particular cardinal sin was. It was rather like when you are asked to introduce someone and you have forgotten their name, extremely difficult to get out of! It was, in fact, the shade of red; there was a slight difference, which was actually due to the fact that the ink was the colour specified but had been purchased from a different ink supplier and was slightly warmer than the red we had used previously. Apologies were duly made and I gave them the assurance that the same ink would not be used on any reprints, and this was accepted.

Colour work has more than its fair share of pitfalls, not least of which being that no two people's interpretation of colour is exactly the same. Four-colour work can be very straightforward and not much of a problem, or a nightmare, according to the subject matter. There are things that are usually a piece of cake, like holiday brochures, and things that are usually considered 'two-ulcer' work, like very specific patterned material, china catalogues, or reproductions of paintings. The fact is that to reproduce a Renoir or Turner accurately, with four-colour process printing, is asking a lot. To produce them together on the same sheet and with no variation on the run is virtually impossible. The criteria and the eye of the beholder being the all-important factors. We took immense care with one particular job, which consisted of an oil painting, and all felt that we had achieved a very good result. When we showed the customer the proofs, we were staggered to be told by him that they were nothing like the original. We were quite upset by this and said that in our opinion we had produced a very good reproduction of the transparency that we had been given. The customer's response was unbelievable; he said that the transparency was nothing like the painting either. We had to point out that, if we were given a transparency to work from and had not seen or been given the painting, there was no way we could be held responsible, especially, as in this instance, where we had achieved a very good match to what we had been given!

The first two-colour litho machine that we installed was not, in the light of our experience, a wise choice and was followed by a learning curve that gave us a difficult time and that only ended when the machine was replaced by a superior one. One difficult situation we found ourselves in was when we produced a large number of small brochures for a religious organisation. It was a nightmare, brought about by variations of the register of the four colours on the print run. When I was checking the job, I had that horrible feeling of an impending disaster. The main areas of worry were that, on one page, we seemed to have some green sheep grazing on some purple grass, and on another page, Jesus seemed to bear a striking resemblance to George Robey, if it had not been for the fact that he had two sets of eyes to go with the eyebrows. I had to come clean and put the MD in the picture; we had a look at a fair sample and came to the conclusion that some were better than others, as they were only dreadful. It was agreed that the customer should come in the next morning and just have a look at a random sample, to make what was referred to as 'a commercial judgement'. I was expecting the worst and I was not disappointed. I joined the MD with our customer the next morning in the MD's office. We opened a number of boxes and took a random sample from them and sat round the table to check them. At this point the customer drew from his briefcase a magnifying glass, and what a magnifying glass, Sherlock Holmes would have swapped his Stradivarius for it! We flew the white flag immediately and said we would reprint the job. I wonder whether he ever had to actually look at any work with that glass, or was it the ultimate ploy!

Another experience related to colour work that I recall, was receiving a phone call one evening from a customer for whom we were producing an upmarket annual report. He asked me if I could take his comments on a proof he had received, and I said that I would be pleased to and got a copy of the proof in front of me, to record his marks and comments. All went well, until he came to a page with a picture of a sea oil rig. His comment was, 'The illustration of the oil rig is out of register!' I looked at it with a glass, and said, as tactfully as I could, 'I am afraid that that is not the problem with that illustration, the register is very good, it is the picture itself – it is terribly out of focus, it looks as if it was taken with a "box Brownie" without a lens in it!' There was a pause, and then the answer came (somewhat icily), 'I took that photograph!' Another photo was eventually supplied to replace it.

It must be said that over the years we got an excellent reputation for our colour work, and more and more sophisticated equipment to produce it. I would not like to give any other impression, as it would not be true, but, even with all the expertise you can get, there will always be some problems in such an exacting area where it is so difficult to make a finite judgement.

In my leisure time I had renewed my interest in football. I had noticed cars driving around the area, with stickers in their windows saying, 'Support the Palace'. I wondered what it was all about, had I moved into a royalist stronghold? The solution was given to me after a while by a neighbour whose car had another strange sign in its window, which said, 'Bring a Pal to the Palace'. It was explained to me that the notices referred not to 'Buckingham' but 'Crystal' Palace, a football team that played at Selhurst Park and was currently in the First Division. I joined the neighbours and soon became a fairly dedicated fan. I saw their last half a dozen matches in the First Division, and followed them through down to the third and back up again. I have supported them for about twenty-five years and have been a season ticket holder for a good number of those years. I must say that I have enjoyed it, even allowing for the times when you felt that you must be a bit of a masochist to do so. It is a sport of swings and roundabouts, if you support one of the smaller clubs, and you have to take the good times with the bad – such as being thrashed by Liverpool in the same season that we knocked them out of the FA

Cup in the semi-final at Aston Villa, and what a day that was. As we queued for our coaches in the car park at Selhurst that bitterly cold morning, we were laughing and remarking that we must have a slate loose to go through it all, to see our team beaten, but what a day it turned into. The team played out of their boots, and we returned triumphant, a memory to cherish.

During my first year with the company the management structure was the MD, the studio manager, sales manager, and myself, the general manager, running the company. The studio manager was, as to be expected, a man of artistic temperament and could be a touch explosive and melodramatic. I remember passing his office and seeing his phone sail out through the window on one occasion. Later on we both used to handle one of the theatre accounts, and I used to drive up to town with him for a weekly meeting. He was not one to hang about and his driving was legend.

We both used to leave our office doors open, to get some fresh air on the very hot days in the summer, and had some problems keeping them open. One morning he said to me, 'I've got a great idea for my door' and showed me that he had hooked one of those rubber straps, with a hook on each end, to the bumper on his car and the door. I thought no more about it until later in the morning, when I was holding a production meeting in my office (which was adjacent to his) with my door wedged back. The meeting was discussing some problem when Ted tore out of his office, leapt into his car, revved up the engine and tore off up the yard. There was an almighty bang, followed by breaking glass and a rubber strap, with one hook on the end, sailed in through my door. People at the meeting said, 'What the hell was that?' I looked at the strap and explained that Ted had forgot about his patent door restraint. He had not even noticed in his hurry, and it was some days before he noticed that his office door had a new window. Whenever he was driving to our meetings, he would drive straight onto a parking meter. When it was my turn, I could never find one empty and would drive about for ages trying to get parked.

The sales manager was a great practical joker; in the summer he used to put on a glove like a werewolf's hand with hairs all over it and fingernails like talons. He used to do hand signals with it on, to see the reaction of other drivers, and he also had a pair of dummy legs in his boot that he would slide under his car when he parked it. One Christmas he bought a plastic nose from a joke shop; it was revolting, the sort of nose that would belong to a claret drinker who was putting away enough to create a boom in the winemaking industry. It was covered in warts and general putrescence, with a good crop of hair protruding from the nostrils. He had a great time with that, until one afternoon, when he went into a block of offices to visit a customer, walked up to the reception desk where the commissionaire was bending down looking for something. He quickly slipped on the joke nose, and to his horror, when the commissionaire stood up, he had a nose that ran the joke one a close second, but was his own!

During the first couple of weeks with the company, I had gone out with Roy on a trip to one of our customers to get the feel of the sales operation. It was a computer company with flashy open-plan offices. We sat in the reception area while we were waiting and, as it was only a few days before Christmas, there was a large tin of 'Quality Street' open on the coffee table. Roy, who had a sweet tooth, lent over to take one, and the chair he was on overbalanced. He was not a light man, and as he crashed to the floor, the toffee tin flew up in the air and it rained 'Quality Street' all over the office. When we got out of the building I said that it was very interesting seeing a salesman at work and could be quite amusing at times. He laughed and said, 'Never mind, they won't forget me in a hurry and that can be a good thing, apart from them hiding the toffee tin when I come in.' He could well be right. When a firm of platemakers called in to us, for the first time, looking for work, their representative had not noticed the difference in his height which had been caused by a king-size helping of dog's muck that he was distributing throughout the company with his shoes. We nearly had to evacuate the building, but he secured work from us and the association lasted for years.

Roy's practical joking caused some embarrassment one evening when Ted answered the phone. The person on the other end of the line announced himself as Lord someone or other. The name sounded a bit far-fetched (like the proverbial bucket of manure from China), Lord Pilkington-Dyke, and Ted answered by saying, 'All right, Roy, I know it's you messing about' (or possibly a more earthy version) only to discover that it actually was Lord Pilkington-Dyke.

Taking customers to lunch was not one of my regular functions, but on occasions I would go with the MD, and possibly Roy and Ted, if the customer was important enough. These occasions could be either enjoyable or a complete drag, depending on the customers. This day we were all present, with a couple of prospective customers, and were trying somewhere new for lunch. Things were not going well, the customers could have 'bored for England' and to make matters worse the service in the restaurant was terrible. I think that Victoria Wood modelled one of her sketches on this place. The waitress, bless her, was knocking on a bit, and she would totter up to us and take our order, taking an interminable amount of time, and then do a passable imitation of Captain Oates. While all this time was passing, keeping the conversation going was not easy with this company. We were all doing our best, and it finally got to the stage where the MD had got round to discussing a caretaker, whom we used to employ, and the fact that he had a strange breed of dog for a pet. This was a topic which only normally surfaced when he was getting desperate. The main meal had at last arrived and I recall that one of the vegetables was garden peas. One of the customers was showing interest. 'What kind of a dog was it?' he asked. The MD said, 'Oh, it was a Mexican hairless dog.' I do not know what brought it on but I could not resist it. I said, 'Oh, yes, they are those dogs that became extinct. They used to breathe out of their backsides and they kept sitting in puddles and drowning!' To be honest, I have had better success with what I thought to be a humorous remark. The best result I achieved was with Ted, who had just taken a large mouthful of the garden peas and had just distributed them around, when he burst out laughing. I can remember thinking at the time, 'There goes another career!'

The period that I worked for the Clapham Company got as close to twenty-five years as it could, taking into consideration the fact that I was forty-one years old when I started with the company. I had taken the position with the intention of not moving around the country at least until my daughter's education was completed. In fact, I stayed on until my retirement. That period of approximately twenty-four years was one of general change. I remember reading at the beginning of that time that you could walk quite a way through a printer's, without barking your shins on a computer. By the end of that period I would say it was down to yards. The trade was in a state of change and in an ever-decreasing timescale, some trades disappearing entirely and others changing out of all recognition. In my early years with the company, I think it would be fair to say that I could cover for just about any of the areas of the trade, but by the finish, with the increases in the use of electronics and the digitalisation of origination and source material, this was no longer the case.

Those same years were ones of continual fluctuation in the national economy and markets. Firstly, there was raging inflation which was so bad that we once had to cancel the purchase of a machine due to the increase in its cost while we were waiting for delivery, which put it beyond our reach. It was a case of a couple of good years, if you were lucky, followed by a couple of bad years. At the same time it was a period of change with legislation and trade unions. A considerable amount of time had to be spent negotiating with your staff. Some of the negotiating got pretty acrimonious, with unions being reluctant to see brought about changes which affected their traditional methods of work. All understandable, but it was very difficult to get over to them the fact that things were such that it was a case of 'change or go under!'

In spite of all that and the fact that the last few years were spent operating in what was a 'buyers' market' (which meant you were under continuous pressure), it was for the most part an enjoyable and exciting way to earn a living. As for more than twenty of those years I was also on the board of directors, I also felt a certain amount of satisfaction that the company was still trading, after going through a time that put many companies out of business. We were also reasonably up to date with the technology and, for a medium-sized independent company, that was an achievement. The capital required to keep up with such an ever changing technology was considerable.

Back when the photocomposition world was making great strides forward, we decided that we had to update our setting system, to keep up with the competition. The system that we had put in was seven years old, and we had only intended it to last for five. We were in a 'Catch-22' situation. The equipment we had was out of date, and we had held onto it to try to be able to take advantage of what amounted to new 'third-generation equipment' coming on the market – skipping one generation. As part of our investigation into the equipment available, the MD had arranged for us to spend an afternoon with an expert in the field, who should be able to update us. He was going to advise us on what was on offer and the strengths and weaknesses of the equipment available, from an independent unbiased position.

The MD, Ted, the studio director and myself set out on a journey to wildest Buckinghamshire. It was quite a trip and, when we arrived, we found that it was an old rectory, situated in a small wood. We parked the car and crunched up a pea-shingle path which wound its way up to the rectory. It was a fairly long path, and as we were walking, I noticed a figure loping through the woods on our left, a tall man, with bushy hair and his shirt hanging out of his trousers at the back. When we reached the front door, which was solid oak with old-fashioned, cast-iron hinges and a 'lion's head' knocker, I looked around and remarked that it would be a good set for 'Hammer Films' to use. We knocked and heard the sound reverberate through the house. There was a long wait and then – footsteps. My imagination was running riot, and I could swear the person coming to open the door was dragging a club foot. I was expecting Boris Karloff with a line like, 'Let me take your hat and throat!', so I was quite relieved to find it was only the wife of the gentleman we had come to see (two normal feet and no bolt through the neck!). We announced ourselves and stated our business, and she said, 'Oh yes, follow the path round the side of the house until you come to the lodge. The door is open, please wait in there, and he will be with you in a minute.'

We followed our instructions and came to the lodge, which did indeed have its door open, and that probably accounted for what we found in there. It was a nice reasonably sized room, furnished with chintz-covered furniture, and with a desk and chair at one end, on a raised platform. What did surprise us was that the room had a number of chickens in it. There was a Light Sussex ambling about on the sofa, a White Leghorn on one of the chairs, and a few Rhode Island Reds scratching about on the carpet. Our razor-sharp minds told us that they were unlikely residents, so we shooed them out, and having checked that they had not left any deposits, sat down and waited. The expert we had come to see entered. He was the same person I had glimpsed through the trees on the way in. A recognition made easier by the fact that his shirt was still not tucked into his trousers round the back. I think it would be fair to say that he was a bit eccentric, and that description could be compared to describing Genghis Khan as 'naughty'. Having introduced himself, he sat down on his desk and boomed, 'Right, so you want to be put in the picture with regards to the photosetting scene. Well, when you talk about typesetting now it is with chips!' At this point in time we were not that well versed in computers, far less microchips, and as the prefix 'micro' was not used – there was some confusion. With the presence of the chickens, we could be forgiven for thinking we had stumbled across a clandestine 'Colonel Saunders' operation.

We were eventually put in the picture and brought up to date by this gentleman. During his conversation with us he was interrupted by one of his employees, who asked if he wanted anything down at the village, as he was popping down there. 'Yes, get me the longest set of darts you can find!' he said, and the lad departed. We then moved to a prefabricated building in the grounds, where he had a small typesetting unit up and running. It was most interesting, and during the demonstration, the lad returned from the village. He handed a set of darts to our host with the passing remark, 'Here's your receipt, they were eighteen pounds fifty.' The instructions to the lad had not included restraints on purchasing power, and, in fairness, he tried to appear as a man would who expected them to cost that much. In actuality, I don't think he would have looked much different if he had just received a kick in the groin.

The next port of call was the studio, and our expert moved over to a drawing board and said, 'I will now show you how easy it is to strip in a correction!' He taped a piece of film to the board, picked up a straight edge and scalpel and with one deft stroke – took the top off his thumb! Now, controlling my amusement is not one of my strong points, and this has been my undoing on many an occasion. With the mind working with great speed, I came to the conclusion that bursting out laughing at this point would not be the best thing to do. I quickly pulled out my handkerchief, clasped it over my mouth and nose, and, I thought, made an admirable job of turning my laughter into a cross between choking and having a seizure. In a trice I had the twitching shoulders back under control and, apart from the tears still running from my eyes, felt I was on top of the situation. A quick look round reassured me that those present were too busy staunching the blood to have noticed anything. At that point I foolishly risked a look at Ted. As soon as our eyes met, we were both in dead trouble. To this day Ted has never forgiven me and swears the only good luck he had was in avoiding a hernia. We did not get back to the company until late that night, and the MD apologised for it being so late. I said to him, 'Bernard, don't apologise – I would have paid for this afternoon!'

It is amazing how you do not realise the passage of time, you notice other people getting older but not yourself The memory plays tricks, such as when someone queries when had we last done that job. You say about a year or two ago, only to find out that it was six or seven years ago. You refer to others as old, only to find they are younger than you, and recall events to people who answer, 'But I wasn't born then.' Eventually, the penny dropped, and I realised that I was approaching retirement age.

I gave the matter a fair amount of thought and the decision was not too difficult to make. It would have been quite easy to work on, no one had suggested that I was 'past it' yet, although June had dropped a slight hint, by saying that it was time I stopped considering myself a sex symbol and started to concentrate on being a 'loveable old fool'. It seemed to me that it would be all too likely that time would continue to slip by, and I did not want to leave it too late to pursue the many outside interests that I wanted to or have the time to visit places that I wanted to see. I decided that at sixty-five it would be best to put my efforts into enjoying retirement.